MICHAEL PENNINGTON

Over the past thirty years Michael Pennington has played a variety of leading roles in the West End of London, for the Royal Shakespeare Company, for the Royal National Theatre, and for the English Shakespeare Company, of which he was co-founder and joint Artistic Director from 1986 to 1992. His Shakespearian roles include Hamlet, Macbeth, Leontes, Coriolanus, Richard II, Henry V, Angelo, Berowne and Timon of Athens, and he has played central parts in the work of Euripides, Molière, Congreve, Vanbrugh, Ibsen, Tolstoy, Chekhov, Dostoyevsky, Bulgakov, O'Casey, Granville Barker, de Filippo, Shaffer, Mortimer, Pinter, Osborne, Rudkin, Stoppard, Harwood, Brenton, Edgar, Poliakoff and Bennett. His one-man show *Anton Chekhov* premiered at the National Theatre in 1984, and has frequently been revived in London, on tour and abroad, and is the subject of his *Are You There, Crocodile? – Inventing Anton Chekhov*, published by Oberon Books in 2003.

His successful *Hamlet – A User's Guide* was published by Nick Hern Books in 1996, to be followed by *Twelfth Night – A User's Guide* in 2000, after his direction of the play for the English Shakespeare Company, for the Chicago Shakespeare Theater and the Haiyuza Company of Tokyo. *A Midsummer Night's Dream – A User's Guide* follows his successful 2003 production of the play at the Open Air Theatre in Regent's Park, described by London critics as 'a captivating Shakespearian experience' (*The Guardian*) and 'riotously funny and genuinely touching' (*The Daily Telegraph*).

In 2004 Michael Pennington delivered the annual Shakespeare Lecture at the British Academy in London – the first time an actor had been invited to do so since Harley Granville Barker in 1925.

D1465368

01279902

by the same author

Hamlet – A User's Guide
Twelfth Night – A User's Guide

Michael Pennington

A MIDSUMMER NIGHT'S DREAM

A User's Guide

WARWICKSHIRE LIBRARY & INFO SERVICE	
Bertrams	31.07.05
822.33	£14.99

NICK HERN BOOKS

London

www.nickhernbooks.co.uk

A Nick Hern Book

A Midsummer Night's Dream – A User's Guide
first published in Great Britain in 2005 as a paperback original
by Nick Hern Books Ltd, 14 Larden Road, London W3 7ST

Copyright © Michael Pennington 2005

Michael Pennington has asserted his right to be identified
as the author of this work

Front cover photo: Peter Forbes as Bottom in
Michael Pennington's 2003 production of
A Midsummer Night's Dream at the Open Air Theatre,
Regent's Park, London. Photo © Alastair Muir

Back cover author photo © Sophie Baker

Extract from *The Wedding* from *Anton Chekhov: Twelve Plays*,
translated by Ronald Hingley (Oxford World's Classics, 1992).
By permission of Oxford University Press

Typeset by Country Setting, Kingsdown, Kent CT14 8ES
Printed and bound in Great Britain by Biddles Ltd, King's Lynn

A CIP catalogue record for this book is available
from the British Library

ISBN-13   978 1 85459 810 3
ISBN-10   1 85459 810 4

CONTENTS

Introduction   I

One
Act 1 Scene 1   16

Two
Act 1 Scene 2   39

Three
Act 2 Scene 1   48

Four
Act 2 Scene 2   68

Five
Act 3 Scene 1   81

Interval Music   96

Six
Act 3 Scene 2   108

Seven
Act 4 Scene 1   137

Eight
Act 4 Scene 2   155

Nine
Act 5 Scene 1   161

Conclusion
Regent's Park, 2003   194

INTRODUCTION

At the beginning of *A Midsummer Night's Dream*, probably the most popular of Shakespeare's comedies, a girl is threatened with state execution if she does not abandon the man she loves and marry her father's choice. In no other Shakespeare play is state coercion applied in quite this way to a matter of the heart. The unexpected savagery of the Elizabethan court anticipates an image of modern brutality: the kneeling figure on television of a teenage Saudi princess waiting for decapitation in the 1980 documentary *Death of a Princess*. She was accused of sleeping with a commoner, Hermia only of being wooed by an unelected admirer, but the punishment is the same. Nobody in *A Midsummer Night's Dream* will question the law (though the silence of Hippolyta, the outsider, is interesting): we have to deduce that it's the norm, and be grateful that before the end of the scene Theseus has the wisdom to moderate it.

The plays of Shakespeare are of course full of irate male parents thundering at their unruly young, with more or less potency. In *Othello*, Desdemona's father Brabantio asks for state punishment for her but is overruled. In *Romeo and Juliet*, Capulet mercilessly bullies his daughter Juliet but is soon manipulated into order. Cordelia faces no more than banishment for refusing to flatter Lear. In *The Winter's Tale*, Leontes orders Perdita, his baby daughter, to be abandoned on a mountainside, but by then he has convinced himself that she is not his. Titus Andronicus does kill one of his sons, off-the-cuff rather, in the heat of the moment; but he is operating in a story in which you might in any case end up cut to pieces and baked in a pie. In truth, none of these children encounters Hermia's extremity, so carefully considered by Egeus, or, by changing the prevailing tone to comedy, survives it more rapturously.

It seems that Shakespeare may have written *A Midsummer Night's Dream*, *Romeo and Juliet* and *The Comedy of Errors* within a year or so of each other, around 1595. In *The Comedy of Errors* it is the father who is the victim of the gallows humour: Aegeon, fallen into enemy hands in a bitter trade war, is given twenty-four hours either to find his twin sons or face death, and this triggers uproarious farce. As with *A Midsummer Night's Dream*, the initial extremity is, like the crack of the starter's gun, more or less forgotten once the action gets going. While *Romeo* looks in its early stages as if it might be a romantic comedy but ends with the piteous overthrow of its star-crossed lovers, the *Dream* and *The Comedy of Errors* present themselves as possible tragedies but develop into wild delight.

Nevertheless the *Dream*'s premise of paternal violence is unnerving, as is much of the play, which threatens its characters with the loss at any moment of identity or hope. At one point, a man famously appears to grow the head of an ass, so convincingly that a supernatural being – the Fairy Queen, no less – thinks that it is real and becomes wildly attracted to him. He is so flattered that he almost comes to think he is indeed a beast; she is deceived even though she knows perfectly well what a human is from her other dealings with the mortal world. Modishly, it might be argued that this adventure of hers represents her subconscious anxiety; but the fact is that she is the victim of a precisely targeted drug slipped to her by her husband, who is – initially, at least – delighted to see her sexually degrade herself with an animal.

Recently arrived from India, she and her vengeful consort preside over a community of fairies, whatever we imagine such things to be. For us their associations have become quite lightweight and prettified, the sentimental end of the older, deeper conceit of 'faerie' which interested and bothered the Elizabethans, for whom it included witches and hags, elves and goblins, incubi, succubi and shamans. But fairy magic still appeals to both the children and the adults within us, as a nostalgically shared memory whose oddity we cannot quite forget. A good ghost story brings its adult listeners together in scary relish: but alone, they dread private visitants, endure bad dreams, and make fascinated guesses at what kind of fantastic life might lie just beyond their vision. In a more mundane way, we become deeply intrigued when infra-red cameras shoot wildlife at night, peering through a veil at a mysterious, shaded world; we watch with a mixture of curiosity and squeamishness, knowing we are not really intended to be witnesses.

Through the medium of King Oberon and Queen Titania, Shakespeare leads us into this unknown, ensuring that we are touched by its discomforts as well as its charms. We are never allowed to see it as something so exotic that it doesn't affect us, and our guides often seem oddly like us. We gather that they have always had direct relationships with men, women and children while also being able to wield unnatural power over them, and their own behaviour suggests there is no real border between supernatural magic and intimate pettiness. Oberon may be able to circle the globe 'swifter than the wandering moon', but much of his career is a matter of correcting simple mistakes he has initiated; he is little more effective as a herbalist than Friar Laurence, more tragically, was in *Romeo and Juliet*. Unable, because of his human dimension, to ignore his morals, we are awed by the cruelty of his trick on Titania; on the other hand his promise of protection for his human clients at the end of the play has a godlike benevolence.

At the threshold of his ambiguous kingdom stands a 'puck', Robin Goodfellow, a figure with long folkloric associations and thought of by many in his original audience as a large, rough hairy devil with a delight in disorder. In an anonymous contemporary play called *Grim the Collier of Croydon* he is described as wearing 'a suit of leather close to his body; his face and hands russet-coloured, with a flail.' Brought to our stage at adult human size, and sometimes smaller, Puck's main pleasure in life seems to be discomforting the vulnerable, booby-trapping old ladies and confusing weary travellers. He watches all the groups that come into Oberon's wood to see what additional trouble he can cause them. The inspirational ass's head is his initiative, not Oberon's, and he would regard it as the best service he does his difficult master. He is a faithful and dependent servant, compensating for his mistakes with exaggerated claims of what he can achieve in forty minutes. Having boasted, he is often next seen dragging around the forest much like the lovers he has been sent to reorganise. At such times he seems more human than not, his self-confidence undone and his relations with the audience frankly confidential. For all that, he remains a slightly unsettling figure from the superstitious recesses of the English memory, and, like his masters, not quite of us.

Into this puzzling world tumbles a group of amateur actors intent on rehearsing a play for a royal wedding. They are nominally led by a carpenter, and comprise a tailor, a bellows-mender, a joiner, a tinker and a weaver called, of all things, Bottom. Bottom especially loves acting, and occasionally becomes vainglorious in his enthusiasm; his fault may be the one defined three hundred years later by the great Russian director Konstantin Stanislavsky, who observed critically that some actors are more in love with what they think they can bring to their art than what art can bring to them.

Puck, in a moment of condescension, calls these actors rude mechanicals, and the name has stuck; the same noun is applied adjectivally by the Tribunes to the Citizens in *Julius Caesar*, and there is no question but that it is contemptuous. But for all their clumsiness, these are decent working men who have discovered a common interest. They speak very much as we might, and bring into the play the easy pleasure of recognition: in the surrounding confusion, their anxieties are agreeably small and familiar.

Although the preparations for their play weave only intermittently through the action, apparently as comic relief, they are doing something their author surely believed in: in fact he is taking us directly into the actors' engine-room in a way that he never did to the same extent again. It is, I suppose, impossible to use the image of theatre in a play without making an audience reflect on why they are sitting there, feeling the cleansing effect of simulated emotions and an eagerness to believe against all odds. Bottom and his friends are afflicted by bad luck rather than incompetence. It may have been a mistake to let Peter Quince the carpenter, who is better at writing and directing than acting, introduce their play, since in his nervousness he nearly reduces it to nonsense; but in any case the production is disabled by the fact of Bottom having been arbitrarily called away by Puck to be part of the fairy world, so that they never managed a complete rehearsal. Even though their work is not so ridiculous, and there is no moment in the text that suggests the author wants the performance to collapse, they are shown no mercy on the night. They are not the last theatre company to find that an upper-class audience can be more vicious than a pub one because it uses such obscure language.

The real mechanicals are four young people who are reduced to the action of puppets by Puck – mostly by mistake. The drug that Oberon uses on Titania is the source of their troubles too – or perhaps, as with Titania, it forces them to enact their suppressed desires. Two of them start the play as consensual lovers and all four seem to be friends, and even seem to be from *Friends*. They might be university contemporaries, not so long graduated, the girls I would hazard in English Literature, one of the men in Drama and Music, and the other perhaps in Business Studies. No sooner has one of the Eng-Lits escaped the threat of execution and run away with Drama-and-Music than he lets her wander round the forest half the night, and on meeting her again turns blankly on her as if she were a loathsome stranger. Her friend, whom Business-Studies has abandoned and who now feels she must be as ugly as a bear, has to endure both men turning on her with an adoration that she knows cannot be real – in the case of one because he is the man who deserted her, and of the other because he really loves her friend. The two women, who have been fond of each other since school, are driven to the edge of violence by these men, and the men prevented from killing each other partly by a supernatural intervention and partly by their own fatigue and cowardice.

This barely comic tale is made possible, and nominally tied up at the end, by two figures from myth re-imagined as the Duke and Duchess of a Renaissance court. As the architects of the play's action, Theseus and Hippolyta might seem to represent the virtues of considered wisdom and humanity. However, apart from Theseus's tolerance of a cruelly anachronistic law, that picture is complicated by the fact that the Elizabethan audience would have recognised them as something less than perfectly matched. Astonishingly, otherwise alert critics have called the pair mature, self-commanding, idealised; still more misleadingly, it has been said that their detachment forms a stable background for the play's madnesses. But the fact is that this royal couple may be as dysfunctional by nature as the lovers are by intoxication. Theseus was known to be a violent military hero with an extremely dubious reputation with women; he emerges from Plutarch's *Lives of the Noble Grecians and Romans*, one of Shakespeare's sources, as a serial rapist, seducer and abandoner, the embodiment of renegade male machismo. The Amazon Hippolyta meanwhile belonged to what he might have feared most, a self-sufficient female community – in Chaucer's *Knight's Tale*, she was the 'Queen of Femenye'.

The general consensus of legend is that together with his friend Hercules, Theseus led the Athenians in a campaign against these Amazons, and that before leaving, he kidnapped Hippolyta's sister Antiope. Depending on which account you read, either Antiope or

Hippolyta eventually married Theseus (and gave birth to Hippolytus, whereby hangs another tale); in yet other versions of the story, it was the Amazons who conquered, whereupon Hippolyta forcibly took Theseus as her husband. The Elizabethans in general were conditioned to see Amazons as barbaric and their female self-government as a bellicose thing, to be subjected at length to male structures. However, this position was necessarily modified by respect for the Virgin Queen Elizabeth under whom they lived: hence the mutedly respectful treatment of Hippolyta in the play, and her implicit link with the equally independent Titania. By the end of *A Midsummer Night's Dream*, Theseus and Hippolyta seem to have come to terms, as improbably as if Mike Tyson and Emmeline Pankhurst decided to marry, but the echoes of the past persist: lurking behind their new genial identities are legendary images of opposition and violence.

*

Needless to say, there is another point of view: that such an account takes matters far too seriously, and that it is faintly ridiculous to allow scruples to play so freely around such a ravishing entertainment. Normally severe commentators roll over on their backs at the blandishments of the comedy, or inquire only half-heartedly into it, as if fearful to compromise the fact that this lovely thing is, after all, only a play. In their more relaxed version of events, not only are Theseus and Hippolyta grown-ups whose union will calm all frenzies, but the lovers' upheavals are impossible to take seriously, first because their characters are barely differentiated, and then because the preponderance of their story is told in rhyming verse, which in English from Chaucer to Hilaire Belloc is a ready instrument of comedy. So all their troubles are like the banana-skins of pantomime when nobody gets hurt, rather than those of life, which lead to fractures.

Undeniably, generations of new theatregoers have jumped with delight at the sight of Bottom in his ass's head, for many people the most enduring Shakespearian image of their lives. The undisturbing and delightful nature of this transformation is, it is said, underlined by the fact that Puck takes the head off as a mere piece of machinery when the joke is over. So Bottom's adventure with Titania should be seen as no more than a merriment, and no erotic deductions made. Puck himself is a jolly figure, imp rather than ogre, and the Mechanicals' play a wonderful example of working-class ineptitude and hubris; never mind the sensibilities of the performers, *Pyramus and Thisbe* must go wrong in a number of hilarious ways, since few things are more enjoyable for audiences than a play within a play that misfires. And as far as a moral register for Oberon and Titania is concerned, there just isn't time to consider it, since the way they speak is so rapturous, so astoundingly beautiful, that that must be more or less their sole purpose. Much else of the play is a superb faunal and floral miscellany that you can almost hear and smell; the magic effects are unthreatening, tongue in cheek. And beyond all this, look at the way the thing has always worked in the theatre: a superb machine that we do well not to tamper with, a supreme imagination on a magnificent riff. Oppression, nightmare and bestiality have nothing to do with it.

In many ways it is difficult to argue with this. Moment to moment, the play gleams like a fish in the water, its intricate and delicate design shimmering with light; it both creates and satisfies desire. The poetry is some of the most brilliant Shakespeare ever wrote, and the most self-generating: it seems often to have no purpose beyond the continuation of delight. The reckless invention upon invention, the breathtaking cadences, the limitless fantastication of an idea which owes virtually nothing to any source, are all executed with a bravado that dares you to suspect it will all fall apart, its various elements impossible to corral. We say it's miraculous that Tom Stoppard can introduce Chaos Theory into a play about landscape gardening (*Arcadia*) or construct another about philosophers and acrobats (*Jumpers*). But at least these are real things; so far he hasn't done fairies, whereas Shakespeare throws them too into a pot that already contains young lovers, amateur actors and their rulers. The play's slight edge of virtuosity, its sense that Shakespeare is celebrating his own gifts, gives it its chutzpah, its arrogant star quality. Like *Hamlet*, a performance of the *Dream* has a tangible effect for good, as if we were all gathered round the same watering hole for a moment. During Oberon's lyric flights audiences often hold their breaths, alert and inspired; then they become helpless with laughter, yelping with it in fact, at the Mechanicals' play. The only bit that tends not to interest people is Theseus and Hippolyta, but we'll see about that. The play has stimulated music as perhaps no other work by Shakespeare; ever since it was reintroduced to the stage in something like its right form in the 1840s, it has been unassailable. Every year a batch of revivals fight it out for our attention; the programming of whole theatres sometimes seems to depend on it; nervous at the thought of *The Tempest,* or even of *Twelfth Night,* they fall on the *Dream* as a dead certainty. Its sheer otherworldliness has led some critics to conclude that it is unstageable and best enjoyed by the fireside, with, so to speak, the eyes closed; yet every year several hundred thousand eyes are trained on it.

But to let the argument rest here – that this play allows you simply to forget your troubles in a world both enchanted and safe – would mean that Shakespeare sometimes wrote great and complex works but at others took the day off. In fact this was a writer who could play bassoon notes on a penny whistle and a line of lyric melody on a tuba. There is no difficulty for him in starting a drama with a matter of life and death and ending it with fairies singing a ditty: he can complicate without strain, execute any number of hairpin turns and articulate whatever you already have deep in your mind. Looking from a distance like a superb fireworks show, at close quarters the *Dream* sometimes has a more acrid smell. Its foray into the unconscious has attracted artists as troubled as William Blake, who used to see angels on Peckham Rye, Richard Dadd, who spent half his life in bedlam after murdering his father, and Henry Fuseli, who swore in seven languages and wept when he read the Bible. The Polish critic Jan Kott, particularly fashionable in the late 1960s, proclaimed the dear old *Dream* to be the most darkly erotic of Shakespeare's plays, as brutal as *Troilus and Cressida,* and saw Titania's fairies as toothless and sniggering ancients; in his view everyone wakes from the dream of the title with a sense of sexual shame, especially Bottom, who has been raped by Titania. Subsequent productions have sometimes concentrated so hard on his lively ideas that managements have had to post warnings to parents in the foyer.

None of this would have surprised the author, mixing and matching with unparalleled virtuosity. At the same time, he was, over twenty years of playwriting, remarkably constant to certain preoccupations. He was always interested in describing a journey for his characters which leaves none of them quite the same at its end. Typically, this involves sending them to an unknown location to re-order their thinking. King Ferdinand's 'little academe' in *Love's Labour's Lost,* the outlaws' forest in *The Two Gentlemen of Verona,* and the labyrinth of Ephesus streets in *The Comedy of Errors* have already been tentative gestures in this direction. The forest that lies at the centre of *A Midsummer Night's Dream* arises from the same instinct for a spiritual journey into darkness and back into a wider light.

It must be said that in this play the outing is circumstantially successful rather than educative. Later, in *As You Like It*, Orlando and Rosalind and even the wicked Duke and Oliver will emerge from the Forest of Arden with an increased understanding of themselves; ahead of them stands Lear on his stormy heath, the deserted seashore of *Timon of Athens*, and Prospero's island in *The Tempest*. Compared with these, it is hard to see what Helena and Demetrius, Lysander and Hermia, quite learn in the wood near Athens. Demetrius receives a sort of shock therapy to remind him that Helena was the girl for him after all; his and Lysander's behaviour plays profoundly on the insecurities of Helena and Hermia but is never explained to them or understood by the men. When all four wake up, their shared dream dispelled by the wave of a wand, they have a beautiful brief exchange to re-cement their friendship, then disappear into virtual silence. Perhaps what they have been through together will temper them, as if they had survived a brush with death; perhaps recognising their frail hold on events will make them into careful parents. But this isn't expressed: we infer it. Actually, their experience has been alarming and cautionary, but hardly instructive.

However, this is almost the first time that Shakespeare has tried such a thing, and soon he will see how much more can be done with it. Oddly enough, curative development is mainly expressed in this play in characters who never leave their natural domain; it is perceptible in Oberon in the forest, and in the seemingly inert Theseus and Hippolyta in the Court. Bottom's group, meanwhile, doesn't need to change, since a secret of their charm is their impermeable stability: whatever happens they will remain their commonsense selves. Bottom does have a great moment of sensibility when he wakens from his dream of being someone else; but then he obliterates it completely and marches back into his old life.

Rather than the commoners, it is the rulers who learn something; especially the males. King Oberon, for all the beauty and rareness of his speech, starts as one of Shakespeare's small men as much in need of change as Leontes in *The Winter's Tale* or Ford in *The Merry Wives of Windsor*: a jealous lover who will sacrifice everything for revenge on a woman for being, simply, what she is. In Shakespeare's early writing he also belongs in the sequence of Richard II, Mercutio, and

Berowne: wonderfully over-equipped men whose articulacy creates mute awe, but who are limited by a disastrous inability to use their talents for any creative purpose. Oberon's fine talk of promontories, dolphin's backs and little western flowers is challenged by the maturity and conscience of Titania, who reminds him of the catastrophic effect of their quarrel on the wider world. His lamentable response is to dream up a sorcerer's revenge; then, no sooner has he seen Titania making an ass of herself with Bottom than he repents and dances with her. As he confronts the limits of his revenge and longs for things to be at peace in all worlds, he seems to be completing an odyssey as Shakespearian as that of Prospero.

Oberon's parallel in the human world is, clearly enough, Theseus. Theseus's presence in a play like this is at first sight surprising, he who moved mountains and was so firmly stuck to his seat in the underworld by Hades that when Hercules pulled him free he lost part of his thigh (giving rise to the belief that Athenians had thin legs). But perhaps he is not so badly chosen for his purpose. His mythic side relates him to the strangely fanciful, intemperate and childish behaviour of classical deities, with its odd mix of embarrassing physical detail and grandiloquence. But he is also the first of such heroes to emerge from the shadows into something like recorded history. Theseus unified Attica and built a fortress on the Acropolis, thus in a way founding the Athenian city state; and in the play, his statesmanlike sonorities give him sporadic authority. Often he is vain, with a disconcerting habit of boasting about his past, especially to his prisoner-of-war bride Hippolyta. But the better side of him understands (with a sympathy that stops short of enthusiasm) the imagination of poet, lover and lunatic, and he has a marvellous final word, if I understand it rightly, on the craft of acting:

> The best in this kind are but shadows; and the worst are no worse, if imagination amend them.

Judge of Hermia but patron of the arts, Shakespeare allows Theseus to be by turns rational and boastful, judicious and self-aggrandising. His contradictions begin to settle at the end of the play, a new relationship with Hippolyta brought about by the simple act of marrying her. Their contentious past seems forgotten, and they speak on equal terms.

Most powerful figures in Shakespeare undergo re-training of this kind, assuming that they live long enough. Very few enter their plays in a state of grace rather than achieving it: Henry V may be the best example of regal consistency, and he, goodness knows, calls for a rather worldly definition of virtue. Others are infected with arrogance and pride (Julius Caesar, Lear); are criminals (Claudius, King John, Richard III, Macbeth) or are at least compromised by their route to the throne (Henry IV). Others again (Henry VI, Duke Vincentio, Richard II) are betrayed by a personal weakness that makes them inadequate for the job but correspondingly sympathetic to us. And if they survive for any length of time, is it not because they learn to listen to voices other than their own? Shakespeare seems very interested in who it is that catches their attention, but profoundly pessimistic about the possibility of any man remaining human while he controls the lives of others.

In general, he seems more hopeful for his women, though they often appear to vacillate between outspokenness and mute stoicism. In the *Dream* female acquiescence is more or less complete, though we are left with the distinct sense that both Hippolyta and Titania could add something if they chose to. Hippolyta's response to Theseus's identification of actors with shadows, quoted above, is quite sharp:

It must be your imagination, then, and not theirs

– and her volubility in this scene suggests she has an undeceived eye on him and is unlikely to hold her tongue. On the other hand, Hermia, who defied the law of the land, and Helena, who regularly tore a strip off both Lysander and Demetrius, keep quiet in the last Act while their new husbands make life difficult for the actors of *Pyramus and Thisbe*; this doesn't seem to suggest disapproval or second thoughts. Titania, dancing with Oberon after he releases her from her spell, may be suspicious of his part in it, but despite arguing violently with him earlier, she raises barely a quibble now, only mildly asking him to explain her aberration when he has a moment. When the two of them come to bless the marriages at the end of the play, it would be wrong to see any resentment between them.

Because of these ambiguous silences – repeated later by Viola at the end of *Twelfth Night* and Isabella at that of *Measure for Measure* – the question of what the women really feel is a matter of preference, and even of changing fashion both in the theatre and outside it. The adjustment in our perception of Shakespeare's heroines during the last half-century – undoubtedly helped by the public articulacy of many leading actresses – is quite striking. It is a long time since Harley Granville Barker, in his *Prefaces to Shakespeare*, could get away with describing Hamlet's mother Gertrude as a 'pretty, kindly, smirched, bedizened woman' and Paulina in *The Winter's Tale* as 'Plucky Paulina – what a good fellow!' Barker's tonality lurked inside a recent article in London's *Guardian* newspaper by Professor Gary Taylor, who proposed, impartially I think, that women serve as props only in Shakespearian tragedy, which is a male genre in which they are mainly present to do men's crying for them. For instance, though he admits that Desdemona does die herself, twice in fact, it is only in order that her tragic husband can exquisitely suffer for having killed her; Juliet and Cleopatra meanwhile are trophy wives, responding appropriately to their men's tragedies, their lives meaningless without them. (He doesn't mention in this context such big hitters as Lady Macbeth and Volumnia, or indeed Hermione, Goneril or Regan.) Rather, I would suggest that Shakespeare regularly proposes that a hero has at least a chance to learn conscience from an eloquent woman. So we surely approve of Emilia rebuking Iago and Paulina Leontes, notice how much of *As You Like It* lies in the hands of Rosalind and what a mess Orlando would make of their courtship were it left to him, and likewise associate Titania with the moral centre of the *Dream*. The female principle in Shakespeare tends to be more comprehensive than the male; and if his women don't become tragic figures with quite the same noisy regularity as the men, that is because they are less like fools. Being a tragic hero seems to involve behaving very stupidly at some point, and Shakespeare seems to see that as a male prerogative.

*

These long arcs of masculine learning are described in the *Dream* in long-shot, so to speak; its foreground business unfolds during the puzzling pause between tiredness and waking, in unconscious absences that hardly seem like sleep at all. For a play so energetic that it seems to move like a wave, flowing this way and that, there is a great deal of slumber: its title, now so familiar that the sense has drained out of it a little, proposes the shortest night of the year as the occasion for the strangest delusions – to borrow Lysander's words, 'swift as a shadow, short as any dream'. Unconsciousness comes in the form of healthy fatigue for Lysander and Titania, but their sleep is corrupted and when they come round they are out of their minds. Hermia goes to sleep in a secure world and wakes in another, then sleeps again and is restored to safety. Helena eventually escapes into exhaustion and awakens to great good fortune. Demetrius drops as if he had been hit on the head and wakes up to his senses. These things happen to the lovers not only because of magic but because justice itself slept and put Hermia's life at risk; eventually Egeus, the source of their troubles, is banished like another bad dream. Only Bottom's sleep allows him a broader vision: he briefly enters a marvellous world, populated by figures hidden from everyone else but visible to us, the audience: and so there is also the hint by the end that the whole thing has been our dream.

These confusions make the play delightful and funny, but perhaps not exactly moving – heartless even, as if the young Shakespeare's infatuation with his talent was slightly distancing it from us. With their awakenings in its last movement, however, each group begins to reach a destination and the register quietly changes. By their strange journey the lovers are brought close not only to their opposite numbers but to their friends; Helena, with ambiguous insight, realises she has found Demetrius, her own and not her own. The translated Bottom stirs and begins to speak of the vision he has had: he thinks perhaps he had something new on his head, that for a moment perhaps he was a king – but the memory begins to slip away. To keep it precious he stops trying to explain it, moving instead into the performance he has long dreamed of giving, which becomes unexpectedly touching. Oberon recovers his largesse as Titania awakens into his arms and trusts him again; by the end of the play Theseus, capable of listening to Hippolyta, seems unlikely to be sentencing any more young women to the block for disobeying their fathers.

All these returns to healthy life, one on top of the other, unexpectedly touch the heart; the play, so dazzling and distracting, moves forward on a succession of deeper notes. Finally, the fairies enter the house like glow-worms to deliver a blessing over the newly-weds, ensuring their future children's safety and health, and the different worlds fall into step. Still more audaciously, Puck arrives to send us home with his benediction, as the couples have been sent by Oberon. It appears that the fairy world can support human life: we feel protected, without knowing quite by what. Soon enough,

Shakespeare will be looking at darker alternatives, at the loss of safety, at the anxieties that press in only very gently at the edges of this play; for the moment he basks in the broad sunlight of a talent able to bring such things together. It is perhaps the last time he thought life could be this good, and for four hundred years we have needed to hear him say it again and again.

*

This is the third User's Guide I have written about individual Shakespeare plays, and it may be the most bluntly opinionated. I've appeared in *Hamlet* a number of times but never directed it; never been in *Twelfth Night* but directed it three times; never been in the *Dream* but directed it once – and have perhaps not even seen it as often as, it being so much a part of the culture, I vaguely assumed that I had. Prolonged exposure to a play leaves you tolerant of infinite interpretations; as a sort of *Dream* novice I see little need to temper my first impressions of it with the dampening qualifications of experience.

What has interested me a great deal is the way the individual plays dictate a way of writing about them. *Hamlet* of course provokes all manner of associations beyond itself – philosophical, emotional, metaphysical; to write about it is to write about most of life. *Twelfth Night*, the least uncomplicated of comedies, is closer than one would think to this tragic masterwork; the light plays irregularly on its surface, darker where the water is deepest, and the commentator has to find a style to reflect the subtle emotional currents beneath its lucid charm. The *Dream* is rather different from both, sufficient to itself, an inspired *jeu d'esprit*: it delights but barely teaches at all, suggesting little outside itself. The voice describing it may therefore become particularly subjective. From a theoretical point of view, there is perhaps not so much to be said about the play – what conclusions can be drawn are generally rather academic, such as the tradition of fairies and what literary precedents are to be found in Chaucer and Ovid. However, I go on the assumption that too much Ovid is bad for you if it prevents such an original piece of music from ringing clearly in the ears.

Meanwhile all the normal rules of these books apply: there is very little here that you can just as well find in any number of annotated texts, all of which explain the more difficult words, more or less well, identify the literary sources and express a wide if not particularly germane range of opinions. Actually, the distinction matters less and less: in my working life textual scholarship has moved ever closer to theatre practice, and the devil take the hindmost. The result is that we practitioners bask in a certain intellectual credibility, not always deserved, while the scholarly constituency shows an enthusiasm for spit and sawdust that quite takes one aback. Many actors now know a Good Quarto from a Bad; and if I visit my friends at the Shakespeare Institute in Stratford the preferred talk amidst the congenial popping of corks might well be some piece of stage business, long forgotten by me, that I intrigued them with twenty years ago. It turns out that there is, after all, no turf war to be fought over Shakespeare: all our interests are the same.

Among a number of such friends I owe a genuine debt on this occasion to Professors Peter Holland, editor of the Oxford edition, Stanley Wells, Jonathan Bate and Anne Barton. I would like to think that this book can be enjoyed whether or not you have a copy of the *Dream* in the other hand; and as far as texts go, I am nominally using the Oxford, but occasionally diverge because it is an opportunistic principle in the theatre to use whichever variant of a particular line suits you best. This is, for better or worse, a report from the front on what happens to the play in the heat of action. It is as much an idiosyncratic machine as Shakespeare's other thirty-six, some parts of it astonishingly strong and intricate and others a little fragile; and if you plan to use it, it is best to have an idea where its stress-points lie as well as its strengths. Beyond that, as always, you can take or leave my views as you wish: their default mode is an endless range of alternatives.

ONE

Act 1 Scene 1

Until they speak, they could be dots on a barely glimpsed horizon;
Theseus, who negotiated the labyrinth, and Hippolyta, the capture
of whose famous magic girdle was one of the twelve labours of
Hercules. But as they approach they shrink rapidly to human size,
collaborating pleasantly like well-matched musicians. Their call and
response seem to belong less to the world of gods and heroes than
to the rituals of courtship, one voice fervent and the other appeas-
ing: perhaps their grand names are disguising familiar transactions.
First, the impatient bridegroom:

> THESEUS: Now, fair Hippolyta, our nuptial hour
> Draws on apace; four happy days bring in
> Another moon. But O, methinks, how slow
> This old moon wanes! She lingers my desires . . .

– then feminine reassurance:

> HIPPOLYTA: Four days will quickly steep themselves in night;
> Four nights will quickly dream away the time . . .

Hippolyta seems to be in tune with the natural rhythm of the seasons:
she knows that even Theseus, for all his heroic interventions, cannot
stop the world turning at its own speed. He can neither delay nor
hurry the moment when

> . . . the moon, like to a silver bow
> New bent in heaven, shall behold the night
> Of our solemnities.

Interpreting Shakespeare is a disreputable business: you must always
be looking for trouble, especially when the surface seems smooth.
So, like prospectors, we start turning these ten elegant lines over and
over, inspecting them for negatives. For instance, did Hippolyta's

final 'solemnities' perhaps fall a little heavily on the ear?[1] Would Theseus have preferred to hear something like 'ecstasies'?

The sober word also halted a line of verse, leaving it short of a couple of beats. These days actors have been trained to spot this sort of detail and identify it as something other than convenience. The best advice is: if a speaker stops short in this way and the next character's half-line supplies the missing beats, the cue should be sharply picked up; but if the next line is of full length, it should be preceded by a silence roughly equivalent to what was missing. This will create a moment quite heavy with meaning, as if the engine had suddenly stalled: it is not often in the prodigal flow of Shakespearian verse that a character falls silent for lack of anything to say.

In this case, Theseus adroitly picks up his cue and moves on, so he has covered up any awkwardness; but his tone has changed a little. He turns to a trusted officer with a slightly ridiculous order; compulsory pleasure for all. Philostrate must singlehandedly generate a holiday spirit, particularly among the young people; he is to

> Stir up the Athenian youth to merriments

and

> Awake the pert and nimble spirit of mirth.

Just as 'solemnities' sounded, well, solemn, 'merriments' and 'mirth' seem a little forced. To boost the cheerfulness, alliteration is called in:

> Turn melancholy forth to funerals;
> The pale companion is not for our pomp.

We are still wondering about Hippolyta: if it is true that she lowered the temperature, there must have been a reason. Theseus's passionate impatience had just been expressed in a striking phrase: as the moon moved gently towards their wedding day, it reminded him of

> . . . a stepdame or a dowager
> Long withering out a young man's revenue.

That is to say, when a second wife or widow gets hold of a father's wealth, the son can't get his hands on it. So to Theseus, counting down the days to being united with his bride feels like waiting for a

---

1. The word, which comes from Latin, really suggests an annual ritual, with overtones not of sadness but of formality. Even so, it is enough to dampen things a little.

rich relative to die. Was this quite the note to strike? A coarse little cluster of images surrounded his idea: stepdames and dowagers can't help sounding like crones, and 'withering' underlined the ageism. Hippolyta, who has a less effortful way with language, elegantly improved on the charmless simile: to her, the moon irritating Theseus was as beautiful as a silver bow in the sky. Her stylishness, concluded by 'solemnities', might have added up to a mild reproach, and Philostrate's mission may be a fast recovery from it.

Philostrate receives his instructions wordlessly, excluded from the self-conscious duet, but the actor needs to have a discreet attitude to them all the same; incredulity perhaps, banked well down behind professionalism. Theseus meanwhile, turning back to Hippolyta, moves smoothly through another gear-change into plain speaking, a certain toughness pressing behind the music:

> Hippolyta, I wooed thee with my sword,
> And won thy love doing thee injuries.

What kind of romance is this? Hippolyta is, it seems, not an equal partner but a prisoner of war. In the manner of certain men, Theseus believes that her affection was provoked by aggression: after all, as an Amazon, she is a soldier herself. But he also knows he owes her something, in 'another key'. To marry her now

> With pomp, with triumph and with revelling

will be considerate, and surely make up for his earlier lack of finesse. He is using the pompous word 'pomp' for the second time in five lines; Hippolyta wouldn't use it once. And she never confirms whether an enormous wedding party – rather than good behaviour in the future – will be to her taste, because there is a sudden interruption.

One man's theory is another's nonsense: none of this interpretation may be 'true' in the sense of piously divining Shakespeare's 'intentions'. Words change their overtones over time; the temperaments of interpreters differ. We try to catch what Shakespeare might have meant, but there is sometimes much to be gained from going our own way, taking him forward with us rather than peering back across the centuries. And the fact is, this exchange started with the silvery moon and ended with a naked sword.

The man who bursts in unannounced, 'good Egeus', starts by routinely wishing his 'renowned Duke' happiness – so the man who killed the Minotaur and then turned into an anxious fiancé now has a Renaissance honorific as well. We are safe and sound in a familiar theatrical world. If Theseus is having trouble organising a marriage, it is nothing compared to Egeus, for whom the question has led to something far worse, a horribly insubordinate daughter. This is Hermia – a shock for the scholars in the original audience, by the way, since Hermia was a famous whore in antiquity much loved by Aristotle. Here she could only be that in her father's mind: for us she is about to become a heroine.

Egeus's unceremonious arrival forces a director to consider the practical context. Is this a normal thing to do in Theseus's world? Are there guards? Is this a big public gathering, or something smaller, like an open hour or levée when the ruler receives plaintiffs? Or perhaps Egeus is presuming on his position as one of the great and good to break in on a *tête-à-tête*. Theseus's reply:

> Thanks, good Egeus. What's the news with thee?

is inconclusive; 'thee', friendlier than 'you', but no more of a welcome than 'thanks'. We are free to choose.

Regardless, Egeus takes the floor. Perhaps he has some legal training, that badge of the establishment: we suddenly seem to be in a courtroom. He has brought with him both client and accused, who have presumably agreed to the arbitration, and are now identified for Theseus and for us:[2]

> Stand forth, Demetrius! . . .
> Stand forth, Lysander!

Seemingly unstoppable, Egeus will combine lucidity with passion, as if he knows he has one chance only to make his points.

---

2 Curiously, in the contemporary texts these two lines were stage directions to the actors. Their absence from the dialogue would have had the effect of wrecking the verse and leaving both men harder to identify.

Already part of Shakespeare's design seems to be to use familiar names anarchically, as with Hermia. Demetrius was a famously bad name, last appearing in Shakespeare as that of a rapist in *Titus Andronicus*. We are quite unlikely to be troubled by something else many Elizabethans would have known, that Egeus was actually the name of Theseus's father, like him a seducer and abandoner of many women. These heroes. The son was the father's undoing: Egeus hurled himself to his death because Theseus, returning to Athens after killing the Minotaur, forgot to change the mourning sails on his ships for those of victory, so that his father thought he was dead.

Philostrate, like Egeus, is from Chaucer's *Knight's Tale*. The name of Hermia's hero, Lysander, is linked to Alexander. And to complete the mischief, Theseus raped Helen, whose namesake is waiting to come on.

His interpretation of events is that while Demetrius has pro-
ceeded with old-fashioned correctness in securing his consent to
marry Hermia, Lysander has gone a devious way to achieve the
same thing. Lysander has been candid only with Hermia herself,
sending her a comically impressive variety of trinkets, poetic *billets-
doux* and love-tokens –

> EGEUS: . . . bracelets of thy hair, rings, gauds, conceits,
>   Knacks, trifles, nosegays, sweetmeats . . .

– and he has also, cutting a somewhat medieval figure, sung songs
beneath her window. All these young man's tactics can suggest to
their seniors insincerity rather than its opposite – particularly if they
have forgotten their own courtships. As far as her father can see,
Hermia's head has been turned as surely as if she had been given
drugs (nowadays it would be that as well). He has been quite
unnerved by all the sexual directness; it is affecting his language, so
that it is Hermia's 'bosom' Lysander has 'bewitched', and he
obsessively refers to her as 'my child' – three times, and twice within
three lines – as if Lysander were up to something illegal as well as
undesirable. Presumably, had the more socially adept Demetrius
done the same thing, Egeus would have found a different word for
his daughter, such as 'young woman of good judgment'.

Egeus's speech, the least equivocal in the play so far, has a
powerful swing to match the paranoid force of its feeling. It is
hyperbole with blood racing through it, full of the furtive suspicion
that a man's womenfolk should be locked up as tightly as his house
and goods. Left to themselves, predatory young males, particularly
if they are musical, will happily ruin impressionable daughters. In
this way an older man condemns himself as well as a new
generation. Egeus's assault has fine verbal choices for the actor:
Lysander is referred to simply as the neuter 'this', and he has not so
much stolen as 'filch'd' Hermia's heart. We look at the girl listening
to it all – mute, and, as the text later demands, small of stature – and
wonder if 'stubborn harshness' is really part of her nature. Her
father resolves his argument with chilling simplicity. Careful to
renew his compliment to 'my gracious Duke', he asks for

> . . . the ancient privilege of Athens . . . ,

which is to give his daughter to any uncongenial suitor he pleases

> Or to her death, according to our law

– a sentence, it seems, with immediate effect and no right of appeal.

This shocking killer punch, sounding like sweet reasonableness, tells us something of the society we are in, and, in view of Shakespeare's intentions, the audacity of his counterpoint. It certainly makes Egeus easy to dislike, but the fact is that he knows no better: he is the victim of his education in that society, whose unpredictability will ultimately baffle him. The calmer and more commonplace the actor can make him here, the more worrying. Certainly the traditional roaring Shakespearian father, benightedly huffing and puffing, serves this play no better than a bombastic Duke Frederick in *As You Like It* or a pain-free Leonato in *Much Ado About Nothing*. For all his passionate bigotry, Egeus is, above all, hurt, made lonely by a breach in nature, and he appeals for Theseus's support not so much spitefully as out of a need for reassurance that the world is after all round.[3] In a certain sense the play will prove him right about Lysander: although the younger man may be on the side of the angels, the confusion he will unwittingly cause symbolises an instability at the heart of his romanticism.

From Theseus's point of view, Egeus's outburst may be an annoying interruption to his own courtship, or he may feel some relief at the diversion: negotiating with Hippolyta is less easy than settling routine matters of life and death. Apprised of the facts, he takes his cue with practised ease, and if he was affronted by the intrusion he quickly gets over it. Hermia seems to him a pretty little thing. It is no more than professional gentleness to explain to her that she has absolutely no identity without her father's approval, and that she risks mutilation if she fails to court it. To do this, he comes up with a little simile:

> To you your father should be as a god,
> One that composed your beauties, yea and one
> To whom you are but as a form in wax,
> By him imprinted, and within his power
> To leave the figure or disfigure it.

This is of a piece with the withered stepdame; no more than half-poetic, its violence only just concealed by the verse. To the warlike Theseus, genetics are a matter of a great piece of metal thumping into unformed human clay, either branding it with its own label or

---

3. Look at the father in the 1999 play and film *East is East*, trying to hold his family to their traditional faith, for a contemporary parallel; take away the satire and you have Egeus.

bashing it out of shape like a condemned motor car. All the same, Hermia must in fairness have a chance to speak, the chance her father has denied her.

She turns out to be more than he bargained for. With her first words she brings about the play's second broken verse line, and, like Hippolyta's, it checks Theseus's easy rhythm. In fact she could hardly be less metrically cooperative:

> THESEUS: Demetrius is a worthy gentleman.
> HERMIA: So is Lysander.

By using a verse opportunity in this way, Hermia briefly sets the terms, even dictating Theseus's manner a little: to keep things going he will swiftly have to match her sharpness, even if he would have preferred to cajole. The alternative, an embarrassing silence, would give her more credit than she is due. So back he comes –

> . . . In himself he is

– and, technically at least, takes the initiative. Rather than getting into a discussion of a man's intrinsic worth which he might lose, Theseus stays in charge by repeating the patriarchal argument:

> But in this kind, wanting your father's voice,
> The other must be held the worthier.
> HERMIA: I would my father looked but with my eyes.
> THESEUS: Rather your eyes must with his judgment look.

However urbane he has tried to be, this is a crackling little argument between equals. There is not only an antithesis in the final exchange, but double meanings. By 'eyes' Theseus means Hermia's appetite, so in need of controlling, but for us the word suggests her unique human intelligence and right to choose. To Theseus, such wayward-ness is meaningless next to a father's 'judgment' – which to him means wisdom, but to us sounds like a legal sentence.

Language, it seems, can be readily manipulated to reinforce authority. Invalidated by like-minded older men, Hermia sees that she will have to play their music if she is to achieve anything. Politely admitting her unworthiness to speak for herself at all –

> I do entreat your grace to pardon me

– she nevertheless invites Theseus to call a spade a spade:

> . . . I beseech your grace that I may know
> The worst that may befall me in this case

> If I refuse to wed Demetrius.

This is a tough one, a leading question publicly fired at a professional diplomat – and in front of his fiancée, who says nothing and whose views are unknown. To his credit, Theseus doesn't shirk it:

> . . . to die the death . . .

Even as he speaks, however, the girl's candour, and her tactical courtesy, has forced him into a compromise. There is a third way that Egeus neglected to mention, if indeed he knew about it: instead of marriage to Demetrius or execution, Hermia could be forced into a nunnery, and there

> abjure
> For ever the society of men.

We look at Egeus, to see what he thinks of this. Has Theseus just invented it? It could be a face-saver, since Egeus, for all his outrage, is surely not that rare thing, a father who positively wants to see his daughter die. Not that the devotional life seems much better: he will surely agree with Theseus's next point, that for a woman to have to do without a man, and instead

> endure the livery of a nun,
> For aye to be in shady cloister mew'd

is much the same as extinction.

We need to pause again: within only sixty-five lines, important decisions have had to be made beyond the strict limits of the text. What did Theseus and Hippolyta and anyone else think of Egeus's sudden arrival; what was the effect on Theseus of Hermia's unexpected toughness; what does Egeus now think of Theseus's emendation; what does the silent Hippolyta think about everything? Unlike in the cinema, a theatre audience's eyes roam at will, doing their own editing: the actors mustn't be caught out in a vague attitude. In any play, to make all these discreet details visible is to respect the spectator's intelligence: it is easy to forget that every character, however 'minor', is on show, all the time.

By this time Lysander will either be bursting to speak or determined not to; while for some reason Demetrius, though on the right side of the argument, contributes nothing. Feeling a manly alliance behind him – Demetrius, like Egeus, will agree about the absurdity of virginity – Theseus laddishly satirises the devotional life, in which a Hermia would have to deny her 'youth' and 'blood', and instead

> . . . live a barren sister all your life,
> Chanting faint hymns to the cold fruitless moon.

This eloquent improvisation surely comes from the heart – the moon seems not to be favoured by Theseus – but any good politician knows that even the rankest devil must be given its due. So, of course, parenthetically,

> Thrice blessed they that master so their blood
> To undergo such maiden pilgrimage

– even if Theseus's own view is that a flower is made for plucking:

> . . . earthlier happy is the rose distill'd
> Than that which, withering on the virgin thorn,
> Grows, lives and dies in single blessedness.

It is quite an adroit manoeuvre, nominally embracing a woman's right to choose while insisting that she shouldn't exercise it. It has also allowed him to close his argument in full rhetorical throttle.

Faced with such elegant suggestiveness, Hermia reinterprets it for what it is – the law of property. She borrows legal vocabulary to debase it: if she granted a 'virgin patent' to Demetrius it would be like putting her head into his 'yoke' as if she were an ox. Just as she gave 'judgment' and 'eyes' a quite different meaning from that of the men, she takes another of their words, 'sovereignty', to round off her argument, giving it an alliterative smack Theseus would be proud of. Demetrius, bluntly, is a man to whom

> My soul consents not to give sovereignty.

In her refusal to negotiate at all, Hermia is closing the door on her own fate. Her linguistic resource and utter resolve have defeated Theseus: with no opening into which to insinuate, he is left with brute force. Faced with the stuff of martyrs, he must hate her at this moment: all he can do is confirm a deadline, a hopeless thing to do to Joan of Arc. He manages one gloss, involving Hippolyta whether she likes it or not. The fateful moment four days hence when Hermia will have to decide will also be

> The sealing day betwixt my love and me
> For everlasting bond of fellowship

– one when all good people will surely be thinking of strengthening society's bonds, not immolating themselves. He is careful to re-emphasise that Hermia still has the face-saving option

> . . . on Diana's altar to protest
> For aye austerity and single life.

It is a request dressed up as a concession: four days are enough for a mind to change with dignity, and it will be a tribute to his exemplary restraint.

Essentially the interview is finished, with Theseus at least having shown a degree of professionalism while Hermia stripped him of his euphemistic camouflage. As it did with Hippolyta, his picturesque talk has fallen away to reveal an iron fist. Egeus's 'child', meanwhile, has proved far more effective than anyone expected; she of course has the theatre audience behind her now, and they will want to be shot of the others and spend more time with her.

However, with the company turning away, Demetrius at last speaks up, the first to do so without an invitation from Theseus. He is almost comically inadequate:

> Relent, sweet Hermia; and Lysander, yield
> Thy crazed title to my certain right.

It is quite a surprise, this singular lack of eloquence from the chosen fiancé; somehow middle-aged, with the clank of weaponry in it. The effort of counterpointing craziness with legal authority seems to wear him out: he will say nothing more for himself until he pursues Hermia into the woods the following night.

In fact this speech undoes him, since it authorises Lysander to break decorum and speak as well. In extreme contrast, he does something almost as brave as Hermia earlier – he makes a joke:

> You have her father's love, Demetrius;
> Let me have Hermia's. Do you marry him.

Everyone freezes, not necessarily without admiration. In this capital court, effrontery like this could send Lysander to execution at Hermia's side; but Theseus, glad to have the heat off him, lets Egeus deal with it. However, the father, like his protégé, has shot his bolt; with the same stiffness he does nothing beyond repeating his position. He calls Lysander 'scornful' and throws in a three-line flurry of possessiveness – five 'my's or 'mine's – and finally turns his daughter into a thing with a chillingly territorial verb:

> . . . and all my right of her
> I do *estate* unto Demetrius.

So just as it was closing, the argument has been forced open by
Demetrius's posturing, Lysander's presence of mind, and the sheer
unpleasantness of the father's argument. It is also, immediately,
frozen: for new blood to flow into it, a more expansive voice needs
to be heard. So, having winded the opposition with a joke, Lysander
swings easily into his case, as logical as Egeus but far more
congenial. Next to Demetrius, he sounds inspired: Hermia has
obviously chosen the right man, if wit and passion make the right
man. Equally at home with practicalities as with serenades, he is, like
her, prepared to argue from the same base as the enemy; but he also
engages with it in a way that Hermia, in her obduracy, wouldn't. As
far as social credentials go, his family is as good as Demetrius's, and
his bank balance as healthy –

> I am, my lord, as well derived as he;
> As well possessed. My love is more than his,
> My fortunes every way as fairly ranked

– and at the heart of the matter is the fact that not only is his love
greater, but it is returned. In all reason, the case should be open and
shut:

> Why should not I then prosecute my right?

Also he has something up his sleeve, a big card Demetrius perhaps
feared he might play, a possible reason he was not more forthcoming
himself. Lysander lets it be known that his rival is already involved
with one Helena, the daughter of a man (or woman) called Nedar.[4]
Demetrius has, in fact,

> . . . won her soul, and she, sweet lady, dotes
> Devoutly dotes, dotes in idolatry
> Upon this spotted and inconstant man.

Here is the scene's big hinge: amused, the audience once again pans
round the company to see what they think of it. There are a number
of possibilities, most of them to do with whether Egeus and
Demetrius saw the accusation coming. If Demetrius was confident
that his secret was safe, he will probably have left Egeus in the dark:
otherwise Egeus might have been less determined to have him as a

---

4. Most probably a man. Shakespeare very rarely writes about mothers and daughters: in his
world young men have both fathers and mothers and women mainly fathers.

son-in-law – better surely to find someone who was free. If so, Demetrius's bad faith has blown up in his face. But perhaps the two men's clubbish compact has been more ruthless than that: in this masculine world, the fact of a seduced and heartbroken girl may be neither here nor there next to a young man's need to make a satisfactory match. However, if that were so, Lysander's point would have little weight; and he would hardly have made it unless he thought it would put a wedge between Demetrius and his patron. These decisions give the audience a chance to sense whether or not there is any decency lurking in a system that cheerfully countenances execution for independently minded young women.

The other critical witness is Theseus, of course. Unwillingly brought back into the argument, he faces another problem; what's more, it seems to be his turn to speak. His utterance is a little ambiguous, or unsettled. Now that he thinks of it, he did hear about this business of Demetrius and Helena –

And with Demetrius thought to have spoke thereof

– but it slipped his mind at this busy time, even during the last few minutes spent dealing with the nub of the case. This was a little careless, to say the least, but such are the pressures of government. He begins to break the scene up, not perhaps out of indifference but because there is a slight risk of his looking a fool, caught with one ducal foot in Egeus's and Demetrius's leaky boat:

But, Demetrius, come,
And come, Egeus. You shall go with me.
I have some private schooling for you both.

It sounds like a reproach, as if the two of them were about to be treated, like children, to some frank words on how they have gone about things. And perhaps some softer bargain could be struck in private which will make Theseus look better in Hippolyta's eyes and his own – better too for the true young lovers, who may secretly have impressed him a little. As is the way with politicians, categorical public statements prepare the ground for backroom negotiation. Let me be absolutely clear about this, he says: whatever route Demetrius has taken to Hermia, he has Egeus's blessing and therefore Theseus's endorsement:

For you, fair Hermia, look you arm yourself
To fit your fancies to your father's will . . .

– otherwise the law is the law,

> Which by no means we may extenuate.

Then he returns more gently to Egeus and Demetrius, as if to reassure them that their 'schooling' will be no more than

> . . . some business
> Against our nuptial . . .

followed by a little discussion

> Of something nearly that concerns yourselves.

He has kept everyone in their place; first the men, then Hermia, then the men again, a little confused now as to what he means. Lysander, impossible to deal with except as part of Hermia, is pointedly ignored. There is also the matter of Hippolyta, and of getting off the stage; so slipped in at the end is a hint that, whatever she feels about what she has witnessed, part of her job is to maintain a good face:

> Come, my Hippolyta; what cheer, my love?

Perhaps he has a deadlock to loosen there as well.

We never learn the outcome of this interview. Egeus, silent now that the high ground has slipped away from him, will later return to the action much chastened. As for Hippolyta, Egeus's commandeering of the scene left her in suspended animation, a lightly smoking gun at most. Because she was so little acknowledged, the audience should have been encouraged to keep as sharp an eye on her as on the rest. She was certainly in Theseus's peripheral vision: hence the moment when he smoothly denounced the celibate life, then judiciously gave due credit to its followers, and then asked her to be cheerful. The hints that he felt her eye trained speculatively on him were small, but, like other such details, worth much.

Put simply, Theseus has allowed the play to happen, both by upholding Egeus and by proposing its four-day span towards a new moon and a new life. With his departure the clock starts: now that the young hero and heroine are alone, things will presumably move quickly.

When their not so distant cousins, Romeo and Juliet, first met at the Capulets' ball, their reaction to each other, far from hesitancy, shyness or any other commonplace, was to improvise a perfect sonnet together. The music of Hermia and Lysander as they face their crisis may be shallower and less devotional, but they too start a literary dialogue that nearly does the same thing. Their language becomes less rather than more 'realistic': where you might expect a gasping mix of shock, incredulity and anger, poetry forms, as a postponement of the problem in hand. Where Egeus had no difficulty in directly expressing his feelings, these two extrapolate, saying nothing specific about what they have just experienced. The play seems to be changing its nature.

Lysander's formal opening is elegant and flattering all right, but far less brilliant than what he has just done with the assembled company:

> How now, my love? Why is your cheek so pale?
> How chance the roses there do fade so fast?

It is oddly off the point: the wit who suggested at the throne of judgment that Demetrius should marry Egeus is now asking his lover, under virtual sentence of death, what the matter is. We need to view this judiciously. At this stage in his career Shakespeare is often less interested in the minute logic of individual reactions than in accumulating stylistic layers in his story. For these purposes, his speakers get the loan of his fluency: rather than 'expressing themselves', they are really swelling an orchestral effect.

However, through this technicality – to the actors' relief – runs the thread of Shakespeare's ordinary wisdom. As well as suggesting the theme of a poem they can compose together, Lysander's question is as human as asking someone in a traffic accident if they're all right. Some problems are too big for language, and what confronts these two, in a possibly new and impulsive relationship, has defeated them for a moment. Adversarially brilliant in company, they are having trouble adjusting alone, paralysed for the time behind self-conscious diction.

Hermia's reply is poetically perfect but still aslant the problem. As far as the roses in her cheeks go, she swiftly obliges:

> Belike for want of rain, which I could well
> Beteem them from the tempest of my eyes.

It is very felicitous. These two have their own kind of intimacy: the long winter nights ahead will be no problem if they can improvise together like this. They continue to rely on what they are good at to reassure each other. In one way it is comic that Lysander should use such a moment to sound off at great and beautiful length –

> Ay me, for aught that I could ever read,
> Could ever hear by tale or history,
> The course of true love never did run smooth

– but the truth is that he and Hermia are trying to write themselves into the history books. Lorenzo and Jessica in *The Merchant of Venice* do the same thing, invoking Troilus and Cressida, Pyramus and Thisbe, and Medea and Aeson, while an interracial scandal swirls around them.

Much as when spoken dialogue breaks into operatic music, poetry relieves the lovers' distress and celebrates what solid ground they have. As if in a chivalrous game of tennis, Hermia is allowed three fine returns of serve:

> LYSANDER: But either it was different in blood –
> HERMIA: O cross! Too high to be enthralled to low.
> LYSANDER: Or else misgraffed in respect of years –
> HERMIA: O spite! –Too old to be engaged to young.
> LYSANDER: Or else it stood upon the choice of friends –
> HERMIA: O hell! To choose love by another's eyes.

The actress, still adapting to the stylised form, may feel that each of these thoughts should be distinct from the last, played with its own heat and colour; but sustaining the pattern is as important as exploring the variations. In any case, Hermia is then massively overruled: as Lysander sees it, the world being so against them, a love like theirs can only be

> Swift as a shadow, short as any dream,
> Brief as the lightning in the collied night . . .
> And ere a man hath power to say Behold,
> The jaws of darkness do devour it up;
> So quick bright things come to confusion.

It is startlingly beautiful, but unhelpful: Lysander is fulfilling his role as masculine interpreter but not his obligation to rescue in a crisis. Perhaps Hermia senses this. Her fatalistic reply is drained of poetry, even banal:

> If then true lovers have been ever crossed,
> It stands as an edict in destiny.
> Then let us teach our trial patience
> Because it is a customary cross . . .

She who faced death with implacability, has, for lack of a plan, relapsed into its poor relation, stoicism. Nothing to be done – there is only death, spinsterhood or Demetrius. Their devices have failed them.

Only inspired action will help them now. In fact Hermia knows this: in a way, her deflation restores traditional sexual balance. And in fact Lysander has an idea, which has either come to him as he versified or was already up his sleeve, like his exposure of Demetrius. Seven leagues away (twenty-one miles) he has a childless widowed aunt, rich and inclined to be on the side of youth: she will surely harbour them as runaways and help them to marry secretly, since for some unexplained reason the 'sharp Athenian law' doesn't extend to her house. All they need to do is to rendezvous a little out of town the following night, Hermia presumably having managed to slip away from house arrest, and camp out in the woods as the first stage of their escape.[5]

The gallant surprise of Lysander's plot, and the existence in the world of such kindly relatives, seems almost to change Hermia's character. Certainly, her excitement gives her a new literary role; the responsive girl matching him with her passionate loyalty, her poetic variety equalling his practical ingenuity. Lysander's strength has made her, first of all, sturdy –

> I swear to thee by Cupid's strongest bow,
> By his best arrow with the golden head

– but her fierce commitment is matched by gentleness:

> By the simplicity of Venus' doves . . .

She intuits the mystery that makes the world go round –

> By that which knitteth souls and prospers loves

– but does not forget the unlucky: her love is the deeper for knowing that Dido burned herself to death at the departure of Aeneas. Finally, she has humour –

> By all the vows that ever men have broke,
> In number more than ever women spoke

5. Lysander's reference to the 'morn of May' they once observed with Helena introduces an interesting little pattern in the play: its shine should unobtrusively appear in the playing, emphasising the bacchanalian side of things. May games were an excuse for young and old to rush into the woods for the night, and it was said that only a fractional number of the virgins who went in came out again. This festival wasn't restricted to May: it could also have happened at midsummer, a time already associated with magic, the presence of spirits and the sealing of love affairs.

– and the playful cadence sets up a simple promise:

> In that same place thou hast appointed me
> Tomorrow truly will I meet with thee.

Halfway through her virtuoso wedding vow, she has also served the play's style by shifting into the rhyming couplets on which the remainder of the scene, and indeed much of the four lovers' action, rests. It was discreet: although the first rhyme – 'doves' and 'loves' – was audible, it was undistracting, slipped in while the listener was waiting to hear what point she was making.

By speaking of literary performances and roles I don't mean that there has been any insincerity. The deep self-consciousness they share is more creative than not, and their affection is beyond doubt. But their style gives early notice of a great challenge facing the four young actors who will sustain so much of the play. They will always speak with great energy, but also, most of the time, much formality – and with exceptional metrical regularity. Just as critics have scrupled to individualise them, they have declared that this is Shakespeare's device to distance us from any real pain the characters might suffer; however, this conceit is no use at all to the actors. Rather, they have to believe that they are people who always speak in this way, instinctively forming their feelings into poetic shapes, well able to complete their thoughts with a rhyming word found a split second before it is spoken. It is their form of jargon: as natural as whistling, and their enjoyment of it is, mercifully, generally free of self-satisfaction. The play will insist more and more on the technical discipline; if the actors can get into this habit of mind and also take care of their breathing, it will become manageable and even triumphant.

A scholar who has squirmed at Shakespeare's cavalier use of mythological names might now be startled by the arrival of a character named after Helen of Troy, but clearly less lucky in love.[6] It is not quite clear why she arrives. Hermia's greeting –

> God speed, fair Helena! Whither away?

– suggests that she is en route somewhere, just passing by chance: but as far as anyone can be sure of Elizabethan nuances, 'whither away' can be addressed to someone heading straight towards you, while 'God speed' didn't carry the suggestion of goodbye that it does

---

6. To the Elizabethans the name of Helen suggested either a great beauty or a great whore, and the play will prove Helena neither. It is in fact a name that Shakespeare will use again, as a marker for constancy to the point of suffocation, in *All's Well That Ends Well*.

now. It is quite a critical point for the actress, of course: getting your first entrance right gives you confidence for the evening. Is Helena seeking out her friends to break her bad news to them, or simply drifting through their eyeline?

Either way, she immediately has to deal with their aggravating happiness. So – a third possibility: she is looking for them and then veers away, to be called back by Hermia. Given a cue – her 'fairness' – she immediately falls in with their music. The rhythms of this new instrument are, so to speak, more rhythmic, the rhymes when they come more pronounced, the end-stops more emphatic:

> HELENA: Call you me fair? That 'fair' again unsay.
> Demetrius loves your fair – O happy fair!

Helena's rattling style, the thoughts tumbling over each other, is that of someone catching up with their emotions: her ingenuity reflects a state of shock. In another way, it is typical of her: she is not always as intelligible as her friends, and will become the play's most garrulous and frequently obscure speaker.

Her opening paean to Hermia's attributes is somewhat overwhelming, and takes a little following; it also seems free of any jealousy of the aggressive kind. Hermia's eyes are lodestars to help lovers navigate the night, she says; her voice is like the lark that tells the countryman spring has come. That is clear enough; but as she links Hermia's beauty with infection, her text becomes a little clotted – hampered as well by a disagreement among editors as to whether she says 'your words I catch' or 'yours would I catch'. The sense then wobbles when she matches 'ear' with 'voice'. It would have been easier to understand if she had matched 'voice' with 'voice' as she then does 'eye' with 'eye' and 'tongue' with 'tongue':

> Sickness is catching; O, were favour so,
> Yours would I catch, fair Hermia, ere I go.
> My ear should catch your voice, my eye your eye,
> My tongue should catch your tongue's sweet melody.

She feels that the best means of negotiating any mistrust of her rival is wit. Once again a duet is begun, this time for two women:

> O, teach me how you look, and with what art
> You sway the motion of Demetrius' heart.

Helena's insistence on a subject is reminiscent of Lysander's announcement of true love's course. Hermia, who might not have chosen this game, responds in a way that could close the argument:

> I frown upon him, yet he loves me still.

But Helena is up to that, and keeps it alive:

> O that your frowns would teach my smiles such skill.

In contrast to Hermia's and Lysander's rally, there are four antiphonal exchanges, not three, and the language is plainer; in the fourth Hermia suddenly defends herself quite firmly (though the familiar 'Helen' keeps matters friendly):

> His folly, Helen, is no fault of mine.

However, she is finessed again – the only advantage Helena has is her speed of thought:

> HELENA: None but your beauty; would that fault were mine.

A point of character, or perhaps atmosphere: these young people seem free of their elders' culture of blame. As Helena describes how she has been traded for Hermia, she attributes no manoeuvring to her friend: she once uses the word 'art', conventionally, and it causes no offence. Her lack of a suspicious mind is as striking as her constancy, come what may, to Demetrius. She knows that Hermia attracts without effort but with no particular instinct for exploiting the fact. It is only what she is, not what she might have done, that has hurt: real loss of trust between them is reserved, hilariously, for later in the play.

If Hermia and Lysander sense that Helena's elaborations are a sign of misery, they could be a little more tactful. Instead, they tell her their idyllic plan for escape:

> HERMIA: Take comfort. He no more shall see my face.
>   Lysander and myself will fly this place.

Hermia does emphasise that it is an unspecified nightmare rather than romance that is sending them away. Observing the prevailing rule of paradox, she pretends it is all Lysander's fault:

> Before the time I did Lysander see
> Seemed Athens as a paradise to me.
> O then what graces in my love do dwell
> That he hath turned a heaven unto a hell?

Lysander is still less sensitive. Wallowing a little, he constructs a gorgeous scenario for the elopement – its unnecessary loveliness, incidentally, prefigures the language of the forest inhabitants they will soon be meeting:

> Tomorrow night, when Phoebe doth behold
> Her silver visage in the wat'ry glass,
> Decking with liquid pearls the bladed grass,
> A time that lovers' flights doth still conceal –
> Through Athens' gates have we devised to steal.

These young people, warm as they are, do have a streak of sublime thoughtlessness. Hermia now does a still more wonderful and oblivious thing. She urges Helena to take comfort from the fact that she and Lysander so love each other that they are about to abandon her for ever – even heading for a place which was once sacred to Helena as well:

> And in the wood where often you and I
> Upon faint primrose beds were wont to lie,
> Emptying our bosoms of their counsel sweet,
> There my Lysander and myself shall meet . . .

They mean to cut all ties, including with her:

> And thence from Athens turn away our eyes
> To seek new friends and stranger companies.
> Farewell, sweet playfellow . . .

The unfolding news, thick with Hermia's pride and love, is unlikely to cheer Helena up. 'Playfellow' seems to consign her to the kindergarten, and being left alone with an annoyed Demetrius will be only a marginal improvement on solitude. Lysander's perfunctory goodbye –

> Helena, adieu;
> As you on him, Demetrius dote on you

– also lacks something, since for Demetrius to be civil to Helena, let alone doting, would be a start. Meanwhile Hermia is absorbed in her exciting plans once more, organising every detail. A brief separation from Lysander will both disarm suspicion and sharpen their fiery feelings:

> We must starve our sight
> From lovers' food till morrow deep midnight.

Their single friend could not have been more effectively excluded, radiant happiness pushed into her face like a cushion.

As their rapid footsteps die away, so does the slight literary competitiveness in the scene; and as always when Shakespeare's stage clears to leave a single figure, we expect confidences. But Helena yields up little that's new, and nothing at all about something we would like to know – how exactly Demetrius handled matters when he fell for Hermia. Instead, she says it all again, much in her previous style:

How happy some o'er other some can be!

In fact, she starts better than she goes on: her first three couplets at least express some sour grapes. It is just not fair, she is known to be as lovely as Hermia, Demetrius is an ass even though she can't help loving him. It is a welcome touch of petty reality after all the poetry. Then things veer off a little. It seems to be characteristic of her to look for a philosophical formula to ease her feelings: her shot at this produces ten lines that need footnotes, as if she keeps exploring one abstract and then abandoning it for another. First:

Things base and vile, holding no quantity,
Love can transpose to form and dignity.

What are these 'things'? Does she mean the erring Demetrius, still adored despite his mistake? Or herself (she was the subject of the previous sentence)? Or even Hermia, no lovelier in God's eyes than she is? Then, another pronouncement:

Love looks not with the eyes, but with the mind,
And therefore is winged Cupid painted blind.

Is this a good thing, since imaginative love is more profound than physical? The opposite, perhaps:

Nor hath love's mind of any judgment taste.

And then:

Wings and no eyes figure unheedy haste.

This is getting difficult: in Helena's mind, is beauty irrelevant next to spiritual grace, or the other way round, and which of the two is it that she, as opposed to Hermia, has? And who is at fault? If there is a real thread of thought here rather than an experimental cluster of conceits, I don't know what it is – at least not without going over it several times, which there is no time to do in the theatre.

The speech could be played in a way that capitalises on this muddle – Helena confused and casting about this way and that – but it will be difficult to do it without laying waste to the verse. Or, for the first time in the play, there is the possibility of a cut: some foliage could be removed and only the more vivid couplets about Cupid kept in. To have written a play such as this at thirty is a staggering thing; it would be odd if there weren't a little overwriting, a few poetic spasms that outstay their welcome.

Mercifully, Helena comes back to us in the end: like Lysander, she has, or finds, a plan, as a soliloquiser should. She will simultaneously repay Demetrius's treachery and make him attend to her again by telling tales:

> I will go tell him of fair Hermia's flight.
> Then to the wood will he tomorrow night
> Pursue her ... [7]

Perhaps, she thinks, Demetrius will appreciate her generous efforts on his behalf, even in the end come to love her for them, feeling that a good pal is better than an unattainable beauty. In any case, being with him as the bearer of bad news will be preferable to not seeing him at all. It is not quite clear from her last lines –

> But herein mean I to enrich my pain,
> To have his sight thither and back again

– whether she intends to wave him off and then wait to welcome him home, bedraggled and undeceived. More likely, she will go with him. This would not be quite the mature Shakespearian heroine's decision to pack her bag and head into the unknown like Rosalind, Viola or Julia in *The Two Gentlemen* – or even the helpless possessiveness of Helena's namesake in *All's Well* – but a pleasantly petty calculation. Imagining Helena trailing after Demetrius through the bracken as he chases loudly after the runaways, we have to wonder, to use her own words, whether her love's mind of any judgment tastes, but we might also admire her for it.

★

Shakespeare is much praised for his long last scenes, multiple threads woven into a single yarn; his openings can be no less virtuosic, and the ground covered in the past two hundred and fifty lines is remarkable. When Lysander and Hermia were left alone, Egeus and Theseus disappeared from the play simply by being banished

---

7. Remarkably, Samuel Taylor Coleridge, a better poet than critic, condemns her 'ungrateful treachery' in doing this, fearing it is 'too true a picture of the lax hold that principles have on the female heart'. (This in a play that continually underlines female constancy as opposed to male.)

from their conversation; when Helena then joined Lysander and Hermia she brought a new culture with her as well as a new story. Since the mode was now romantic comedy, it didn't occur to us that she never got the important information that her friends were running away not as a picturesque choice but as a desperate emergency. That initial crisis, so alarming at the time, was no longer needed by the play.

So far as 'character' goes, we have had to snatch hints from the pitch and roll of different habits of speech. Only for a short passage in the middle, when Egeus spoke with so much passion and so little grace, did we hear the spontaneous pulse of mature Shakespearian verse. Everything else was idiosyncratic manner; the tense equivocations of Theseus, the pointed terseness of Hippolyta, the charm and self-determination of Lysander and Hermia, the odd mixture of rarefication and girl-next-door in Helena. All this was achieved through musical counterpoint, until Helena introduced a new device: the solo instrument with its narrative promise essentially no different from when Hamlet shares his secrets with us and makes his plans.

Just as his style kept changing at will, the geography has been that of Shakespeare's first, unlocalised stage, across which ideas of place scudded like passing thoughts. When Helena arrived we seemed to have moved so far from Theseus's palace that we didn't ever wonder how she'd got in. To all intents, we had moved somewhere else, much as if Hermia and Lysander, in a movie, had got on their bikes and started travelling. Now, as the scene ends, it no longer feels like ancient Greece, if it ever did. There is, however, no particular sign that the proceedings will involve the unseen world, or, despite a certain insidious comedy in the air, that they will be particularly funny.

TWO

Act 1 Scene 2

What happens next could not be more improbable or more interesting: just as the play is beginning to form itself, six working men arrive to discuss putting on a play. Breaking across Helena's rhymed couplets, they talk in the most ordinary way, with a preponderance of monosyllables. The very first line is oddly direct, entirely in context but including the audience in a new way:

> Is all our company here?

So if we are ready as well, another story is about to start.

Shakespeare often juxtaposes high rhetoric with the vocabulary of trade: watching the most elevated dramatic action, we become aware of a commonplace of life beneath it. High culture can be refuted by a word as normal as rain, as ordinary as a headache; an eloquent protagonist is regularly tripped up by someone going about their daily business, a Gravedigger, a Fool, or a Player. The second scene of *A Midsummer Night's Dream* gently helps its audience to reconsider what went before, much as in a medieval Mystery Play the high-minded Virtues were regularly routed by demotic Vices. In Theseus's spasmodically formal Court, meaning and manner strained against each other: even Hermia, who was capable of seeing things for what they were, became part of a musical trio. Now, with a pleasant rush of air, all the codes collapse like cards.

A moment later a second voice will refer to a 'scrip' – near enough the familiar word for what actors hold in their hands in order to rehearse. This theatrical reference is a subtle, cunning and habitual little trick. The wooden O of *Henry V*, Lear's great stage of fools, the poor player that life becomes for Macbeth: even in extremity Shakespeare remembers the boards under his feet, reminding us of his artifice even as he grips us with it.

The announcement by Peter Quince, a carpenter, that he holds in his hand written confirmation of the men

> thought fit through all Athens to play in our interlude before the Duke and Duchess

may be hard to understand immediately. It is quite difficult to think of Hippolyta as a Duchess, and 'interlude' is a quaintly denigrating word for the play they are planning for her. Also, Philostrate must have worked remarkably fast in rounding up possible entertainments for the great day. Although the selection process is unclear, Quince seems to be confirming that the job is theirs. His friend Nick Bottom, a weaver, translates him for us:

> First, good Peter Quince, say what the play treats on; then read the names of the actors . . .

The work chosen to charm the newly-weds is not credited with an author (the suspicion will grow that that is Quince himself) but it has a substantial and improbable title:

> 'The Most Lamentable Comedy and Most Cruel Death of Pyramus and Thisbe.'

We have four centuries of advantage here, and a guaranteed laugh. The announcement of a profound tragedy that was also a comedy would not have seemed particularly unusual to the Elizabethans. They were used to Shakespeare's contemporaries trying to have it both ways with titles such as *A Lamentable Tragedy Mixed Full of Pleasant Mirth, Containing the Life of Cambyses King of Persia*. It is, in a way, an early marketing strategy – the tragedy not too heavy, the comedy rather deep, something for everyone, and performed by a company such as the one described by Polonius in *Hamlet* – 'the only men' for 'tragical-comical-historical-pastoral, scene individable or poem unlimited'. So Bottom's reply –

> A very good piece of work, I assure you, and a merry

– is less a piece of silliness than the endorsement of a sales point. His first audience might have been more amused by the fact that the story chosen is that of two famously star-crossed lovers, well enough known to have featured in popular ballads. At such a celebration, it might go down as well as *Romeo and Juliet* at an interracial wedding.

Bottom seems to be as much in charge of events as Quince: to help Quince to 'grow to a point', he now asks the company to 'spread' themselves. They may have been eagerly crowding around, or not concentrating at all, but he at least is very serious about what comes next: the casting process should have the momentousness that, as the keenest of amateur actors, he would expect. No need for bustle, nobody will be leaving without a part: Quince's list of those 'thought fit' is precisely this group, no more nor less.

The allocation of roles in the public way that follows is almost unheard of nowadays among professionals, who generally consider their options in an inviolable privacy. Among amateurs, I dare say, as at school, it still happens, and perhaps it did in Shakespeare's company. In this context it makes possible a helpful naming of names, which Shakespeare undercuts with further mischief – though the jokes this time are more for the groundlings than the scholars. Peter Quince, sounding like a fruit, is a carpenter, and a 'quine' is a kind of wedge used by carpenters. 'Bottom' quite probably did not have its obvious meaning then, being equally familiar as the wooden core in the centre of a roll of thread used by himself as a weaver. Flute mends bellows, which would cause a church organ to make a fluting sound on its high notes. Snout takes his name from the spout of a kettle, to be found on a tinker's cart. Starveling just suggests sickliness, also the condition of his fellow-tailor Francis Feeble in *Henry IV Part 2*. A snug fit between timbers is what joiners such as Snug aim at.

The accumulated Anglo-Saxon ordinariness of the names seems to fill the air with wood-dust, the clatter of pans, bolts of fabric and particles of thread. With friendliness, too – part of the charm of all this lies in its sudden warmth, the first evidence in the play of companionship uncomplicated by romance or crisis. These men work in parallel trades, perhaps with their own professional alliances and interdependencies, and out of hours they are united by the same enthusiasms; shared effort will reveal their idiosyncrasies and, on the whole, their best sides. Character, a little compromised by style up till now, quickly blooms. Bottom, first in line, immediately demonstrates, albeit as an amateur, something of how actors express themselves. First, the snapping to diligent attention:

Ready! Name what part I am for, and proceed.

Then, having secured one of the title roles as of right, he professes an ignorance of the play which he has just described as a good piece of work and a merry. Having not quite read it, he doesn't really know what the 'lamentable comedy' calls for:

What is Pyramus, a lover or a tyrant?

Here he is like a certain kind of theatrical old-timer who speaks of 'straight' and 'character' parts, of 'juveniles' and 'fifth business', remembering such terms more easily than the names of the plays. Shakespeare himself worked in a theatre that called on its actors for their own specialities, rather as if they were tenors or baritones, Wagnerian or bel canto.

As it turns out,

A lover that kills himself, most gallant, for love

is not really Bottom's preference –

... my chief humour is for a tyrant. I could play Ercles [Hercules] rarely

– but he is at pains to reassure his colleagues that, once into Pyramus, he will break the audience's heart – let them 'look to their eyes'. He already knows which interpretative hat to wear: as Ercles you must tear a cat, whereas love scenes like these will require 'condoling', a special tender word he keeps repeating. Before relinquishing his tragic status, he takes the trouble to give them a taste of what they might have had from him as Ercles:

The raging rocks
And shivering shocks
Shall break the locks
Of prison gates ...

This is a tilt at a contemporary translation of a play about Hercules by Seneca, and its alliteration and onomatopoeia are standard enough. The style is old-fashioned, certainly, but not necessarily ridiculous, and not so far from what Shakespeare himself put into the mouth of the tragedian who comes to visit Hamlet, with his story of Pyrrhus 'Roasted in wrath and fire ... o'ersized with coagulate gore, With eyes like carbuncles'.

What the moment does require is for Bottom to show his colours a little. Is he, in fact, any good? To make him a hopeless actor is, in my opinion, a poor option; his energy is admirable, and if his delivery, like the writing, is a little outmoded, it might still earn the same respect as a cylinder recording of Henry Irving or John Barrymore does from us. It is also typical of the aspiring actor, as opposed to the successful, to be slightly out of date, since nobody has taken him in hand and shown him the better, more difficult options. Bottom's technique is impressively unapologetic; if the effect is funny, it is because it is so very different from the way he normally speaks.

Overall, in fact, Bottom is not an ass, despite his future association with that animal: his choice of 'condoling' as a lover's manner is good. His linguistic slips and malapropisms[1] are legion, but they are part of the normal repertoire of a Shakespearian comic, even if we find them less hilarious than they once were. Already he has confused Quince by instructing him to assemble the company both 'generally' (altogether) and 'man by man' (individually); he will shortly promise to 'aggravate' his voice when in fact he means to moderate it, do an actorish variant on Phoebus ('Phibbus'), and constantly set a bad example by mispronouncing 'Ninus' tomb'. From the point of view of establishing his talents, none of this matters much. What he certainly is is an enthusiast; his tendency towards arrogance and control comes from over-eagerness, and is mitigated, I would say, by a certain bonniness of disposition. His attempt from now on to take over every other actor's part is prompted by excessive zeal for the cause; and he generally falls back into line when called to order by Quince.

The bellows-mender is summoned next. Flute, by the sound of him, is not cut in the same cloth as Bottom: for a heroic actor his name is against him for a start, and it may be that the voice Quince recommends him to use is of a piece with his gifts:

> . . . you may speak as small as you will.

Much as Flute would wish his 'vein' to be the fashionable wandering knight of early Elizabethan theatre, he is more like the unfortunate at a boy's school who always has to play the woman. Not that this was a disgrace in 1595: all female parts were played by men.[2] In fact, Flute's objection to his casting marks him down as a

---

1. The term flatters him a little: 180 years were to pass before Sheridan brought this particular misapplication of language to a comic epitome in *The Rivals*. Shakespeare's efforts seem perfunctory next to the glories of Mrs Malaprop in that play; and Bottom's malapropisms are quite mild compared to those of Shakespeare's two benighted policemen, Dogberry in *Much Ado About Nothing* and Elbow the Constable in *Measure for Measure*.

2. The speciality must have been as highly respected as that of the onnagata, the female impersonator in Japanese kabuki, was about to be, not to mention the best drag artists later on. As part of an odd timeline, at the time of this play female actresses were approaching their apogee in kabuki – the Japanese government was to ban them from the stage in 1629 for their sexual notoriety, opening the way for the onnagata, who has held sway ever since. In Britain, by contrast, the Puritans closed the all-male theatres in 1642 and actresses first appeared on the public stages when they reopened in 1660.

true amateur, a civilian so anxious about his virility that he claims to have a beard on his chin when, fairly clearly, there is not so much of one as would be a problem, least of all behind the kind of mask that ladies wore to balls.

The idea of wearing such a mask, and Flute's reluctance, gives Bottom a new idea: if Thisbe's features are not to be seen, he himself could hide his condoling face behind one and lend his talents to that part as well. His demonstration this time is a little less impressive than his Ercles was:

> 'Thisne, Thisne!' 'Ah Pyramus, my lover dear, thy Thisbe dear and lady dear.'

Apart from his general tendency to approximate, it isn't clear why he says 'Thisne': perhaps it is a pet name he is devising on the spot, or more likely his attempt at a feminine lisp. The performance seems to be aimed at getting a laugh from his colleagues, and may be less amusing for Quince: this sort of horsing around doesn't much please directors, and authors even less. Bottom is only allowed a single line of it before he is tersely interrupted:

> QUINCE: No, no; you must play Pyramus, and Flute, you Thisbe.
> BOTTOM: Well, proceed.

The speed of acquiescence, with or without a minor sulk, suggests that the actor knows the limits.

So far the carpenter-turned-director is being tasked at every turn. But relief is in sight. Bottom's bottomless capacity for showing off and Flute's squeamishness are immediately contrasted with the good company behaviour of Robin Starveling and Tom Snout, who accept their casting as the lovers' parents without a murmur; Starveling with particular nobility since he is to play not even the main female part like Flute but her mother. Snug gets Lion, a funny idea to us since we may not be aware that the plot of *Pyramus and Thisbe* depends as crucially on the lion who tears Thisbe's dress as *Romeo and Juliet* does on Friar Laurence's magic potion. Anxious to please, Snug wants the part written down as he is 'slow of study'; Quince's explanation that it is the one role which surely could be improvised –

> You may do it extempore; for it is nothing but roaring

– may not entirely satisfy him. In any case, the chance of animal impressions as well as female impersonation is too much for

Bottom, who seems to have a lion speciality up his sleeve as well, and even visualises an encore:

> I will roar that I will do any man's heart good to hear me. I will roar that I will make the Duke say 'Let him roar again; let him roar again'.

For a moment Quince seems to entertain the idea of Theseus becoming overexcited in this way, but he has a flattering reason for Bottom to forgo the opportunity. Being so gifted at lions, Bottom might terrify the ladies – and in this somewhat peculiar culture that would lead Theseus, chivalrous gentleman that he isn't, to hang them all as high as Hermia. Everyone is agreed on the danger of that:

> ALL: That would hang us, every mother's son.

However, Bottom would not have got where he thinks he is today without becoming an expert on audience tactics, and he sees a way of adjusting the performance for the occasion – a gentle version of the ravening lion he could so easily have delivered:

> I will aggravate my voice so that I will roar you as gently as any sucking dove. I will roar you an 'twere any nightingale.

In other words, not a lion at all.

Quince now shows real class as an impresario. He knows that in Bottom he is dealing with a theatrical archetype: the actor who needs to be ritually persuaded even when he has every intention of accepting the job. Quince understands that leading actors sometimes need to have it purred into their ears that they are the only possible casting for some outstanding role, and that without them the production might as well be cancelled:

> QUINCE: . . . Pyramus is a sweet-faced man; a proper man as one shall see in a summer's day; a most lovely, gentlemanlike man. Therefore you must needs play Pyramus.

It works like a dream, as it generally does:

> BOTTOM: Well, I will undertake it.

As if there had never been a problem, Bottom now riffles through some practicalities: should he wear a straw-coloured beard (presumably youthful); an orange-tawny one (in which he could perhaps still double as the lion if circumstances change); one dyed red ('purple-in-grain', possibly more suitable for a virile lover), or a perfect golden-yellow one (this one dropping a hint of what he would have made of Thisbe). Presumably he has them all at the ready, in his box. It is not as silly as you might think: there were occasions when Laurence Olivier would plan a false nose or a new vocal register well before reading the play through with his colleagues. Bottom's last suggestion, a 'French-crown-colour beard' – that is, in the gold of a French coin – allows Quince an uncharacteristically salty joke about venereal disease, which can cause baldness – and which the English associate with the French as the French cordially do with the English, the Italians with the Spanish, the Russians with the Poles, and the Arabs with the Christians:

> Some of your French crowns have no hair at all . . .

This is not such a surprise. Just as Bottoms and Dogberrys make their verbal slips (Bottom is about to propose rehearsing 'obscenely' where he means 'seemly'), most Shakespearian characters, apart from the very noblest, become helpless pawns of the author if he sniffs a good *double entendre*.

On the evidence of this brief introduction, its length judged to whet the appetite, the prospect of Quince's company going into rehearsal is enticing, and its composition is fairly clear. Quince can be played avuncular and bumbling, innocently self-important or strict and obsessed, and Bottom more or less insufferable, but they are vividly differentiated, and their earnestness makes them vulnerable, as serious approaches to the theatre always are. The balance of power is judged nicely enough: Quince may be chairman, producer, director and perhaps writer, but the energies of his main actor prove that it is one thing to hold a controlling share in a dramatic society and another to handle its personalities.

There is at least a hint that Flute might be someone's son, a new arrival who has not yet earned his spurs. The patient rump of the company, Snug, Snout and Starveling, has fallen into what is probably a characteristic formation. Their silence sometimes leads directors who don't mind patronising the working man to see them as disobliging or dim, but the fact is they could hardly have got a word in anyway, and may all be temperamentally disinclined to enter into artistic debates which always end in the same way.

Having opened with bravura, the scene ends with breathless fur-tiveness. Overriding all of Quince's other anxieties is the fear that, in these days before copyright, his winning idea might be stolen. Work this good must be kept secret, so his tactical plan is to meet at the Duke's Oak, out of town, deep into the next evening – even though that may not necessarily be what the others, for all their enthusiasm, would choose:

> . . . meet me in the palace wood a mile without the town by moonlight. There will we rehearse; for if we meet in the city we shall be dogged with company, and our devices known.

You would think he had devised a new story line for *Star Wars,* or some other high-grossing enterprise so nervous of 'leaks' that the actors are only supplied with the pages that concern them and asked to put them through the shredder at the end of the day's work.

There is no evidence yet as to whether this version will be good, not a line having been heard, but it should at least be getting the benefit of the doubt. And Quince, in his quietly insistent way, has won the day in all respects. He has made no concessions on casting or script, and even Bottom, probably his main investment, is satisfied. As the group scuttles off to catch the last bus home, they are, in Bottom's eyes at least, like dashing pirates, their cloaks flung around their faces, uttering mysterious passwords:

> Take pains; be perfect. Adieu . . . At the Duke's oak we meet . . .
> Enough. Hold, or cut bowstrings.

There will be many times with *A Midsummer Night's Dream* when you ask yourself, What is it, what exactly, that causes such delight and excitement, what is the secret of the play's profound charm? It is with this scene, marvellously stuffed with the real matter of life, that it begins to open like a flower, and its audience becomes infected by the author's joy and impatience. At the point when we should surely be rushing three miles into the forest after Hermia and Lysander, we have been deflected sideways. Now Quince has energised his friends into heading for the same forest, suddenly reported to be only one mile away. There, presumably, they will collide with the lovers whose story, surely, is to be resolved there. Not a chance. The flowering has only just begun: when both parties arrive at that apparently featureless place, they will be stopped in their tracks by something absolutely astonishing.

THREE

Act 2 Scene 1

In *Romeo and Juliet* Mercutio, off the cuff, conjures up Queen Mab, the fairies' midwife, who gallops through the night in a chariot made of a hazelnut. Its wheels, coverings and whip are the legs of spiders, the wings of grasshoppers and a cricket's bone; it is drawn by atoms with bridles made of moonlight. For a moment the invisible becomes rapturously real: barely thirty, Shakespeare is indulging an uncontrollable talent for language, wild, gleeful and fantastic. It just pours out of him: at this point, if you asked for a quick fourteen lines about the jaws of a stag beetle, it would be in your hand within minutes, in rhyme and metre.

Now he goes further and conjures an entire fairy kingdom out of thin air. The astonishing world of the forest near Athens in *A Midsummer Night's Dream* owes little to any literary precedents, only lightly drawing on English folklore for Puck, a little bit of Ovid for Titania and a mid-sixteenth-century romance, *The Book of Duke Huon of Bordeaux*, for the beginnings of an idea for Oberon, although in that story the King of the Fairies is only three foot tall. Using, as ever, only what he thinks he can improve, Shakespeare removes from his fairies one unsettling association, that they are inclined to pinch and torment mortals when they can; a prejudice he himself had drawn on in *The Comedy of Errors* and would again later in *The Merry Wives of Windsor*. In the *Dream*, apart from a sadistic streak in Puck's humour, they are entirely human-friendly, a little fascinated by our world and inclined to intersect with it to the final benefit of both sides. And all-seeing: while the play's human communities are mostly unaware of each other's existence, the fairies are assumed to see everyone but be seen by none, except briefly by Bottom in a most rare vision.

And this, of course, is where the real difficulty of staging the *Dream* arises – the point, in fact, when directors decide whether they want to take the play on at all. These mysterious beings are so effortlessly imagined by Shakespeare but so hard to square with our picky literal-mindedness. With them, we know that we are being given a licence to play but don't quite know how to. They inhabit a seemingly unstageable microscopic world where they can hide inside acorn cups or wrap themselves in shards of snake-skin; they also compete with humans on at least equal terms. It is such a puzzle that the normally perceptive writer William Hazlitt, returning in some distemper from a night at Covent Garden Theatre in 1816, famously wrote that this play

> . . . when acted, is converted from a delightful fiction into a dull pantomime . . . the boards of a theatre and the regions of fancy are not the same thing . . . Fancy cannot be represented any more than a simile can be painted

– continuing to miss the point by complaining that fairies are not themselves incredible but become so when they are six foot high. Though we may reject his intolerance of the theatre, or at least the highly un-Shakespearian theatre of his time – the production he had seen ended with a pageant of an inordinate number of Theseus's mythical triumphs – the problem remains. Something has to be done about these fairies, and as interpreters we know we are standing or falling by it.

From a literary and historical point of view, they are easy enough. Chaucer (in *The Merchant's Tale*) had already had them quarrelling over humans as Oberon and Titania are about to do; for the previous twenty years, Queen Elizabeth had become used to seeing and being greeted by benevolent 'fairies' dancing and giving her presents at court entertainments; and Edmund Spenser was at this moment preparing *The Faerie Queene* for publication. In the production history of this play, necessity being the mother of a range of inventions, the variations have been wide: sometimes the whirring of gossamer wings has been heard, at others the dark shadow of the jabberwocky has seemed to flap over the play. Huge *corps* of little all-singing and all-dancing angels dominated the Victorian stage (fifty in Frank Benson's production of 1889, ninety in Charles Kean's of 1856). They have worn different-coloured sashes to demonstrate their allegiance to either Titania or Oberon: both Oberon and Puck were, for some reason, generally played by women from 1840 until 1914. The twentieth century proposed mischievous children and gilded birds, ballerinas, punks, Roedean-jolly girls, gypsies or acrobats on trapezes, the last originating in Peter Brook's ground-breaking production of 1970. They have been infant-small or large and lumpen, worn Doc Marten boots and spiky hair, or been the black and slithery contortionists Robert Lepage made of them in his 1992 'mudbath' production at London's National Theatre. It seems that these fairies can be pretty much anything we want; but also that whatever decision we take may leave us feeling that we've missed something important.

To dwell too much on precedent is, obviously, to come at the play from a bad angle. Instead we have to open the script in a state of purposeful amnesia and listen as innocently as possible to Shakespeare's strategies. So: at the outset, Puck meets a figure called the 'First Fairy', and from a rhythmic point of view Shakespeare seems to be sharing some of his reader's hesitancy.[1] Puck's opening line is only just an iambic pentameter, and would sound silly if treated as one:

How now, spirit, whither wander you?

In fact, just as Quince's prose clashed with Helena's rhymes, this unorthodoxy is a metrical bridge into something new. The Fairy now starts in a jingling verse, in performance probably two beats to the line rather than four. It is not particularly impressive though obviously alliterative and musical; in fact, it is a style as old as medieval English balladry:[2]

Over hill, over dale,
Thorough bush, thorough briar;
Over park, over pale,
Thorough flood, thorough fire . . .

1. This Fairy starts as a confection of literary influences. Puck asks it a first question directly lifted from John Lyly's *Gallathea*, published three years before, in which Cupid interrogates Diana's nymph about her quarrel with Venus; the Fairy's answer echoes *The Faerie Queene*, which Shakespeare may have just seen in manuscript. These are really the last moments in the play for which any external sources can be detected.

2. It is the same form, though with a jauntier feeling, as the beautiful and still popular carol, 'I Sing of a Maid':

He came all so still
Where his mother was
As dew in April
That falleth on the grass.
He came all so still
To his mother's bower
As dew in April
That falleth on the flower.

Inside it is a welcome link: the moon, watched so impatiently by Theseus, looks down on this world too. As if in recognition, the metre becomes a little more up to date – four beats, with more of a Shakespearian swing –

> I do wander everywhere
> Swifter than the moon's sphere . . .
> I must go seek some dewdrops here

– before switching into his standard five stresses:

> And hang a pearl in every cowslip's ear.

It has been a gentle move through the gears: if fairies, so remote at first, are able to speak in the same register as everyone else, the road is open before us. From now on they will address us with great clarity: what seemed like Shakespeare getting into his stride was his way of acclimatising us to the fantastic.

The daily round of duty described by the First Fairy at first seems to be all pictorial cuteness – rubies, freckles and dewdrops – but is in fact enriched by a sly humour: it is a mischievous tour of the tiny, to include a little biochemistry and a topical joke. The 'orbs' the Fairy must water 'on the green' are scientific facts, small circles of nitrogen-enriched grass still known as fairy-rings. The 'pensioners' (far from the modern, enfeebled kind) hint at the men of Elizabeth I's bodyguard in their gold and jewelled coats. Candidates for this élite cadre had to be tall and good-looking, so they are particularly nice to reimagine on this minute scale, their official red markings turned into 'fairy favours'. The inventory ends with the Fairy's urgent mission to find a dewdrop and hang it on a cowslip, rather as an Elizabethan courtier might choose his earring.

So two bargains have been struck. First, the fairies are as witty as pretty; and second, our sense of scale is to be interfered with at will. Since the First Fairy, even if played by a child, is clearly much too big to do the things described, we must get used to looking at one dimension while imagining another. The effect is so absorbing – not to mention how they might look – that an audience would find it hard to catch the exact relationship between Puck and this fairy even if there were much of one provided. The greater need has been for an introduction: if the two of them simply stood side by side and announced themselves to us, it would have been almost as good theatrically.

The Fairy, busy as the White Rabbit, needs to get going –

Farewell, thou lob of spirits; I'll be gone . . .

– but fortunately leaves the scent of a story behind:

Our Queen and all her elves come here anon.

This allows Puck to let us in on some facts, not all of which the Fairy may know. There is a King in this forest as well as a Queen, and a quarrel raging between them because of – listen hard – a 'lovely boy', a 'changeling', whom the Queen has stolen, Puck says, from an Indian king. (The language is a little inaccurate, since a changeling is normally the runt from the fairy world exchanged for a human child, rather than the actual child they have snatched.) The question here is who should have the child's custody and upbringing, a matter which, as always, defines the taste of the parents. Should the boy become a manly knight born 'to trace the forests wild' with his new father, or an exotic love-object forever swaddled in flowers by the Queen? Now, as well as matters of size, two emotional perspectives are being shuffled together: the passions released by the quarrel are so big, so 'human' perhaps, that the tiny creatures of this world have to

Creep into acorn cups and hide them there.

Hearing this, the Fairy realises that Puck is close to the centre of events, and suddenly recognises him as something more than a 'lob' or bumpkin. In fact he is a celebrity, the famous Robin Goodfellow whom country wives have to pacify with offerings of milk and bread, as if he were a hedgehog, if they want help rather than hindrance in their daily work. Suddenly a great splay of country words sketches rural borders into the fairy world – an interface with Warwickshire, you might say. They celebrate the fact that Puck's sense of humour is on the unkind side. It seems he likes to scare the 'maidens of the villagery', but, more than that, to steal the cream off the milk and watch the 'breathless housewife' wear herself out with fruitless churning that produces no butter. Likewise he keeps the beer from developing its head ('barm') and snags the action of the 'quern' (the corn-grinder). His other joy is to make travellers who have lost their way at night more desperate by some goblin equivalent of turning the signposts round. In his tiny reign of terror, the only insurance is to address him as he prefers:

FIRST FAIRY: Those that 'Hobgoblin' call you and 'sweet Puck',
You do their work, and they shall have good luck.

Puck's own elaboration of these activities is even more malicious. He boasts: since he is Oberon's magical Fool, even able to morph into a 'filly foal', he has earned the licence to amuse himself as he will. And of course, he can change size as well as shape. So he might hide in a 'gossip's' (housewife's) drinking-cup, disguised as the roasted crab-apple she uses to spice her winter's drink, bouncing about so much that she spills it; or, should another one tell a sad story, he will dispirit her further by impersonating a stool on which she can settle before leaping away to cause her a bad fall. All this, he says, is much appreciated, greatly increasing his credit with 'the whole choir', the assembled company of watching, invisible fairies.

If the First Fairy painted a new world of miniature delicacy, Puck, both attractive and off-putting, has rudely augmented it. Drawn in by some of its familiar features but startled by its range, the audience's imaginations balloon. Whether the tone is pitched as high as the upper air or as low as pantomime, it is curiously accessible: and throughout the play, if the language ever threatens to become archaic – Cupids, vestal virgins, Corin and Phyllida – it will quickly be grounded again by natural smells and sounds as familiar to us as to the countryman-poet.

> PUCK: But room, fairy; here comes Oberon.
> FIRST FAIRY: And here my mistress; would that he were gone.

The extreme good sense of allowing this little discursive exchange to get us attuned to fairy life becomes evident: what happens now happens fast, and we have to concentrate. It is a critical moment visually: however Puck and the Fairy look, the new arrivals will look, so to speak, more so. There will also be a number of them, since Titania and perhaps Oberon have attendants. Therefore, if the designer is not very disciplined, there is a real danger of being distracted from what is immediately a complicated and vicious argument. However, this is also an opportunity not to be missed: the moment when the fairy world fills up the stage should indeed be wonderful. In a traditional production it could become as populous as a beehive; in another, the inanimate could come alive; in one favouring a rougher form of magic, some sleight of hand or impudent conjuring could do it. Behind each choice lies the same excitement.

As the Fairy and Puck scatter, one perhaps to an acorn cup and the other to his position as Oberon's lieutenant, a bell rings out, silencing the fairy village:

> Ill met by moonlight, proud Titania . . .

Most people have an idea of what the best Shakespearian poetry sounds like: it may be hard to analyse, but the unique cocktail of sound, meaning and presence is instantly recognisable. With Oberon's and Titania's entrance, it arrives fully in this play for the first time. What makes Oberon's opening statement magically typical, seeming to shimmer with the moonlight it describes? A soft heavy beat lies underneath a melodic line that tugs a slight counter-rhythm across it. The alliteration is subtle and internal: the first half of the line – 'Ill met by moonlight' – uses only four vowels and five sounded consonants, with one of the vowels repeated and three of the consonants; if the line had been 'well met', the addition of a new value, the 'w', would have flattened its music as well as changing its sense. The line's second half – 'proud Titania' – hammers with plosives; all the more so because Shakespeare would have been hearing the Elizabethan pronunciation of the Latin name, 'Tietainia'; ugly for us, too like the Titanic or titanium.[3]

The cadence of 'moonlight' and the ring of the Queen's name, heard for the first time, is so impressive that you might take this for a warm greeting rather than its opposite. But the quarrel in hand is fundamental. It tumbles headlong onto the stage in a wave of sound: there was every reason, it seems, to hide in acorn-cups. Titania, resisting the rendezvous, retaliates, adjective for adjective:

> What, jealous Oberon? Fairy, skip hence;
> I have forsworn his bed and company.

In a way that is becoming familiar, the ethereal is lying alongside something more candid: if Shakespeare's intentions had been simply decorative, Titania could have forsworn Oberon's 'arbour' or his 'fairy bower' rather than, bluntly, his bed. In fact, the question of Oberon's and Titania's sexuality, and whether it in any way relates to ours, is one Shakespeare will be at cunning pains never to answer. Instead, he insists that we look at the two of them through alternate lenses. Through one, the human male can be glimpsed pulling marital rank –

> Tarry, rash wanton; am not I thy lord?

– while the female deflates his domineering instinct:

---

3. In Ovid, Titania is a generic name for any goddess descended from the Titans.

Then I must be thy lady . . .

But as they wrangle about who is being taken more for granted, a more rarefied picture forms in the other eye: Titania is accusing Oberon (able to alter his shape as readily as Puck) of changing himself into the shepherd Corin and sitting in a field to play music to Phyllida the shepherdess. These are completely conventional names for a pastoral lover and his lass, and the whole picture a sixteenth-century cliché; its purpose is to return us to arm's length at the very moment we were thinking Oberon and Titania might be easily accessible.

To Titania, the lapse of taste with Phyllida was simply to do with Oberon's ever-wandering eye. Her more important grievance (which also keeps us at a distance, intrigued) is elaborate: he has come all the way from India – the limit of the Elizabethans' known world – to see his 'bouncing Amazon' Hippolyta married to Theseus. The oddity is that she is not accusing him of planning to interrupt the banns to pursue his own interests with Hippolyta, far from it, but of blessing the human union with 'joy and prosperity'. It seems that while Puck interferes with the rural community, Oberon and Titania have some proprietorial relationship with the grander end of the mortal world; its meaning is skewed for us by the fact that Oberon's at least is entirely benevolent, like that of a patron rather than a lover. It is his guardianship of Hippolyta that enrages Titania, making her as jealous as if the offence were sexual.

Oberon is more brutal in reply, and more conventional. When it comes to human clients, he knows that desire may be involved as well as protection, and Titania so loves Theseus that she has already intervened to break up no fewer than four of his love affairs – if that is not too creditable a word for his rape of the nymph Perigouna, whose father he killed by tying him between two bent pine trees and then letting go; or his affair with Ariadne, whose spool of thread helped him get out of the Minotaur's labyrinth and whom he then abandoned; or with Aegles, for whom he abandoned Ariadne; or with another Amazon, Hippolyta's sister Antiope, whom he then left for Phaedra.

The whole mélange – fairies with semi-human dynamics entangled with a badly behaved classical world – now takes an unexpected turn. Rather than countering Oberon's accusation, Titania broadens the argument to describe the comprehensive damage their current quarrel is doing to their environment. In the play's longest speech, she describes a catastrophe in nature that speaks clearly to a later generation peering guiltily at the holes in their ozone layer. The language she uses is graceful, passionate, richly imagistic, and it puts her, as is often the way with the Shakespearian heroine, way ahead of her consort. She confronts Oberon, in fact, with the moral authority of a much later victim, Hermione in *The Winter's Tale* countering the destructive pettiness of Leontes, or of Queen Katharine facing Henry VIII.

For the actress, however, there is a large technical difference. In those later plays she would find a far more flexible approach to verse than anything in the *Dream*, where almost every line, even if not actually tied to a rhyme, is end-stopped – that is, the word that momentarily clinches the sense always arrives on its last beat. And in Titania's thirty-seven here there are only three examples of a verb at one line's end leading to the completion of the thought during the next. So the imagination that ranges easily across river and sea, human and animal disorder, disease in nature, wintry cold, a malevolent moon and all manner of seasonal disruption remains as tightly tied to its structure as the notes of a minuet. And in fact, in the paradox well understood by Shakespeare and Bach, it is the fierce discipline that secures the sense; fail to observe the rules, and the argument unravels.

Of course all blank verse, while being the rhythmic form closest to conversation, is an unnatural way to speak; Titania's outburst is one for which both brain and lungs have to be ready. It is not only athletic but cultural: we are simply unused to sustaining our accumulating thoughts with the vigour of a Shakespearian hero. In very general terms, it is typical of English conversation to start an idea, then monitor it as it goes along, qualifying and even neutralising it – it is a form of apology for having an opinion.[4] Random words en route may be emphasised – especially the pronouns and possessives, in a way that doesn't suit Shakespearian verse at all – but the energy of the whole may drain progressively away. However, in Shakespeare, ideas are developed in an unfurling domino effect that can extend for as many as twenty or thirty lines. In a speech as

4. Again very generally, this is where Americans have an advantage. Not only did they inherit Jacobean language so quickly they are in some ways closer to it, but there is a characteristic in American speech to start strong and stay strong to the end, even if a certain amount of local colour is lost on the way.

intellectually formidable as Titania's here, a word that seems about to complete an argument may be only a stepping-stone to a more convincing one:

> Therefore the winds, piping to us in vain,
> As in *revenge* have suck'd up from the sea
> *Contagious fogs*, which falling in the land
> Hath every pelting river *made so proud*
> That they have *overborne their continents* . . .

The forensic energy is accompanied – created in fact – by great precision of thought: Titania is forcing us to see the world exactly as she does from her privileged vantage-point. Her draughtsmanship is sharp and practical; and Shakespeare has planted an earthy root in her from which language of great beauty happens to blossom.

She is not especially conscious of the richness with which she speaks; to her, the picturesque grievances are no more than reality. Wherever she dances on the sand in delicate circles with her women, the hoodlum Oberon breaks in, brawling like a molesting drunkard; the embrace of the crimson rose by the hoary-headed frost seems to her as grotesque as unmelting ice would be in the heart of a fire; winter suddenly looks like spring and autumn like midsummer.

When Shakespeare describes the breakdown of social or natural order, it is usually part of a political complaint, or at least a means of persuasion. The Duke of Burgundy in *Henry V* and Ulysses in *Troilus and Cressida* both do it, one to reproach the invader for turning his country into a wasteland, and the other to cajole the Greek military establishment into line. But this is different: Titania is aiming at herself as much as at Oberon. Simply, the world is upside down because they cannot stop quarrelling. The wind sucks up the sea-water and returns it as an overwhelming flood; the harvest rots in the fields; cattle are poisoned; the human race has lost the sanctuary of hymn and carol while darkness falls at midday; and it is all, emphatically, their fault:

> And this same progeny of evils comes
> From our debate, from our dissension;
> We are their parents and original.

They have become less the changeling's guardians than the mother and father of catastrophe.

And what does Oberon have to say to this vivid, self-punishing analysis? The fairy equivalent of Nothing To Do With Me:

> Do you amend it then, it lies in you.

Her conscientious despair is thus, shockingly, dismissed. Instead he ingratiates –

> Why should Titania cross her Oberon?

– then wheedles:

> I do but beg a little changeling boy
> To be my henchman.

As far as he is concerned, the world will right itself – harvest, weather and all – if only he gets what he wants, a boy on whom his only claim seems to be that he too comes from India. Faced with this version of leadership, the disgusted Titania leads him on for a moment –

> Set your heart at rest . . .

– the better to frustrate him:

> The fairy land buys not the child of me.

As far as the rights and wrongs of this go, it is hard to know if Titania's position is any more defensible than Oberon's. Perhaps this sort of random kidnapping is all in a day's work for them: perhaps many human families have been shocked to find a fairy runt in their child's bed. But her implacability is supported by deep feeling, and the story behind it is personal. She used to know the changeling's mother, 'a votaress of my order': in the thick-scented evenings they would sit on the beach together, watching the merchants' boats on the water. The pregnant woman would laugh at their sails as they grew

> . . . big-bellied with the wanton wind

and imitate them as she ran to find gifts for Titania, gliding across the sand as if through the waves of the sea. Then she would return to her

> As from a voyage, rich with merchandise.

These memories are childish, affectionate and humorous – a startling new tone of fairy voice – and they form a picture far more graceful than the libidinous Oberon serenading Phyllida. As a story of friendship, in fact, it is more full-hearted than Helena's sentimental description later on of her schoolgirl alliance with Hermia.

And it demonstrates a frailty: there are limits to the fairy deities' control of events. Titania may be able to see into the heart of nature's darkness, but once joined to the human world she is powerless to hold on to a friend. The loss of her votaress in childbirth soon afterwards was a matter for real human grief, not passing melancholy:

> But she, being mortal, of that boy did die

and all Titania can do is look after her interests now she has gone:

> And for her sake do I rear up her boy;
> And for her sake I will not part with him.

The monosyllabic drumming tells the actress what to do: the more pain and devotion there is in this bleak repetition, the better.

Next to such a burst of feeling Puck, who attributed outright theft to her, seems blindly prejudiced, and Oberon pettier than ever. For the moment, with nothing to say, the King of the Fairies sulks feebly:

> How long within this wood intend you stay? . . .
> Give me that boy, and I will go with thee

– and is brushed aside by a rhyming couplet before he can manage anything fine:

> Not for thy fairy kingdom. Fairies, away;
> We shall chide downright if I longer stay.

Titania's has been a magnificent performance, deeply felt and voluble, and its lack of compromise is humiliating for the man in Oberon: he engineered the parley, and she has simply walked through it and over him and continued on her way. It doesn't feel good, especially in front of all her fairy attendants: it is as if he had tried to force her off the road and ended up in the ditch himself.

His rage begins to make him creative, though too late for winning the argument by fair means. Like all of us who think of our best retorts after the event, once Titania has gone Oberon finds an extravagant poetry, and his vicious drive to get even kicks the play into new splendour:

> My gentle Puck, come hither. Thou rememb'rest
> Since once I sat upon a promontory
> And heard a mermaid on a dolphin's back . . .

The famously virtuosic speech that follows, as extraordinary as Titania's but serving quite a different purpose, is a form of pure creation, like a dream: where hers was ruthlessly informative, the

writing now has little purpose except to be itself. By the time
Oberon reaches his real subject, the little western flower purpled by
love's wound, we seem to have travelled through as many worlds as
he has. There was a time when he and Puck sat on a promontory like
father and son, listening to a mermaid's song as she perched (like
the mythical poet Arion) on the back of a dolphin; but this is not his
point. Her music pacified the tides and brought the stars tumbling
out of the sky to listen; but that isn't it either. The point is to remind
Puck that it was just at that moment that Oberon, seeing further
than he could, glimpsed the figure of Cupid wheeling with his bow
and arrow through the huge space, ready to strike at his natural
enemy, a vestal virgin (a nod here to the reigning Queen Elizabeth
I, though that won't matter to us), but, untypically, missing his aim.
This is the real story: the 'bolt' fell instead on a tiny white flower
which, wounded by the impact, became Love-in-Idleness, the wild
pansy also called Heart's-Ease that Puck and everyone else knows
of. What we and Puck didn't imagine – because the play invents it[5]
– was that this modest blossom, erotically bruised, had the power to
infect any sleeping man or woman, mortal or fairy, with the most
slavish infatuation for whatever he or she first sees on waking.

Over these delicate bones, of course, stretches a speech of
intoxicating beauty, recklessly mingling different scales; the cosmic
vastness between moon and earth, the diminutive figure of Cupid
firing his arrow, the even smaller wild flower. The dimensional
bargain struck by Puck and the First Fairy is thus continued, more
deliriously. The extravagance of it excites Puck, who feels for a
moment his master's power to compass the limits of the world, even
if he can't sustain the poetry so well. To bring this flower, he will

> . . . put a girdle round about the earth

in, what shall we say,

> . . . forty minutes

– no more than the time, according to Oberon, that it takes a great
whale to travel a league.

As with Titania's speech, the challenge for Oberon is not to be
seduced by his own poetry, above all noticing how it naturally bends

5. More or less – there is a hint of it in John Lyly's *Euphues and his England*, which
Shakespeare knew, where the herb Anacamsoritis is credited with the same effect – but the
victim has to touch this herb themselves rather than having it applied to their eyes.

and contracts in the heat of his needs. The actor has to handle its vertiginous potentials with Titania's precision – shifting in and out of close-up as if examining one thread before looking again at the tapestry it belongs to. And all with eyes and voice, so that it is as demanding as acting on radio: this is not the time for anxious miming, suiting invented actions to the wild words. We have to see every detail Oberon describes through language alone.

Meanwhile Puck's job is to mitigate the extravagance with simple punctuations. At a certain point, Oberon leaves him behind: Puck may have seen the mermaid and the shooting stars, but not Cupid and the flower. Oberon is at home in this wider dimension between moon and earth, but 'gentle Puck' remains in the hedgerows, his limitations marked by the touchingly simple:

> I remember.

The difference between what each can see underlines the interest of their relationship. There is something of the human father and son in it, and this will sharpen later on when they briefly and painfully quarrel. But there is something less readable as well. The audience was able to handle Oberon's and Titania's strange argument largely by catching its human element – the weight and flow of a marital row, with its shaming pettiness, and even the weather as a symbol of unhappiness; but by contrast, the mystery of Oberon and Puck is sustained exactly because it is only just humanised. How did they come to be bound together? Was it always so, or was Puck at some point inducted into the higher fairy world? How are they physically with each other? Perhaps there is something animal, unabashed about them; perhaps Puck clings to Oberon with a thoughtless sexuality. His dependence will always be something deeper and less traceable than a servant's on a master or a son's on a father; each production will invent its own language for them.

Oberon, meanwhile, has become very interesting – not only the idea of such a figure but what goes on inside him, especially his ugly, debasing jealousy. His eagerness to see Titania humiliated, her heart set

> on lion, bear, or wolf, or bull,
> On meddling monkey, or on busy ape

would be shocking were it not expressed in such a lovely way; we are finding that in this world the devils sometimes speak like angels, while the angel, Titania, is quite daunting. It is very clear that were it not for his non-human status and our uncertainty about the rules governing it, Oberon would be the smooth-tongued villain of the piece. His voice, breaking through the fairy strings like a burnished bassoon, set a new musical standard, and as a master of ceremonies he has been surprisingly seductive.

His true journey through the play begins now. Engrossed in his vengeful plans, he sees two young humans chasing towards him:

> But who comes here? I am invisible,
> And I will overhear their conference.

A practical choice in performance: should Oberon affect his invisibility with some invented fairy gesture, or is the phrase simply an explanation to the audience of how things stand when fairies meet humans? Better the second than the first, I would say: devised rituals of how a fairy might disappear plunge us into something like ballet, one of the risks always lurking within the play. There is nothing wrong with Oberon talking to the audience with the same simplicity as everyone else: the theatrical aside is a great leveller, and allows us the same relationship with both fairies and humans.

What Oberon observes unobserved is a human variant of his and Titania's quarrel. Helena has pursued Demetrius into the wood as she planned, after breaking the news to him of Hermia's and Lysander's flight. The chase has been at least as much as her self-punishing nature could have hoped for: the steady rhyming patterns of her earlier scene have broken down into breathless blank verse, while Demetrius speaks almost for the first time. He might as well not have uttered in Theseus's court for all he revealed, and in one way he makes up for it now:

> I love thee not, therefore pursue me not.
> Where is Lysander, and fair Hermia? . . .
> Thou told'st me they were stolen unto this wood
> And here am I, and wood [mad] within this wood
> Because I cannot meet my Hermia.

Now that Helena is faced with 'plainest truth', the dynamic of the scene lies in her desperate efforts to quibble out of existence the bluntnesses he hurls at her – 'I love thee not . . . *fair* Hermia . . . *my* Hermia . . . Hence, get thee gone'. Having dumped her, Demetrius is, with the injustice of comedy, infuriated by her overwhelming devotion. It makes him unnecessarily rude:

. . . I am sick when I do look on thee.

No, no, Helena declares, on the contrary: she is the one who becomes ill when he is out of her sight. Rather than that, she is happy to be punished like a fawning dog. Look – she will suit the action to the word, down on all fours as in some fetishistic game: the sight makes Demetrius and us almost look away, he in disgust and we somewhat delightedly. However, the more she abases herself, the more high-faluting her language becomes. Prostrate, her blue-stocking side investigates the properties of metals, not even scientifically but as an almost impenetrable conceit:

> You draw me, you hard-hearted adamant!
> And yet you draw not iron; for my heart
> Is true as steel. Leave you your power to draw,
> And I shall have no power to follow you.

A girl like a dog speaking like Edmund Spenser, rejected by a weak and desperate master: it could split a fairminded audience into two. A reasonable male spectator might take the view that Helena's candid self-exposure commands respect, while Demetrius repre- sents men's worst side in its brutal, cut-to-the-chase purposefulness. The women, on the other hand, might admire Demetrius's courage- ous honesty and find Helena's refusal to let him follow his heart – or even take a step past her – a dismal controlling tactic. Making your- self into a doormat, after all, is the opposite of love: insisting on driv- ing your lover to the airport even if it's not welcome is a selfish and asphyxiating act. But both sides also know that a man's inability to return devotion can make him unreasonably enraged. At this pitch of comedy, Helena is becoming less than a lady and Demetrius no gentleman.

What, his sympathisers might say, is Demetrius to do? There is nothing Helena won't put up with, no unkindness she will not bear; she would cheerfully lie down in front of his car, which might or might not have time to stop. The answer is simple: he must run away – it is easy enough to lose someone in a forest if you try – but, protesting and paralysed, he stays to listen. Perhaps he is flattered by the attention: certainly some combination of inhibitions is working on him. He may be fascinated by the sight of a girl pretending to be a dog and asking to be kicked: these are not the kind of women, or dogs, he grew up with. There may also be a little conscience behind his hostility: he must know he has treated her badly. An interesting nuance slithers into the scene when he points out the risk she is taking:

> You do impeach your modesty too much
> To leave the city and commit yourself
> Into the hands of one that loves you not;
> To trust the opportunity of night
> And the ill counsel of a desert place
> With the rich worth of your virginity.

At first sight Demetrius seems to be saying that her danger is himself: his are the hands she is in, and who knows what his hands might do? But in the second half of the speech he disappears as the subject and seems to be warning her of shadowy men worse than himself. There might be a little solicitude here, in acknowledgment of times past: 'modesty' is a compliment, and her 'virginity' has 'rich worth'. This small outcrop of protectiveness, if played, deepens and humanises the scene. On the other hand it could be merely self-regard, masquerading as concern: Demetrius may no longer love Helena, but he would prefer to imagine her tucked up in her bed thinking kindly of him than, wild with disappointed love, exposing herself to night-wanderers.

If it is kindness, it is of a sort that rarely works under these circumstances. It draws still deeper commitment from Helena, who suddenly becomes calm and unstrategic:

> Your virtue is my privilege. For that
> It is not night when I do see your face . . .
> Nor doth this wood lack worlds of company
> For you in my respect are all the world . . .

No more smart word games, just her belief that he will not harm her, he who brings the sun up and makes her life worth living. Whatever Demetrius does now, he will sound bad: her martyrdom is leaving him no room for manoeuvre. Shamed, he begins to bale out –

> I'll run from thee and hide me in the brakes,
> And leave thee to the mercy of wild beasts

– and as he does so, the dialogue urgently flicks this way and that. Helena deals easily with the idea of his flight, by literary means:

> The story shall be changed;
> Apollo flies, and Daphne holds the chase;
> The dove pursues the griffin . . .

This sort of thing might be appreciated by Lysander and Hermia, but Demetrius doesn't get it at all:

> I will not stay thy questions; let me go.

Stumped, he threatens the terrors of the earth if she persists:

> Or if thou follow me, do not believe
> But I shall do thee mischief in the wood.

But she holds all the cards that matter:

> Ay, in the temple, in the town, the field,
> You do me mischief . . .
> Your wrongs do set a scandal on my sex . . .

His exit is absurdly silent, words having failed him once again.

Neither has done well, but at least Helena can feel a tinge of heroism, running after a departing back. And of course, they have not been alone. It could all have been played with Oberon melting into the shrubbery; but the plan he is about to perfect will be more satisfying if he has been an unobtrusive third party to the quarrel, and we will surely have looked for a reaction from him as it raged. Obviously enough, this is one of the new interconnections: how do fairies view humans? Do they laugh at what we laugh at, is Oberon curious about all the undignified behaviour, or does he take it in his stride? What, in fact, was the effect on him?

To turn him briefly into a feminist, strangely enough. Minutes after losing his battle with Titania, he finds himself, perhaps without sensing the irony, favouring the distaff side. He calls Helena 'nymph', a high compliment, almost a goddess; he is clearly taken with this girl who thinks herself no better than a dog, and sees her as a fellow-victim, to be included in his somewhat warped attempt to put the world to rights. His best offer will be to give her not the fulfilment of her dreams, but a variation on the kind of revenge he favours. He promised Titania 'torment' for having injured him; now Demetrius will suffer the same and Helena be a little appeased:

> . . . Ere he do leave this grove,
> Thou shalt fly him, and he shall seek thy love.

So far Oberon seems to prefer conquest and advantage to reconciliation: but it will not always be so.

Puck returns with the flower, perhaps out of breath, seemingly out of nowhere, but again with great simplicity –

Ay, there it is

– and once more Oberon finds sumptuous language for his malevolence:

> I know a bank where the wild thyme blows,
> Where oxlips and the nodding violet grows,
> Quite overcanopied with luscious woodbine,
> With sweet muskroses and with eglantine.

The monosyllables of the opening line slightly snag its standard rhythm, offbeats succeed each other at the end of the third line and beginning of the fourth: emotion nags at the beautiful music. Oberon is again unaware of its beauty: it is only a natural description of what he is remembering.

What has changed now he has the magic flower in his hand, causing the new brilliant speech to be different from the first? There is a more intimate feeling in it, something between nostalgia and resentment. The past was all pleasure; the present is vicious. Oberon used to love Titania's bower as part of his life: lying there oblivious to time, he could watch a snake shedding its skin and fairies wrapping themselves in it. Now the memory symbolises everything that is painful and disharmonious, like thinking of a house you were once happy in but had to leave. As his language becomes more angular –

> I'll streak her eyes
> And make her full of hateful fantasies . . .

– Puck, sensing the vexation, wisely remains neutral and waits for instructions. Since the humans are secondary to Oberon's design on Titania, they come in a mundane form, almost as an afterthought, just the facts of the case and no poetry:

> A sweet Athenian lady is in love
> With a disdainful youth – anoint his eyes . . .

Identification will be no problem – how many males in Athenian clothes will Puck find in the forest, especially with a trace of disdain about them as they sleep? It's a simple job to be done before curfew, which in the fairies' case is the beginning rather than the end of daylight.

★

This remarkable third scene has contained an experiment. It would be hard not to feel excitement at the arrival of Demetrius and Helena in what for the time being seemed to be Oberon's play. The *Dream* – like *Twelfth Night*, another great piece for several instruments with an equal claim on our attention – has held back its intentions as long as it can, and now the constituencies have to mingle. After half an hour, it seems likely that we have met everybody; and two of the protagonists have appeared twice. All four lovers have been seen in action, responding feebly or brilliantly to their individual pressures, and the outsider Demetrius has emerged as a character: the glimpse he had, perhaps influenced by Egeus's brandies, of a brighter future than as old Nedar's son-in-law has proved to be one of the play's motors. The world of the forest has been conjured, and a connection made between it and ours – much of this due to Puck, whose rumbustious practicality we can recognise. Oberon and Titania, spirits clashing in the pale light of the moon, have been as breathlessly unreasoning as we ourselves might be. Having dutifully puzzled over how these unprecedented fairies are to be presented in performance, we find it increasingly easy to move among them, their foreignness and familiarity being so finely judged.

There is of course another group to be drawn into this intriguing place; but also quite an urgent narrative need which has nothing to do with them, flagged up by Puck as he signs off:

Fear not, my lord; your servant shall do so.

The action could either follow him and his flower to Demetrius, Oberon and his to Titania, or it could move sideways for a new inevitability: Bottom among the fairies. For the writer, everything is to play for. Having started with a premise that would not have shamed a tragedian, he has added a dribble of amateur theatricals and a dash of magic and folded in some romantic delusion; the flavours are beginning to feel inseparable, and his trusting audience is caught in the oldest, most childish excitement the theatre can offer – where to next? The moon, if he says so.

FOUR

Act 2 Scene 2

Since everything comes at a cost, Titania, worn out, is calling for music, and in a moment her fairies will sing to her, at some length. We could become as disheartened as she has. As with the First Fairy at the start of the last scene, the text suddenly seems decorative and the narrative pulse, so urgent a moment ago, fades a little.

Shakespeare generally uses music in a disciplined and selective way: when Feste in *Twelfth Night* or Ophelia in *Hamlet* breaks into song it feels inevitable and semi-improvised, sprung by the action rather than a desire for embellishment. For this reason, a folk-song convention we can believe to be familiar to the characters may be much more useful than any setting in which a composer's hand can be felt.[1] As far as its motivation goes, the fairies' song for Titania –

You spotted snakes with double tongue

– does pass the implied test, just about: it is intended as a lullaby after her quarrel, though I doubt whether Shakespeare would have dealt with the situation in this way later in his career. However, we will soon recognise his need to get Titania asleep so that the plot can go forward.

Being on the long side, the song needs as brisk a musical treatment as a lullaby can bear, and a fairly simple one if it is not to sound like a conventional elaboration. And since Titania's call for 'a

---

1. It seems that Shakespeare sometimes borrowed both words and music from composers such as William Byrd and Thomas Morley – for *As You Like It*, *Twelfth Night* and *Othello* particularly. At other times, fairly clearly, he took familiar melodies and gave them new words. Feste's 'Come Away Death' in *Twelfth Night* may originally have been sung to a very old tune, brought to England by Huguenot weavers. Much of this is speculation – not a note of music from Shakespeare performances in his own time has indisputably survived. It is frustrating: musical settings for plays produced shortly after this period are abundant, perhaps because Court performances were by then more closely documented.

roundel and a fairy song' risks archaic tweeness, it will be best to apply to it the sharp logic we are already using with the fairies: what is it that Titania needs at this point, how is she feeling, and how well do her attendants understand it? She has survived a savage row with Oberon in which her appetite for good government has been so thwarted that she was driven to bleak defiance. Still, she kept her dignity under the insults, her voice never wobbled and she remained completely unyielding. Now she is home, and can let go. Calling for a song is her equivalent of coming through the front door, kicking off her shoes and putting on a record: music comes into its own when intense feelings are unsatisfied by language. Titania's need for it, though lighter, is essentially no different from Desdemona's absorption in the Willow Song to distract her from the approach of death towards the end of *Othello*.

While the fairies warm up, Titania issues instructions for afterwards; picturesque missions wittily adapted for fairyland by the fact that they will only take 'the third part of a minute', twenty seconds, to perform – rather swifter than Puck's circuit of the earth in forty minutes. But they contain a slight sting, if we care to feel it. Two of her orders are characteristic, as unsentimental as the eye she cast on the malfunctioning landscape. First, the rose trees must be cured of canker – her need is the same as that of a human gardener, and the fact that these are fragrant musk-roses only idealises them a little. Secondly, the 'clamorous owl' that the Elizabethans found so ominous (see *Macbeth*) must be kept at bay, but this is only a practical precaution to stop intrusive noise – what with the owl and Oberon, peace could be hard to secure. However, Titania's third order – to strip 'the reremice' (the bats) of their wings in order to clothe her elves – is surprisingly brutal, not like her at all, as if an animal-lover were calling for a cull. Just as our instinctive liking for Puck was suspended as he revelled in the damage he did to old ladies, Shakespeare avoids too much lyricism here by pointing out how savage nature is even in the tiny tooth and claw of the Queen of the Fairies. Hers and Oberon's practices are at least as predatory as the human hunting culture Theseus will celebrate later.

So, frazzled as she is, Titania has the energy to organise her own soirée, though not to specify the song. The one the fairies choose, or improvise, is concerned with royal security: it is meant to repel nocturnal danger and put a ring of fire around their Queen. It is constructed, like a hymn, on a sequence of verses punctuated by an affirming chorus. The lyric nicely combines things we too fear in sleep with others which, with the passage of four centuries, have lost their power over the imagination. No one would want to wake up eye to eye with a spotted snake or lie on a hedgehog; but it is difficult to be quite as frightened as the Elizabethans seem to have been of spiders, daddy-longlegs, worms and snails. No wonder they were: a near-contemporary of Shakespeare's wrote a standard text[2] which claimed that a blindworm (which of course is not blind at all) could poison a cow that made the mistake of lying on it, and that a newt could swell up like a puff adder and stare gorgonically at its enemy.

In one way Shakespeare's intention, as often in the play, is to paint as vibrant a word-picture as possible, and the texture of this incantatory song is indeed beautiful. It also has the tension and release of good folk music; the images topple rapidly over each other in the verses and can then be released by a melodic 'hook' into the open, emotional sound of the chorus:

> Never harm
> Nor spell nor charm
> Come our lovely lady nigh.
> So goodnight, with lullaby.

This chorus invokes the unfortunate Philomel, raped and turned into the most rhapsodic of all birds, a nightingale; and in mid-flow it resolves into pure, non-verbal music:

> Lulla, lulla, lullaby; lulla, lulla, lullaby.

Whereupon Titania, like a baby, sleeps – somewhere on the stage where she will not be in the way for the next three hundred lines.[3]

Again, the play has linked the intimate and the metaphysical. Titania has interpreted the world, attributed responsibility and seen off her psychopathic partner; now she is being sent to sleep with wordless crooning, like a child. The 'humanity' of it overrides any need for a pictorial tableau; and to secure that, Titania needs to bring into the scene a great sense of effort expended on Oberon – and of

---

2. Edward Topsell, *The History of Serpents* (1608). Blindworms and newts crop up again in *Macbeth*, in the witches' brew.

3. It was all much easier on the Elizabethan stage, with the fairy sentinel on its upper level and Titania tucked away underneath on the inner section, where Oberon could sneak up on her. In one of those moments when four centuries shrink to nothing, a property list for 1598 has survived from the papers of the Lord Admiral's Men, rivals of Shakespeare's company, which includes 'Two Mossy Banks', quite possibly wheeled on for comparable scenes in their repertoire.

the open wound of her lost votaress – so that her need for rest is completely real.

Surrounded by her solicitous team, she makes the solitary Oberon, skulking onstage now, seem like a stage villain. There seems to be a difference between her court and his. Although Shakespeare gives him, like her, a 'train' of attendants for his main entrances, Oberon never, unlike her, addresses them: to all intents and purposes he walks by himself, or at the most with Puck for company. But she never seems to be alone. At this point the fairy appointed to watch 'aloof' over her immediately (and mutely) vanishes from the action – scared off by Oberon perhaps, or frozen in deference – so that Oberon can hiss an imprecation in Titania's ear as vicious as the fairies' was benevolent. Whether she wakens to

> . . . ounce [lynx] or cat or bear,
> Pard, or boar with bristled hair

it will immediately become the object of her desire.

This four-beat rhyming verse, used originally by the First Fairy and later on by Puck for similar activities to Oberon's, has, like many magic spells, an element of doggerel in it – it is a nursery rhyme with a kick in the tail:

> Wake when some vile thing is near.

There is something of the pantomime about this; the last line (the fifth rhyme in a row) sounds like an unnecessarily vicious afterthought. A young audience may hiss, which is quite all right: Oberon's childishness is being held in the same frame as his potency. In fact, much of the audience's response to this moment will depend not only on how it is staged but on the size of the theatre. There is a point on any acting area downstage of which a figure seems bigger than life-size, and upstage of which it begins to shrink into the surrounding space. Powerful as the latter place can be, especially for rhetorical purposes, it can be easier to influence an audience from close to them (as we know in general from contemporary studio productions of Shakespeare). I would be prepared to bet that when Oberon bends over Titania a long way away it is easier for his audience to be amused: closer up, he could be quite frightening.

The need for sleep is human as well. So Hermia's and Lysander's exhausted arrival on the scene, en route to his aunt, echoes the fairy world as wittily as its King and Queen mimicked mortal emotions. Their fatigue is appropriately mundane: the intrepid eloper Lysander has lost the way. He only admits it after pretending their need for rest is a matter of Hermia's lack of stamina –

> Fair love, you faint with wandering in the wood . . .

– and perhaps as a result of the beady look this might provoke from her. To be lost in the middle of a forest as darkness begins to fall is not quite what Hermia signed up for. She gets ready for bed as best she can, lightly punishing Lysander by leaving him to fend for himself and addressing him without an endearment:

> Be it so, Lysander, find you out a bed,
> For I upon this bank will rest my head.

She probably knows that she will also have to engage in a perennial tussle, now blessed with new opportunity. Since they are away from home, Lysander implies, could they not sleep together under God's sky?

> One turf shall serve as pillow for us both;
> One heart, one bed, two bosoms and one troth.

The gentle implacability she applies to this idea suggests that, though ready to admire his heroism, her grip on their arrangements is tight:

> Nay, good Lysander, for my sake, my dear,
> Lie further off yet; do not lie so near.

She is as principled now as when she determined that they shouldn't see each other for twenty-four hours before their flight: in her own way, she has Titania's implacability.

In pursuit of his interests, Lysander riddles very prettily, and in fact they both do, composing a sequence rhymed first alternately and then in couplets. The slightly distancing effect of this suggests not artificiality but a familiar routine, which Hermia would probably miss were it ever to stop: it is, after all, a part of courtship. Everything is right and normal: she proper even at the risk of loneliness, he pushing his luck as far as good humour will allow. There is an easy flow between these two, and little at stake: the punitive older generation, Egeus and Theseus, have evaporated in the new setting, and the lovers no longer seem to be on the run.

Even in his roguishness, Lysander pleads transparency –

> O take the sense, sweet, of my innocence;
> Love takes the meaning in love's conference

– and gives up with conspicuous good grace:

And then end life when I end loyalty.
Here is my bed; sleep give thee all his rest.

Hermia, meanwhile, won't allow any darker pun on 'lying' to come
between her and her 'gentle friend':

LYSANDER: Then by your side no bed-room me deny;
    For lying so, Hermia, I do not lie.
HERMIA: . . . Now much beshrew my manners and my pride
    If Hermia meant to say Lysander lied.

Their verbal scrupulousness is a measure of care: knowing what lies
ahead for them, Shakespeare is at pains to emphasise a chastely respectful partnership. As they settle at an appropriate distance – perhaps synchronising their actions as they do their speech – a fragile
peace hangs in the air.

There is, in fact, little doubt whose is the true love in the play
whose course, though not running smooth, will finally steady itself.
Coming after Oberon's ominous jingle, this short exchange has
rippled with light and, beneath the routine gestures, mutual understanding. And now everyone sleeps, each of them destined for their
own midsummer dream. For Hermia it will be a waking nightmare,
for Lysander a deceptive delight, and for Titania, in a sense, both.
There needs to be a bar or two of silence as the play moves quietly
through another door.

If Hermia had only stretched a point and let Lysander sleep next
to her, Puck, trailing though the forest rather than putting a girdle
round the earth, would never have mistaken him for Demetrius and
the four lovers would have been spared their painful rite of passage.
As it is, he arrives sounding a little fed up and fatigued: his fairy
verse, factual where Oberon's was boding, suggests he has been
muttering discontentedly to himself for some time:

Through the forest have I gone,
But Athenian found I none
On whose eyes I might approve
This flower's force in stirring love.

Lysander and Hermia are far enough apart for him to see them as if
in separate beds, and to deplore it: Hermia is on 'the dank and dirty
ground', a billet good enough for the man, Puck thinks, but not for
such a 'pretty soul'. Half-versed as he is in human behaviour, he sees
this amicable arrangement as proof that the Athenian maid has been
horribly spurned:

> Pretty soul, she durst not lie
> Near this lack-love, this kill-courtesy.

Conversely, he doesn't ask himself why they are asleep so relatively close together when things are supposed to be going so badly between them.

His confident misreading of what he sees is the first stage in a lengthy central joke, and interestingly in character. Just as Oberon favoured Helena in her struggle with Demetrius, the inquisitive Puck is sympathetic to Hermia and critical of the sexually negligent male: his pagan assumption that Lysander should fall in with female desire contrasts pleasantly with Hermia's actual modesty. Like Oberon (as long as his own interests are not threatened), Puck will always take Jill's side rather than Jack's: practical jokes aside, his sensibility is instinctive and feminine.

Indignant at the lack of gallantry, he administers erotic correction, and springs the trap. With the magic flower, Love-in-Idleness, applied to his eyes, the 'churl' Lysander will at last be harrowed by desire:

> When thou wak'st let love forbid
> Sleep his seat on thy eyelid

– an ironic mistake, since the capacity for desire is the surest thing we know about Lysander. Exits and entrances now begin to take on the precise rhythm of farce, and its perverse logic. Helena and Demetrius arrive as if on a passing train, with him trying to push her out of the carriage door:

> I charge thee hence, and do not haunt me thus.

To him, Helena's crime now is to be there at all, and still talking –

> O wilt thou darkling leave me? Do not so

– but he does manage to find a tone that settles matters:

> Stay, on thy peril; I alone will go.

After all his panic, this is firm enough to make even the most devoted spaniel sit.

What is about to happen is rather clear, stage-managed by Shakespeare with a tongue-in-cheek patness that is funny in itself. Although Hermia is lying not far from Lysander, Helena, remarkably, doesn't see her; and Lysander's infected eyes are sure to open now that his victim has arrived on cue for the purpose of being fallen in love with.

Shakespeare is ordering his play in such a way that accident is allowed to be at the heart of things. It always is: on his recent record is the unlikely loss of a vital message to Mantua which brings the heavens down on Romeo and Juliet; one day he will invent the equally absurd device of a statue coming to life in *The Winter's Tale*, and the unlikely change of heart for Edmund which comes too late to save Cordelia and Lear from extinction. The *Dream* is afloat on shallower but similar waters.

Before the inevitable, Helena, the play's only true soliloquiser, confides in us again. The toothless envy she used to feel for her beautiful friend may have sharpened a little –

How came her eyes so bright?

– and overall, her feelings of bad luck have deepened into those of real inadequacy. Whereas before –

Through Athens I am thought as fair as she

– now:

No, no – I am as ugly as a bear . . .

However, what you believe makes you unattractive may, acknowledged, become almost its opposite. So Helena's tough judgment on herself is funny and appealing: we would like to reassure her that she is wrong to think that

. . . beasts that meet me run away for fear.

Not that she would accept our help: she just feels all wrong, paralysed by self-doubt and clumsiness – even metaphors don't help her now. The merest furrowing of a stranger's brow would strike her as a sign of disgust. How could she have been so stupid as not to grasp that her defeats are part of the natural order?

What wicked and dissembling glass of mine
Made me compare with Hermia's sphery eyne?

Under these circumstances, the surprise that awaits her when Lysander awakes will be awful as well as delightful. His sweet words will bring a spasm of joy – brief, as he would say, as lightning at night – but then plunge her into deeper despair. This time, though, she will at least have someone to blame.

As she approaches him, her tone is plucky and helpful, as if she were the heroine of a melodrama:

> But who is here? Lysander, on the ground?
> Dead, or asleep? I see no blood, no wound.

The shared heartbeat of rhyme and metre is preparing the best possible version of the joke. The technical requirement for Lysander to complete a couplet, as if he had heard its first half in his sleep, will force him into a fast awakening with no time for naturalistic wooziness. No one could have guessed that Oberon's terrible invention would be as funny as this:

> HELENA: Lysander, if you live, good sir, awake!
> LYSANDER (*wakes*): And run through fire I will for thy sweet sake.

If that is how the love-juice always works, this will be a great evening. The only grace-note Shakespeare has added to the comic predictability is Helena's initial politeness – 'good sir', almost as if, rather than being his friend, she had never met Lysander before. All of it is delightful; but the laughter falters as Helena begins to realise she is a victim, for the second time, of male instability. To her discomfiture, Lysander claims to see right through to her inner beauty much as if her chest was naked –

> Transparent Helena, nature shows art
> That through thy bosom makes me see thy heart

– but the vision makes him immediately want to make not love but war:

> Where is Demetrius? O, how fit a word
> Is that vile name to perish on my sword!

Staunchly loyal, Helena ignores his fulsome compliments as if they were a foreign language, as such talk must be to her. She assumes that it is Demetrius's pursuit of Hermia (her fault again) that is stirring Lysander to violence:

> What though he love your Hermia? Lord, what though?
> Yet Hermia still loves you . . .

Lysander's marvellous backflip has thus been done for a sterling girl who sees her job as cheering up her friends. At the same time the darker meaning of Oberon's trick begins to show itself: the newly enchanted don't simply forget the past, but turn uglily against it. Lysander harshly dismisses as 'tedious minutes' the tender exchanges we have watched him share with Hermia; he attributes his change of heart to 'reason' rather than its opposite; and he insists that the sight of Helena has, in a moment, turned him from a child to a man, rather than the other way round:

> . . . I, being young, till now ripe not to reason.

There is quite an ugly determination in this; within a dozen lines he even calls Helena a dove and Hermia a squawking 'raven'.[4] It stalls the comedy: it is as if, in *As You Like It*, Rosalind were to dump Orlando for Oliver and abuse Orlando into the bargain, and it also has the malevolent energy of Claudio disgracing Hero at the altar in *Much Ado*.

Victim of two male changes of heart and the beauty of a school friend, exhausted by pointless exertion and a galloping loss of self-esteem, what is Helena to do with this? Half amused only, we hold our breath for her reply. Instead of the old, slightly schoolgirlish tone of complaint, she now seems to have the full Shakespearian engine behind her:

> Wherefore was I to this keen mockery born?
> When at your hands did I deserve this scorn?

It stays within the comedy pattern – just – because of the restraining rhyme; also because her next line is as endearing as when she pictured herself as a great brown bear. Now she feels old as well as ugly, so she might as well develop the *hauteur* to go with it:

> Is't not enough, is't not enough, *young man* . . .

Apart from this slightly spinsterish moment, her language is powerfully stripped down. The riddler who ran rings around Demetrius (the only rings she could) becomes almost monosyllabic, her feelings too strong for styling:

> . . . That I did never – no, nor never can –
> Deserve a sweet look from Demetrius' eye
> But you must flout my insufficiency? . . .
> But fare you well. Perforce I must confess
> I thought you lord of more true gentleness.

We are reproached too, having lacked the gentleness not to laugh.
As Helena leaves, Lysander makes a stage joke:

> She sees not Hermia.

Like Oberon becoming invisible, he is simply informing us of the rules – she just didn't, don't ask questions, that is how things stand.

---

4. Romeo describes Juliet as a dove; Orsino shockingly calls Olivia a raven as he threatens to kill Viola towards the end of *Twelfth Night*.

Indeed, most people who arrive at this spot – even Puck – become a little unobservant. As Lysander then turns to the unprotected Hermia, his tone darkens like the approaching night: he sounds less like a Romeo than an embittered Troilus, speaking biliously from the gut. He says the unsayable, his curse more vicious than Oberon's over the sleeping Titania. The very fact of Hermia's existence causes him violent sickness, like too much sugar; she has been, in his life, an early mistake (a 'heresy') that he will continue to detest long after he has shaken it free. He punishes her not only with his own loathing but that of the world:

> So thou, my surfeit and my heresy,
> Of all be hated, but the most of me.

This is some drug. He turns to his new love, and his shift into romantic courtliness –

> And, all my powers, address your love and might
> To honour Helen and to be her knight

– is at once funny in its quaint medievalism (the minstrel under the window again) and deranged. Laughter at his fantasy wavered as its impact reached Helena; it dries up entirely as he leaves, a stoned Sir Galahad trotting in silly bliss behind her, while Hermia wakens to learn what being a victim means.

It seems there is more than one kind of night in Oberon's wood: thick with erotic harshness, the play turns a little swampy. As they do for anyone left alone in them, the woods deepen and darken, hissing with unknown life:

> HERMIA: Help me, Lysander, help me! Do thy best
> To pluck this crawling serpent from my breast!

As well as being a nice psychological idea, this unconscious serpent was no more than strict fact: it was her lover. Standing over her, blaspheming, he created the play's least summery dream. Hermia's trust in him is such that for seven lines she assumes he is still with her; she begs him to get the snake off her, to share her shock:

> Lysander, look how I do quake with fear.

The worst part, of course, was the fact that throughout the dream Lysander

> . . . sat smiling at his cruel prey

– as in fact we have seen him do. Then she turns to find him gone.

It takes courage to call for help. It means broadcasting a private terror to the wide world, and the fear is not so much of not being taken seriously as of giving the unknown a name. Now the threat, acknowledged, can hear her too. She manages to call out, four or five times in various pitches, coming to know the deep silence that follows; the trees rustling, the air heavy with some diabolical refusal to reply. Who hasn't lost their way in the countryside while the sun was sinking fast, far from any road and before the days of mobile phones? A primitive cell in the brain has one purpose only: to get you home, to bring the injured climber out of his crevasse, to find a way of surviving the stare of a wild animal. It tells Hermia what is at stake: simply, one thing or the other. Fight and flight combine as she plunges into a deep, noisy darkness:

> Either death or you I'll find immediately.

Unexpectedly, it is not Helena but Hermia who is having the worst time: what seemed such a blessing in life is bringing her nothing but trouble.

★

It is increasingly easy to see what a disservice lazy-minded critics have done us by saying that these four lovers lack individuality. The feckless argument goes that Shakespeare has made them much of a romantic muchness, interchangeable verse-vessels with little personality, and conventional in what they have. The exact opposite is true. I've occasionally heard Hermia grudgingly described as a spitfire, headstrong and wilful, in that male vocabulary reserved for a quick and opinionated woman. The fact is that she is brave, though her courage in risking her life doesn't make her more able than most of us to deal with separation and bad dreams. Helena has been called an ugly duckling, after her own assessment, but in truth she deals open-heartedly with a very raw deal. The men too are far from interchangeable young bucks. There is a wilfulness in Lysander, emphasised by the drug, and Hermia will need to keep an eye on him. Thus far Demetrius is more conventional; but he will end up as the quartet's eloquent spokesman when called upon to account for the night's events.

It is important that these differences are established now: the lovers' tendency to mistake one for another as the plot thickens shouldn't be shared by the audience. Ahead of them lies their toughest challenge: a prolonged and brilliant dance that teems with distress without losing its wit. Their earlier scene called for the actors to rattle off rhyming couplets with unembarrassed relish. Now the madness of Lysander and the women's pain flag up a further need: they are going to have to be good enough for the dramatic torments of Strindberg as well.

FIVE

Act 3 Scene 1

When his team first met back in the city, it was Peter Quince who sounded like the director:

> Is all our company here?

Now, at the Duke's Oak, Nick Bottom seems to have taken over:

> Are we all met?

His tone of voice banishes all shadows, as if a bank of lights had suddenly flared. The perilous clearing in the forest where in some other dimension Oberon wrangled with Titania, the dank and dirty ground where Puck pranced, is now just a stage waiting to be used again; the seething bushes in which Hermia, scared half out of her wits, hoped to spot Lysander are now a 'hawthorn brake' which will serve as an actor's dressing-room. A play that deals in exceptional illusions once more sets about anatomising how they are created.

Quince's cheery talk of 'this green plot' may be meant to reassure his colleagues, a full league away from home. But why he would think the middle of the forest in the middle of the evening is a marvellous convenient time and place for a rehearsal remains a mystery to them. Before they even sit down, rebellion stirs. Ostensibly, the problem is the script:

> BOTTOM: Peter Quince . . . There are things in this comedy of Pyramus and Thisbe that will never please.

The supporting cast cluster behind their leading man, his expertise unquestioned. Bottom's objection is not so much aesthetic as practical –

> First, Pyramus must draw a sword to kill himself, which the ladies cannot abide

– and if those grand consorts were to disapprove of naked violence, and the lords besottedly side with them, what would it lead to for the players?

It happens that forty years later an actor was to be put in the stocks for playing Bottom (in his impending asinine role) too convincingly on a Sunday in front of the Bishop of Lincoln. And the temperature of the times can be taken from the fact that Shakespeare's company, the Lord Chamberlain's Men, would shortly sail close to the wind themselves by reviving *Richard II* at the invitation of the supporters of the Earl of Essex. These patrons, who were involved in a rebellion against Queen Elizabeth, thought that a play which dealt with the demotion of an unworthy king would make good propaganda. In the ensuing fracas, the actors got away with it, but it had been a considerable risk: the Deposition Scene in that play had already been cut from all three printed versions as being too dangerous a hint of Elizabeth's vulnerability. So Bottom's fears for his company, more humbly hired but governed by the same rules, are not so far-fetched.

He might have added that beneath the expediency lies an artistic point: after all, the question of stage violence such as Pyramus is to commit was much pondered by the ancient Greek tragedians, who always kept such things from view, generally sending a Messenger forward to deliver an account of the offstage calamities. In another way, Bottom's chaste objection to perpetrating such things on stage is rather surprising, since such blood-boltered pieces as *Tamburlaine the Great* and *Titus Andronicus* were great current favourites with Elizabethan audiences. Perhaps, as a lover of language able to move storms and roar a lion's part as gently as a turtledove, he doesn't care so much for Senecan melodrama and hankers for more refined methods. What goes without saying in it all, of course, is that his acting will be convincing enough to frighten the ladies in the first place.

From Quince's point of view, this is not a good start: a revolt from the centre, implying a danger vague but huge enough to affect everyone's confidence. He might have preferred his star to confide his worry in private rather than to expose him in this way: there is a certain etiquette in such things, and it was only yesterday that Bottom proved himself a public handful over the casting as well. Best for the moment for Quince to wait and see: he is silent.

The vacuum is quickly filled by Snout and Starveling, who, having contributed nothing to the earlier meeting beyond meekly accepting their roles as Pyramus's father and Thisbe's mother, now become relatively verbose. It seems Bottom carries the company with him. He might not be able to do so in a professional set-up, where it is one thing for the star to take a stand, but another for his less secure colleagues to support him openly, however much they may egg him on in private. But these actors don't fear Quince in the same way: they rightly assume that in a co-operative of amateurs anyone should be able to speak his mind, and they can always go back to the bellows-mending. In fact, Snout is so overwhelmed by the problem Bottom has identified that he swears, by the Virgin Mary ('our La[dy]kin'); while Starveling goes further, impulsively wanting to cut the suicide altogether – thereby disabling the play as effectively as if Juliet woke up before Romeo arrived in the tomb.

Perhaps they know in advance that Bottom already has the answer, and the orator's trick of talking up a difficulty so that he can provide a brilliant solution; and it may be that, for him, establishing his supremacy is a necessary preface to collaboration. He insists that he has

. . . a device to make all well.

There must be a speech written in which it is explained that the actors are only acting and not really the people they say they are – what's more, that the player of Pyramus is good old Bottom the weaver. This to an audience, who apart from almost certainly not knowing who Bottom is, are presumably quite used to watching all sorts of plays and courtly entertainments: the risk seems more likely to be their condescension than their outrage.

It continues to be a remarkable thing that Bottom, for all his bullishness, never comes across as a pain: if he did, these scenes would be intolerable. Self-confidence rarely takes such an attractive form or so obviously arises from naiveté. His is a face that rarely clouds over: perhaps he sings 'Oh What a Beautiful Morning' in the bath and whistles all the way to rehearsals. Alongside his self-promotion runs a softly courteous border: in the earlier scene his director was always 'good Peter Quince', and the play 'very good' and 'merry'. His own acting he described with the affable superlative 'lofty', and his roaring would 'do any man's heart good': he is refreshingly free from self-doubt, filled with the glorious enthusiasm of the amateur.

Quince, seeing how the land lies, accepts the emendation to his text with alacrity, but swiftly reasserts himself in his own, literary way. He proposes for the new speech a peculiar metre, 'eight and six' (syllables), the pattern typically used for a ballad: 'di-dum di-dum di-dum di-dum/di-dum di-dum di-dum'.[1] Bottom won't have it: 'eight and eight' (close to the four-stress, generally seven-syllable metre used by Puck and Oberon), will give such an important passage more gravity.

The discussion now flares up as if the wind had got to it. Quince, obliged to be patient with Bottom, might well be losing enthusiasm for the Snout/Starveling axis: if it is left to them, soon there will be nothing left of the play at all. Whether by prior agreement with Bottom or not, they are pressing an advantage:

SNOUT: Will not the ladies be afeard of the lion?

Again, this is terror of official displeasure veiled as tender-hearted-ness: a petrified female audience will once more hold their lives in the balance. It may be, though, that Starveling is worried about the lion anyway:

I fear it, I promise you.

This is, I would say, intentionally ambiguous: he may only mean that he shares Snout's tactical fears, but it is difficult to resist the idea that he is personally tremulous as well.[2]

Bottom is completely at one with them about this lion, but this time he doesn't seem to have a solution: it may not be a problem he has considered. He makes a show of egalitarianism – it is not for him to decide:

Masters, you ought to consider with yourself, to bring in – God shield us – a lion among ladies is a most dreadful thing . . . [3]

Snout, who has learned fast, suggests another explanatory prologue, which will say much the same about the king of the beasts as its

1. 'The Lion and the Unicorn
   Were fighting for the crown.'

2. The comparison with the ladies' tailor Francis Feeble in *Henry IV Part 2* continues. Feeble tries to escape the military draft ('I would Wart might have gone, sir'), but his cowardice is redeemed when, resigned to his fate, he becomes a wonderful cut-price Hamlet –

   I care not; a man can die but once; we owe God a death.

Starveling will achieve a comparable heroism when he faces down the mocking Court at the end of *Pyramus and Thisbe*.

3. His odd comment after this that a lion is a 'wild-fowl' has some mythical basis in the griffin, a fabulous bird that was half-lion and half-eagle. But to us it is another linguistic blunder.

predecessor did about the suicide of Pyramus. But one sentence is
all he gets out before a familiar voice breaks in:

> BOTTOM: Nay, you must name his name, and half his face must
> be seen through the lion's neck . . .

On the basis of his two suggestions so far, Bottom seems to be an
early proponent of Bertolt Brecht's *Verfremdungseffekt*, the 'alienation
effect' whereby the audience is encouraged not to identify with
individual characters but to consider them part of an ongoing
dialectic.[4] Thus ahead of his time, he now confirms that the action
should be stopped at the crucial moment of the lion's appearance for
an explanation, at some length, of his purpose; also that this lion
should have a purely nominal costume that reveals the actor's face
while he delivers his lecture and names himself. Lion being another
part he once angled for himself, he shows a certain generosity here
in assuming that its ghastly effect will be safe in the hands of Snug
the joiner.

The plan is slightly compromised by the fact that Snug is known
to be 'slow of study' (dyslexic?). Since he cannot be trusted with
anything too literary, his tremendous effort to absorb Bottom's
elaborate phrasing of his speech –

> . . . 'ladies', or 'fair ladies, I would wish you', or 'I would request
> you', or 'I would entreat you not to fear, not to tremble . . . '

– brings him nicely into the scene. Although he has nothing to
contribute to the stylistic debate, he will be feeling anxiety at the
tough rehearsing, and, worse, memorising ahead.

Quince lets all of it pass. In the earlier scene he was the one who
worried that misjudging the lion could get them all hanged, and he
can see that Bottom has probably found the right solution:

> Well, it shall be so.

He also knows that, around the next corner, the writer has caused
the director bigger problems. As if he were helpless before his own
inventiveness, he acknowledges, with authorial pride,[5] two great

---

4. Brecht's views on the theatre were rooted in the Elizabethans, and what Bottom proposes
is a travestied version of Brechtianism in practice. Certainly when the style arrived in England
in the 1960s, it led to quite a number of Pierrot-like figures holding up irritating signs in
Mother Courage or *The Caucasian Chalk Circle* to announce the contents of the ensuing scene.

5. Somewhat like that of a much later playwright of my acquaintance who once presented his
director with the terse stage direction 'Hannibal's Army Crosses the Alps'.

scenic difficulties: the need for moonlight, since on the night Pyramus and Thisbe met the moon shone; and for a wall between their houses with a cranny through which they can communicate. Whereas a Shakespeare might announce the first with a line or two of ravishing verse and the second by simply stating it was there, Quince, with the zeal of the amateur, feels the need to do something. The inspired suggestion of taking advantage of the real moon if it is shining on the night comes (according to both Folio and Quarto) from 'Sn.' The routine academic debate as to whether this is Snug or Snout could be re-enacted with some feeling between two actors who already have too few lines. Without this, Snug has nothing in the scene apart from mute worry over doing justice to Lion; on the other hand Snout, a longer name, was perhaps more likely to have been abbreviated by the printer. There are benefits both ways. If it is Snout, he is abandoning his role as agitator to make the scene's most creative suggestion; if it is Snug, it is a flash of sudden brilliance from an improbable quarter, and likely to be much admired.

A calendar is called for, and by (very) lucky chance Quince has brought one. It confirms what we already know: that on Theseus's wedding-day the moon will be shining. Bottom, no longer a Brechtian, is delighted with this verisimilitude: it doesn't involve scaring anyone, and it will be a fine thing to see real moonlight pouring through the casement of the Great Chamber to bless their endeavours. Who knows, it might even bring them luck with the ladies. Quince, meanwhile, has taken up Bottom's earlier position: there must be yet more explanations. It would be better to write a third great aside in which the actor appointed to 'disfigure' the moon announces that this is what he is doing, presumably going on to explain his cumbersome and arcane props. The lantern he will carry is obvious enough, but the 'bush of thorns' has an obscure folkloric meaning (a man who was once banished to the moon for stealing firewood on the Sabbath). Understood or not, it will be a charming addition, like the dog that eventually materialises, for equally obscure reasons.

Pyramus and Thisbe could be a show with a very long exposition. Perhaps for this reason, Quince's idea gets no response, though in the event it carries the day. Moving on to the problem of the wall, Quince welcomes suggestions, but Snout for one has reached the end of his tether:

You can never bring in a wall . . .

This delightful pessimism, making the tinker less actor than Eeyore, is also like that of a manager harassed by impossible artists: you can still hear it at production budget meetings. Bottom's answer should be obvious by now; a man dressed as a wall, thankfully without an introductory speech this time, but ready with a reasonable mime:

> . . . and let him hold his fingers thus, and through that cranny
> shall Pyramus and Thisbe whisper.

Like it or not, Snout ends up in the part, perhaps bounced into it by Bottom – no lines as yet, but an appearance at least, and probably preferable to his original casting as Pyramus's father.

A spoken disclaimer about the suicide and the lion, the mime of a wall and a bit of luck over the moon: good enough, and enough already. It is time to rehearse. The company has been a little unruly, but all momentary ill-humour has been absorbed: the weaver and the tinker, suspiciously in cahoots as if they were conspiring to exploit a customer, seem pacified. Quince has survived as ringmaster, even salvaging a little pride, Bottom has discharged his obligations, Snout and Snug have improved their casting, while Starveling (unless he was implicitly awarded the part of Moon on the spot) is still stuck with Thisbe's mother. As Thisbe herself, Flute, the unwilling female lead, has been silent and uninvolved, either sulking or harvesting his energies for the hard times ahead.

The best joke of all is that it seemed they would never get to the point of getting started, like a modern cast gossiping about last night's television as a way of postponing picking up their scripts to rehearse. For seventy-odd lines Shakespeare has delicately satirised theatrical procrastination and its tendency to formless debate, and it is noticeable that all the production methods finally agreed are those he habitually embraced himself. His Choruses are always decrying the theatre's inability to bring on the vasty fields of France, to which they might well add lions and suicides who have to be carried off and walls that have to be carried on. As for the moon, it must have been an automatic reflex in the open air theatres to acknowledge the weather: the sun must, some afternoons, have come through as Romeo said

> But soft; what light through yonder window breaks?

It has been a matter of practical opportunism, a little too much theory, a willing suspension of disbelief and limited means. As ever.

Within a moment the rehearsal has an invisible audience of one; Puck, on his way back to Oberon after what he imagines to have been a successful mission. For the first time we see him watch walking, talking humans; and he suddenly seems as protective of Titania, to whom he is supposed to be causing maximum trouble, as one of her attendant fairies might be. His snobbish worry is that working-class characters ('hempen homespuns') are

> swaggering here
So near the cradle of the Fairy Queen.
What, a play toward?

He clearly knows what such a thing is, and uses a rather stiff word – 'auditor' – for himself as its witness. So Puck, drink-spiller and cream-thief, has become for the moment another kind of Shakespearian commentator, making lumpen asides to the audience about the action; conservative, sententious and not particularly interesting. However, he is about to surpass himself.

Bottom would hardly be Bottom if he didn't start with a baby malapropism. Ever cavalier about the subject of the play in hand, he is now careless with his text, as if his main job was tearing a passion to tatters and to the devil with the detail. His mistaking the textual 'odours' in his very first line for 'odious' is obviously typical,[6] though a bad example to be setting the younger actors: when, a few moments later, Flute does the same thing, offering 'Ninny's' rather than 'Ninus'' tomb, Quince's deepening despair may be funnier than the mistakes themselves. Quince can be slapdash too: his mistake when Bottom leaves –

> . . . he goes but to see a noise that he heard

– will start another running joke, clinched at the eventual performance when Bottom says:

> I see a voice.

Each of the actors, in fact, has his problems. Flute, at the other extreme of experience from Bottom, just doesn't spot his cue –

> Must I speak now?

– while his tendency to

> . . . speak all your part at once, cues and all

shows that he doesn't understand the way an Elizabethan play (or for that matter a script in England's weekly repertory system as late

---

6. It is probably better, as recommended in some texts, for Quince to correct him with 'odorous' rather than 'odours': the three syllables of 'odorous' are funnier and clearer to the ear.

as the 1950s) was laid out. Each actor's copy contained only his own lines plus his cues, so that he would have no idea how long or short the intervening speeches might be.[7]

The lamentable comedy turns out to be stylistically quite varied. It starts as a mixture of blank verse for Pyramus and yet another form, hexameters, to be intoned by Thisbe, once Flute gets the hang of it. Just as the conventions the group have agreed are Shakespearian, the language, though laborious, is not ridiculous, and it serves a story no sillier than *Romeo and Juliet* would be without the linguistic genius. What is supposed to happen is that Thisbe replies to Pyramus's opening four lines and exit (to avoid an approaching voice, perhaps that of Thisbe's mother) with four lines in her own style, whereupon:

> PYRAMUS (*re-entering, the 'danger' past*): If I were fair, Thisbe, I
>   were only thine.
> THISBE: I'll meet thee, Pyramus, at Ninus' tomb.

What would therefore have been a charming enough opening exchange in which the lovers pledge their faith is interrupted by one of the most famous entrances in Shakespeare.

It eclipses everything of course. Instead of Bottom as Pyramus, Bottom wearing the head of an ass: even in these animatronic days, a young audience is taken aback by the daring of it. Professor Jan Kott, startled from a turbid dream, points out that of all four-footed beasts an ass is the best-hung; a recent critic finds an echo with the myth of the Minotaur, half-man, half-animal; there has even been talk of the legend of Diana and Actaeon. It is so famous that some of the subsequent text forms part of a TV commercial for Levi 501 Jeans; the image is on the cover of the most recent Arden edition of, for some unfathomable reason, *Twelfth Night*. It is as reckless an inspiration as making the hero of a tragedy talk to a Gravedigger, or an asp-seller outstay his welcome with jokes as the Queen of Egypt prepares to kill herself. But what does it mean?

A little and a lot. It is both mysterious and banal, a hint of nightmare and a joke. Whatever darkness is suggested by it fails to threaten its essential charm. It is also rather logical: clearly Puck,

---

7. And therefore, at least until repetition made them familiar, be inclined to stand woodenly and wait – in the very way I don't recommend to the Court in the first scene of this play. At Dulwich College you can see the remains of one of these scripts, its pages stuck together in the form of a scroll, for Edward Alleyn's part in Robert Greene's *Orlando Furioso*. Its original seems to have been some six metres long.

whose initiative it is, has seen the ass in Bottom and decided to make an ass of him. If Bottom, a silly ass, has been played with the right kind of boorishness, the audience swiftly gets the point. This is an animal that can bite fiercely and perform all kinds of bestiality; but its daft prettiness, its face, ears, mournful eyes and apparent innocence guarantee affection even if it remains a not necessarily friendly mystery.

Intriguingly, there is a hint that this head, like Titania's grassy mound, was a stock prop in Shakespeare's company – 'Enter Piramus with the asse-head', says the First Folio, as if it were a familiar enough requirement. There is no evidence of such a thing being used in other parts of their repertoire,[8] but then who knows what has been lost.

The design of the thing is crucial, of course. There have been frightening heads and cuddly heads, remote-controlled heads and heads operated with strings to make the ears twitch and the eyes roll. Increasingly, it is made as a form of half-mask that leaves the actor's mouth – and better still, eyes – quite free: an extremely practical consideration. If the head is complete it is very difficult for Bottom to remain audible from behind his protuberant nose; and an actor's eyes are his great asset.

At the end of it all, the magical thing will be revealed for what it is: the most functional of props. But for the moment it seems like an outgrowth, something from Bottom's subconscious which has burst out through him; were it not for the predetermined key of comedy, we could be as unnerved as if he had suddenly turned into the Elephant Man. As with Pinocchio, there will be beguiling moments when Bottom's and the donkey's character will merge. It is generally this way when actors play animals: neither the human starting point nor the metamorphosed figure is as intriguing as the moment, on a half-lit threshold, that they begin changing from one thing to the other.

We watch securely: the sight is enough to cause Bottom's friends, already a little tense in this marvellous inconvenient place, to panic and flee. As if punishing their cowardice, Puck rises to some fearsome transformations: his alliterations may be reminiscent of the First Fairy –

---

8. There is a play from the 1570s with the oddly modern title of *The Cradle of Security*, in which three ladies put a pig's snout on the King's face while he sleeps, ho-ho.

> I'll follow you, I'll lead you about a round
> Through bog, through bush, through brake, through briar

– but his shapes are drawn from contemporary reports of diabolical manifestations. Looming up at the frightened actors is a pig, a dog, a bear without a head, in a forest turned to a booby trap of snagging thorns, swampish damp and sudden fire.

For Bottom, all this is a puzzle: he was simply hiding behind a bush, in listening posture, waiting for his cue. Entering at the correct moment, he gathers that he is the victim of some unkind joke: instead of the concentrated attention he was expecting, a disrespectful plot has been hatched and everyone pretends there is something wrong with him. It is a 'knavery', the sort of unprofessional fooling about he thoroughly disapproves of. What, otherwise, is the explanation? Does he have an unseemly branch stuck on him, a tangle of ivy, or burrs? Irritatingly, Snout and Quince return for another peek at how their trick has worked, giving unconvincing performances of shock. Snout's assumed incredulity –

> . . . what do I see on thee?

– is no better than Quince's poor impression of awe:

> Bless thee, Bottom, bless thee, thou art translated.

Do they really think he of all people can be taken in by such bad performances?

> What do you see? You see an ass-head of your own, do you? . . .
> This is to make an ass of me, to fright me, if they could . . .

For the second time, an innocent party has been left alone in this wood. Hermia's reaction was to plunge after the real Lysander, hoping to forget the cruel mocker; Bottom, unaware of any mystery, stands his ground. When his pretend-aghast friends return in triumph, tired of their prank, he must be sure they find his dignity intact; but in the meantime it is a little alarming out here on your own, like being abandoned in a room during a game of blind man's buff. In order not to crumble, best to walk up and down and sing, as anyone would, especially a weaver[9] – loudly too, to face down any sniggering in the bushes around him.

9. Weavers were well-known singers at their work, and since they were often Puritans their taste tended towards the liturgical. Hence Falstaff's delightful and apparently incongruous line in *Henry IV Part 1* as he laments the cowardly state of the world:

> I would I were a weaver – I could sing psalms, or anything.

Bottom's taste in music will gradually decline with his asshood until all he wants is the percussive 'tongs and bones'; but for the moment his song, invented or otherwise, has a gentle charm. It is full of the reassuring sounds of familiar birds: the 'ousel-cock' (male blackbird), the 'throstle' (thrush), the tiny treble of the wren. However, it doesn't work: something alien is breaking through the comforting tune, a piercing sound from the night sky:

TITANIA: What angel wakes me from my flowery bed?

Perhaps he imagined it, or perhaps this is another practical joke, best ignored. In the theatre there will be a laugh (we have probably forgotten about Titania), so it is just as well that Bottom needs to think for a moment before answering. To have him then sing a second verse before giving in to the new experience is cunning – it provides a bridge between his old life and the new and obviates some awkward questions about what he thinks has happened. So, another verse, in, near enough, eight and six, the birds jostling still more noisily together –

The finch, the sparrow and the lark,
The plainsong cuckoo grey

– with perhaps a giveaway sound on the song's last word:

Whose note full many a man doth mark,
And dares not answer nay.

But even the churchy cuckoo doesn't calm him: he runs out of words and a bad silence falls. To fill it, he contrives an uneasy gloss on his lyric, its muddle a measure of anxiety:

. . . for indeed, who would set his wit to so foolish a bird? Who would give a bird the lie, though he cry 'cuckoo' never so'?

The landscape is changing around him as if he had been spun like a top, and when he recovers his balance what will he be?

TITANIA: I pray thee, gentle mortal, sing again . . .

The Queen of the Fairies and Bottom as an ass: we marvel at them as much as they at each other. Perhaps she smiles for the first time, her heart lost to this marvellous form of centaur with his royal flush of attributes. He seems to her a new design of being: a wonderful mix of musicality, 'shape' (the sheer figure he cuts) and indefinable 'virtue', that hint of a man's unique soul.

His prose comes thumping in on her music: to him she is simply
'mistress'. Not that he takes her for granted: he is trying for
philosophy while really gabbling, filling the silence again:

> TITANIA: . . . thy fair virtue's force perforce doth move me
> On the first view to say, to swear, I love thee.
> BOTTOM: Methinks, mistress, you should have little reason for
> that. And yet, to say the truth, reason and love keep little
> company together nowadays . . .

Bottom seems to have become modest, even self-denigrating, in his
new character. His easy sententiousness, as if he were propping up
the bar or chatting on his doorstep with a new friend, is exactly the
thing to increase Titania's admiration – such imperturbability, such
intellectual range:

> Thou art as wise as thou art beautiful.

In reality, Bottom's nerve is going fast: feeling he is being sucked in,
he would just as soon, all in all, be on his way, 'out of this wood' as
fast as his legs will carry him. As he makes a run for it, the
relationship suddenly toughens. This Queen is more powerful than
the seasons, and he is love's prisoner:

> Out of this wood do not desire to go.
> Thou shalt remain here, whether thou wilt or no.
> I am a spirit of no common rate;
> The summer still doth tend upon my state . . .

But, on the other hand, look at the benefits:

> I'll give thee fairies to attend on thee
> And they shall fetch thee jewels from the deep,
> And sing, while thou on pressed flowers dost sleep.

A powerful female blatantly soliciting a stranger is allowed in comedy
as its reverse is not. Meanwhile what is Bottom making of Titania
through his ass's eyes, long-lashed and trusting? We don't know, and
he himself will never say whether he was captivated by a tiny thing
on a leaf or something almost human. Of course not: no ass can do
justice to such a thing.

Suddenly they are all around him, mad illustrations from some
picture book, and he the giant in wonderland. He watches the fairies
as he swims in their leader's words, as luscious as what they describe:

> Hop in his walks, and gambol in his eyes;
> Feed him with apricots and dewberries,
> With purple grapes, green figs and mulberries . . .

A world small enough to hide in acorn-cups is finally up against a full-sized one, huge-headed and hairy. From moment to moment, though, the fairies and Titania seem to shrink and swell. As they are sent on more violent errands even than before, the fairies remain small enough to steal honey-bags but big enough to carry armfuls of apricots and figs. While the airy King Bottom eats this full-sized fruit, bees' thighs lit by glow-worms will be his tapers to escort him to Titania's bed, a butterfly's wings protecting his eyes from bright moonlight. The ravishing prospect of living on these twin scales, a tiny army satisfying his farmyard desires, relaxes him and provokes an easy, homely wit we didn't expect. He ignores Moth (who could be the First Fairy returned to the ranks), but tailors a greeting of the utmost gallantry to each of the others. Since cobwebs were thought able to close gashes, Cobweb will staunch his wounds; he immediately senses that the parentage of someone called Peaseblossom must be an unripe pea-pod (a squash) for a mother and a ripened one for a father, and civilly sends them his regards; he very much respects the stoicism of Mustardseed, who loses so many of his relatives to the grazing cattle but has the retaliatory gift of provoking violent sneezing. Titania takes the idea of Bottom's eyes watering in just this way and turns it into something rich and rare:

> The moon, methinks, looks with a wat'ry eye,
> And when she weeps, weeps every little flower,
> Lamenting some enforced chastity.

Much now depends on how you interpret 'enforced'. The word is more likely to mean 'obligatory' than 'violated' (as it would if the flowers were bewailing a rape): Titania is ushering Bottom into a place without rules, where chastity is not much prized and nature must follow its course.

This can involve fairies sleeping with mortal gentlemen: so the weaver must be taken to paradise. Titania's sexual encouragement is extremely lyrical; but beneath its restraint it burns with desire. It certainly has its effect on Bottom. In his own person a chivalrous and chaste amateur actor worried for the ladies' feelings at the play, he is now a famously well-endowed brute with full licence. Perhaps he drops a big vocal hint that he is beginning to become as he looks, some terrible braying eruption in contrast to Titania's beautiful words, so that he has to be subdued before being unleashed again:

> Tie up my love's tongue; bring him silently.

In a play which already brilliantly counterpoints the music of dreams with the sounds and smells of the working world, high poetic suggestiveness has now been laid next to carnality. It might well be the moment, as writers used chastely to say, to 'draw a veil' over proceedings, and have a pause.

INTERVAL MUSIC

His hands black with engraver's ink, William Blake – 'poor Blake, still poor, still dirty' – looks up to see the dead members of his family gathered around him. Then he walks in the countryside, and angels and demons join him as he goes; a thistle transforms itself into an old man and warns him never to return to London. He habitually talks to Michelangelo and the Angel Gabriel, and towards the end of his life he summons up the ghost of a flea in a picture as unnerving as one of Goya's late 'black' paintings. Feared and viciously underrated, tormented and transcendent, Blake produced images which just about fed his family for a month but are now out of the reach of some millionaires. He fought bitterness as if it were another visible demon in his road, sometimes successfully and sometimes not; when he died (as he used to claim he had done several times since his birth), an artist friend closed his eyes to keep his visions in.

He was a hard man to please, but he very much liked and admired his fellow-artist Henry Fuseli:

> The only man that ever I knew
> Who did not make me almost spew.

The face of Fuseli, a Swiss with an assumed Italian name, was crowned by a mane of hair blanched pure white by a fever, which had also left his hands chronically shaking. He only turned to painting in his late thirties (improbably, he had trained as a priest), not so long before he met Blake. Unlike many artists – and unlike Blake – Fuseli rather resembled what he produced: the theatrical witches and pop-eyed heroes rendered by his shaking hands, their nostrils flaring and limbs wildly out-flung, would ultimately inspire Edgar Allan Poe and Salvador Dalí. His *Nightmare* (1781) has a young woman lying spread-eagled on her bed surmounted by an incubus under the milky and voyeuristic eye of a great horse, and at the time he met Blake, who had agreed to do some engraving for him, it had already made him the talk of the town, in spite, or because, of its lurid misogynism. What fire and fury the man has, marvelled Goethe; according to the writer Johann Lavater, he was like a wild warrior travelling on the wings of the wind. The pugnacity and vicious humour that accompanied Fuseli's talent – his laughter was described as the mockery of hell itself – was so alchemised that he became the Establishment's darling (and incidentally that of Mary Wollstonecraft, who tried to interest him in a *ménage à trois* with her husband), and in due course Professor of Painting at the Royal Academy. The same qualities in William Blake earned him mostly humiliation and neglect.

Their meeting was in 1787, when Fuseli was 46 and Blake 30: and though Fuseli's love was said to be like a deadly flash of lightning, he genuinely returned Blake's wary affection. Apart from diminutive height – both nearer five foot than six – what they had in common was a love of the theatre and a special fascination with Shakespeare. Their friendship is the more remarkable since just before this moment John Boydell, a London alderman with an entrepreneurial streak, had hand-picked a group of fashionable artists to contribute work to his grand new Shakespeare Gallery in Pall Mall – essentially with an eye to selling subsequent engravings of it abroad, but in the process bringing Shakespeare into an intense public spotlight. He pointedly excluded Blake while welcoming the equally revolutionary Fuseli with open arms. The special salt in this wound is that the older man and established star often comes across as the unfortunate Blake's pupil – the Blake perhaps of *Jerusalem* or *Europe*, from which Fuseli's Constance in *King John*, aghast and dejected, could easily have come, just as his Lear could be Blake's Job.

Blake, prone as he was to seeing the aisles of Westminster Abbey fill up with imaginary monks and priests, especially favoured Shakespeare's Ghosts – Richard III's consciences, Caesar with Brutus, Hamlet and his father. (Later he did a superb *Pity* based on *Macbeth*.) Fuseli's Shakespeares, meanwhile, are nothing if not violent – they often look as if a hurricane were blowing through them, stripping the flimsy garments from overmuscular bodies that strain and grimace against its force. His study of Margaret taunting York with the paper crown in *Henry VI* is really a pile of hysterically striving nudes; his plumed Henry V discovering the conspirators also shows an excessive interest in anatomy for such a moment.

Both artists, being men who saw visions themselves, loved *A Midsummer Night's Dream*: but their treatments were very different.

Blake brings to his many studies of the play a childishly vivid colouring. His *Oberon and Titania on a Lily* is the least threatening image you could hope to find for the fairy world. His 1786 *Oberon, Titania and Puck with Fairies Dancing* has Oberon as a little bearded old man looking on as if leaning against a lamppost, cuddled cosily by Titania while her fairies dance in a flowing, musliny circle. It is all very pleasant and pastel, and a half-naked Puck is caught in an all-purpose merry-devil pose best avoided on the stage: his hip is swung and he looks as if he had a belly-dancer's bells on his fingers.

Henry Fuseli did the exact opposite with Puck, who becomes a frightening harpy causing a horseman to fall into the river. When he came to paint *Titania and Bottom*, one half of the schizophrenic picture is all light and airy figures, but the other features a young woman leading in a wizened old man (youth conquers age?), a witch holding a waxen changeling and a group of childish warlocks. In another picture, *Titania's Awakening*, there are three witches, and a little monster between Bottom's naked and spreadeagled legs.

If Shakespeare was essentially an excuse for Blake to endorse his private world – some of his paintings are almost unrecognisable from their Shakespearian titles – for Fuseli the playwright's own imagination was the magnet, and he remains his best-known interpreter on canvas. In the case of the *Dream*, his temperament immediately grasped the sharp twist from light to dark and back again that has vexed and exposed the play's later interpreters in the theatre. It would be nice to think of the two artists returning home from Drury Lane discussing the latest production – Fuseli developing visions to anticipate Jan Kott and Robert Lepage, and Blake dreaming in pink and blue, like a visual Mendelssohn. However, it didn't happen; for the extraordinary fact is that neither artist ever experienced the play in any form that we could accept.

It is indeed hard to grasp (though Blake would have sympathised with the author) how underrated or ignored many of Shakespeare's plays were for the first two hundred and fifty years of their life. When the Puritans closed the public theatres in 1642, effectively pouring cement over the repertoire, the *Dream* disappeared with the rest. Under the ministration of Shakespeare's godson (or perhaps illegitimate son) William Davenant, who was allowed to form a theatre company on Charles II's succession in 1660, nine of the plays showed their heads again – some familiar titles but also, oddly enough, *Measure for Measure* and even *Henry VIII*, a play some might think well buried. The *Dream* was briefly revived at this time in a version that may, unusually, have quite resembled Shakespeare's play (Davenant was much inclined to make the texts 'fit' for the new age). It was seen by Samuel Pepys, who called it 'the most insipid ridiculous play that ever I saw in my life' – so insipid in fact that, like a lazy critic, he took to looking at the audience, where he saw 'some handsome women, which was all my pleasure'. (He had, earlier in the year, said much the same about *Romeo and Juliet.*) However, he also reported some good dancing on the stage, a first clue to the play's commandeering by music. Pepys might have had a better night at the underground 'droll' which had been doing the rounds even during the Commonwealth years and was now being published openly as *The Merry Conceited Humours of Bottom the Weaver.* To suit the *Zeitgeist*, the lovers were absent from this version, leaving things to Oberon, Titania, Theseus, 'Pugg', and particularly the Mechanicals, some of whom had to double as fairies. Or perhaps he would have preferred, in his middle age, the 1692 opera composed by Henry Purcell to celebrate William and Mary's fifteenth wedding anniversary, *The Fairy Queen*. Again, no lovers; but fairies called Tanterabogus and Trash, as well as the little Indian boy, make their debut here. There is no Shakespeare text, but masques at the end of each act feature swans and dragons, Chinese dancers, monkeys and the goddess Juno drawn along by peacocks.

Beguiling travesties like this set the tone for a further century and a half in which the play will only appear swamped in music, with at least one group of characters omitted and a new title such as *Love in a Forest* or *A Fairy Tale*. Then, in 1840, Queen Victoria married Albert, and Elizabeth Vestris, joint manager of Covent Garden, feeling, like Purcell, that the play was suitable for a royal event, put on a spectacular – and Shakespearian – *Dream* with herself as Oberon. Judging from her diary, Victoria was not much amused.

To credit Vestris with allowing the play at last to speak for itself is to ignore the much vaunted 'restoration' of Shakespeare that had supposedly taken place in Fuseli's and Blake's time under the eye of the great actor-manager David Garrick. Garrick arrived at Drury Lane in 1747 with the stated aim of respecting the plays' original identity, but he is a highly ambiguous figure. In practice, his boast –

'Tis my chief wish, my joy, my only plan
To lose no drop of that immortal man

– is a flat lie, since he cut and rewrote the texts almost as heavily as previous adaptors like Nahum Tate (happy ending for *Lear* with marriage for Edgar and Cordelia, a royalist revision of *Richard II*, an anti-Commonwealth *Coriolanus*). For his part, Garrick gave a moment of reunion to Romeo and Juliet, cut the Gravediggers from *Hamlet* and left Laertes and Horatio alive to run Denmark. His three versions of the *Dream* were essentially musicals, with songs imported from *The Tempest* and non-Shakespearian sources: the one most generous to Shakespeare still only contained a fraction of the text and was very unsuccessful. This urge to contradict the play is very surprising, but Garrick's misapprehension was shared even by the textual critic Edmund Malone, who has survived as one of Shakespeare's most important editors. He was making his complete edition of the plays as Fuseli and Blake were walking the streets of London: to him, the *Dream* was 'puerile . . . a forced connection of various styles . . . a meagre and uninteresting fable'.

So Fuseli and Blake were responding to the resonances of the written play in innocence of its theatrical fact, and had no need to qualify their introspections. Absorbed in the fairy hinterland, they were deaf to the counterpoint of Mechanicals, lovers and Court. With most subsequent artists too, also fascinated by a quarter of the original, you learn more about the painter than the play. It would be hard to argue that Joshua Reynolds' 1789 Puck – a horrid little naked child with pointed ears sitting on a mushroom as if it were his potty – has much to do with Shakespeare. No more so, among the Victorians, has the beautifully done meeting of Oberon and Titania by Francis Danby, so drenched in moonlight it could be under water; or Joseph Paton's vision of their quarrel, with Puck obliviously mounting the First Fairy; or Edwin Landseer's swooningly beautiful Titania with her sweet-faced ass. Neither do the ravings of the poor parricide Richard Dadd (who could hardly be expected to have a merry view of fairyland), or, by contrast, the twentieth-century prettiness of Arthur Rackham. The main claim that could be made for all these paintings is that they contributed to a general interest in fairies that may in turn have sharpened curiosity about the play.

In 1825 Henry Fuseli died in Putney and was buried in St Paul's Cathedral; soon afterwards, his widow destroyed the erotic drawings of which she had been the subject, as being unfit for public consumption. In 1827 Blake, singing joyful hymns to his wife up to the moment of death even though he felt 'all strings and bobbins, like a weaver's loom', passed away and was interred in a common grave, on borrowed money, in the Dissenters' burial ground in Bunhill Fields off the City Road. In the year between these departures, Felix Mendelssohn, seventeen years old and in love with *A Midsummer Night's Dream*, sat down in his parents' summerhouse in Berlin to imagine an opera of it, which would of course require an overture – which is all he did for the moment. The famous result is utterly infectious, and quite remarkable for a schoolboy: the play's mysteries are extroverted into romantic gladness, and the scurrying fairy violins, the brass, the braying of the ass (which he almost cut as being too blatant), are impossible to dislike even if you wanted to. Sixteen years later, famous by now, the composer was invited by the King of Prussia to extend his ideas into a full incidental score for a revival of the play in Potsdam. Despite the resulting work's popularity, I think he might as well have declined. The score famously includes the Wedding March, a silly, martial, brazenly insistent theme more suited to a Coronation or the opening of Parliament than a wedding: the story of Theseus and Hippolyta, no longer human, feels like some great public event glimpsed in long shot on television. The stately Act III Nocturne for horns is lovely, but it is hard to imagine where to put it in a production except, God forbid, as a five-minute entr'acte near the end, as the lovers sleep. Oddly enough the funeral march for *Pyramus and Thisbe*, though intended satirically, is, with its slight Eastern motif and bent tonalities, more intriguing. The music at its best is too much for the play, at other times not enough: it often overwhelms Shakespeare with its romanticism, or rather proves that Shakespeare was much more than a Romantic. Incidental music should never do more than half the work, but the Mendelssohn *Dream* is like a tidal wave. No wonder the Potsdamers, unable to detect the play, preferred the music to the production it accompanied; no wonder it more or less held sway in English productions for a hundred years; no wonder it is rarely heard nowadays, when the play is so loved for itself, except as a wedding march in life.

There was never to be a Mendelssohn opera of the *Dream*, but Benjamin Britten and Peter Pears completed one in 1960 – at the start of a decade in which George Balanchine and Frederick Ashton were to use the Mendelssohn for ballets and the Beatles would perform Shakespeare's *Pyramus and Thisbe* scene on television. In this opera Puck is a spoken part, the fairies boy-sopranos and Oberon a counter-tenor – the first operatic part written for this vocal range since the eighteenth century. By giving the maddened Thisbe a great parody of Donizetti, Britten allows opera to mock itself as roundly as the theatre does in the play. Elsewhere he concentrates on the fairies and the lovers: there are some ravishing moments, particularly a quartet when the lovers awaken and repeatedly overlap the phrase 'I have found . . . mine own and not mine own'. The opera is very popular, but it does raise the question of whether even Britten's genius can add anything to a play that makes such distinctive and varied music of its own.

The one place the Mendelssohn *Dream* can still be heard is in the movies: the overture ushers in the film most people associate with the play, Max Reinhardt's 1935 version for Warner Brothers, co-directed with William Dieterle. The score is in fact so insistent that long balletic sequences for the fairies are often devised as a fore-ground to it while the play awaits its turn. This only really pays off in their final departure from the wood to become distant stars in the night sky – technically, in fact, the film is extremely advanced. (The fairies are most of all like Munchkins from *The Wizard of Oz* in gauzier costumes.) Reinhardt had staged the play a dozen times in Germany between 1905 and 1934, his accounts naturally darkening in tone up to the point that Hitler came to power in 1933 and Reinhardt then fled the country, all his theatres lost to the Nazis. Rather as Olivier's *Henry V* adjusted the play to Britain's wartime spirit, Reinhardt's Hollywood *Dream* – his last major work, as it turned out – takes a lighter tone, to distract from the continuing Depression, the New Deal not fully dealt. It is in many ways hard to take now: some of the acting is excruciating, both clangorously loud and cruelly slow; the lovers are winsome, fluttering their eyes charmlessly as the potion works on them; and a Hollywood choir edges proceedings close to *Snow White and the Seven Dwarves*. There is much archaic diction of course, some of it very unmetrical – Hermia's father is pronounced 'Eejus', perilously close to 'Eejit'. Titania sings her lines at every opportunity, and Lysander and Demetrius wear those plumed helmets that look like silver coal-scuttles – once they are removed, they become extremely lightweight gentlemen. Quince has difficulty reading in the first scene but not in the last when he prompts continually from the script. A manic James Cagney, as if on speed, overplays in a good cause as Bottom, demonstrating every word with an action; Snout seems to have laughing sickness and cackles like a hyena – quite a good idea but very irritating after a while. In fact laughter rather than Mendelssohn is the besetting sin of the production: everybody roars with mirth all the time. When the lovers awaken they immediately start chortling and speak not a word for the rest of their scene; Mickey Rooney's Puck screeches throughout like a nail on a window – but then he was only fourteen years old, and there is at least a good youthful obnoxiousness in his average-kid's disgust with the grown-ups' love-stuff.

However, Reinhardt's accumulated knowledge of the play is evident from the nicely edited text and from his intelligent view of Hippolyta: she is neutral to displeased (Theseus, though, remains a decent chap, sounding all the more so because he is Hollywood English). In the same tone, there is a distinct moment of resentful tension before Titania, wakened from her dream, accepts Oberon again. Above all, the film has an enormous virtue; the scene in which Bottom is translated. Although they arrive in the forest like Robin Hood and his merry men, the coaching of the actors by Quince is inventive and good, and he and Bottom quarrel viciously before compromising on the female lead's name – 'Thisnebe'. Then Bottom rushes into a bush where Puck sprinkles him with what looks like pollen, and a cinematic dissolve transforms him into the most affable but melancholy ass. The Mechanicals flee not hysterically but in hushed tones of awe, and are pursued by a real pig and dog and flames of fire. Then Bottom, horrified, notices the ears on his head (at which Puck has thrown an apple): he crawls on all fours to a pool to see his reflection and falls into a profound sadness, weeping with shame and confusion. (He reverses the effect later when, transformed back, he rushes trembling to the same pool for reassurance.) Titania approaches him and joins him in his song about the ouselcock; the little Indian boy whom she has cosseted till now is abandoned, weeping his heart out at his rejection before being whisked away by Oberon. Bottom then gets the benefit of Mendelssohn's Wedding March as the fairies carry him away, wrapped in cobwebs, to Titania's bower.

This is something the theatre has no time or means to do. The first sight of Bottom as an ass, emerging from the bushes in cool mid-shot in a very realistic forest, is extraordinarily affecting: it's as if he were simply part of the landscape, the focus is so restrained. The same unnerving naturalness applies as he struggles to eat his

hay in Titania's bower with human hands and ass's mouth. Whenever he sinks into panic and alienation you can glimpse, beyond the
soft focus and majestic kitsch, the depths Reinhardt's versions of the
play on stage must have reached as darkness closed over the Weimar
Republic. With the human spirit sinking into brutality and despair,
such moments feel thick with grief for a lost identity and terror of a
new one.

The strains of Felix Mendelssohn are heard again, and Reinhardt's
fireflies glimpsed as well, in (at the time of writing) the most recent
film of the play, directed in 1999 by Michael Hoffman. They serve
as a sort of whoomph factor for the rather uncertain magic of this
fairy world. The traditionalism is quite surprising, as the action is set
in the present on Monte Athena ('somewhere in Italy'), on the eve
of a high society wedding. The film is remarkably respectful of the
text, making the disclaimer 'after the play of Shakespeare' unnecessary; but like many stage productions it succeeds brilliantly in some
areas while faltering in others. The Theseus-Egeus scenes are very
successful, their wrangling over Hermia conducted as tensely and
privately as at some inner conclave of the Mafia: for once the threat
of death, delivered by a Theseus acutely aware of his responsibilities
as well as of their cost, is strikingly believable. Down in the village,
the Mechanicals, led by Roger Rees's Quince, sit around on the
steps of the (closed) church in siesta hour, killing time and hoping
for the best from the grandees up the hill. The movie wobbles somewhat in a dank woodland setting which even the most uninitiated
can see is in a studio (less impressive, even after all these years, than
Reinhardt's), into which the lovers blunder on their bicycles – which
have a starring role throughout. In contrast to Reinhardt's misty
forest glistening with fairy lights, this world of dwarves, furies and
fawns looks like a fancy dress party, or *Caligula* without the sex, and
I thought for a moment I heard Oberon refer to 'such dulcet and
Armaniist breath'. Apart from the Theseus story, the real interest is
in Kevin Kline's Bottom, a white-suited dandy in panama hat in love
with opera and acting, clearly on the run from vengeful husbands all
over town. *La Traviata*, *Norma* and *L'Elisir d'Amore* regularly swathe
him; but for all his bravura, he is utterly crushed by being doused
with wine in front of his admiring colleagues as he does his
turtledove version of the lion. Scorned by his long-suffering wife as if
he were some down-at-heel Macready, and quite unable to remember
the name of Thisbe, his co-star, he will certainly never forget

Titania's love, and given half a chance will clearly be revisiting fairyland.

As fireflies flicker again, Mendelssohn's overture crashes over the credits of Woody Allen's 1982 *A Midsummer Night's Sex Comedy*, prefacing the perverse swirls of sexual desire during a weekend house-party in, perhaps, New York's Hamptons. The Shakespeare play is like a faint default setting: only the Mendelssohn and the film's title owe much to it, though there is occasionally a sly advantage in the alliance. So the moon, toadstools and a barn owl are very evident; the women traipse around in the long grass talking about sex while the men challenge each other in the woods and practise their archery.

Woody himself is sometimes seen with a bow and arrow as if he were Cupid. He presides as – I suppose – an unlikely Oberon; an inadvisable investment adviser who at weekends turns 'crackpot inventor with a spirit box', insisting that it can penetrate the unseen world on any summer's night. The trouble between him and his Titania (Mary Steenburgen) is simply that 'we have a bad sex life, that's all'; he often transgressively rides his flying machine outside Mia Farrow's window, but as often, in homage to Buster Keaton, falls into water just out of shot a moment later.

The Theseus figure (Jose Ferrer) also goes hunting. He is a great scholar intent on a little fling, inclined to sing German lieder while Hippolyta fans herself, and in his overbearing meanness is more reminiscent of Serebryakov in Chekhov's *Uncle Vanya* than of Theseus. (In another quotation from Chekhov, one of the lovers inconclusively shoots himself.) Eventually, unprotected by fairy blessings, he passes away 'at the height of lovemaking' and is transformed into a swarm of, yes, summer fireflies. Meanwhile, violently reunited with his wife at the expense of their kitchen furnishings, Woody joyously declares that she has cleared his sinuses for the summer.

It is easy and ungenerous to pick off these films like Shakespeare's policeman, laughing at the shortfall as if parity with the original were ever intended. What they all of course do is testify to the play as Great Suggestion, and each pulls off something good in one or other of the play's worlds. Doing so, they prove its essential elusiveness. Probably more derivatives have been inspired by the *Dream* than by any other Shakespeare apart from *Romeo and Juliet* and *Hamlet*. However, *Hamlet* stretches generously: Shostakovich, Walton, Olivier, Kozintsev and Ethan Hawke all seem, as it were, included in the play. But alternatives to the *Dream* often seem to be tipping their hats to something that really belongs far away in the theatre; none really capture the play's mercurial heart, its peculiar mixture of innocence and danger. Sometimes, indeed, the distance is comically exploited: when in *A Midsummer Night's Sex Comedy* the prevailing wooing style is summed up by one of the men begging his favourite to 'Gimme ten minutes, ten lousy minutes', the echo of Shakespeare's courtly elaborations seems part of the joke.

The musicality of the *Dream* is likewise a mixed blessing. Shakespeare is not only musical in himself but the cause why music is in other great men; but when you hear Purcell or Mendelssohn or Britten you think fondly of the play, and if their compositions are used in a production the result can be cumbersome and digressive. Mendelssohn falls enthusiastically into some of the traps the play sets; Britten is surprisingly bland in the face of it. Purcell's music is as beautiful as you would expect, but *The Fairy Queen* is really a series of baroque masques ordered by Titania to be performed by 'supernatural' singers while the human parts are played by non-singing actors. In visual art, the great contribution of Fuseli and Blake was that they broke off from delivering portraits of famous actors in great roles (Fuseli did Sarah Siddons and Garrick as the Macbeths and Blake covered Garrick's production of *As You Like It*) to draw attention to the play's inner life. Of course there are no great star parts to paint in the *Dream*: even Bottom compares badly to Falstaff as a study for portraiture, since at his best moments you wouldn't even see the actor's face. Conversely, what we get in a flash from a portrait of Garrick as Richard III, say – the real odour of the play, Shakespeare's hot, discernible breath – we lose looking at devilishly imagined pucks, wizened fairies and priapic asses.

So the talents of artists outside the theatre have formed a kind of alias for Shakespeare, to be entirely enjoyed for being no other than it is. Woody Allen meanwhile must have known that in 1939 Louis Armstrong appeared on Broadway as Bottom in the musical *Swingin' in the Dream*, written by Jimmy van Heusen and Eddy de Lange and choreographed by Agnes de Mille. The action was set in 1890s New Orleans, and it flopped expensively. But it did produce a hit song for Billie Holiday, the strangest impersonator, you might think, of Helena or Hermia confronting Demetrius or Lysander. She finds in the simple lyric of 'Darn that Dream' the first premise of the blues – look the truth in the eye: that voice compounded of honey and absinthe curses the fantasy that makes her think the man might truly love her. Rather than go on enduring such a fool's paradise, she would prefer to live through a real nightmare. As they are about to do.

SIX

Act 3 Scene 2

For all the speculation, little recorded fact and much wish-fulfil-ment, there are still many things about Elizabethan theatre practice that are mysterious to us. How odd it seems that Shakespeare's plays were generally performed in the noisy afternoon in the middle of London, in the open air – one step away in unpredictability, it might strike us, from street theatre. Then there is the time taken. The Chorus introduces *Romeo and Juliet*, one of Shakespeare's longest texts, by referring to 'the two hours' traffic of our stage', making present-day directors feel inadequate – how can that have been the playing time without the most extensive cutting? So, what really is the relationship between the published texts we now use as gospel and the actual words spoken at the time in the public theatres? There are certainly plenty of occasions when Shakespeare seems to be providing us with two or three similes in a speech when in the theatre one will do, as if, as far as he is concerned, we should choose between them. Best perhaps to remember that the Chorus's phrase sits pleasantly in a blank verse line and from an alliterative point of view is better than 'three hours' traffic'. We also don't know whether in their race against sunset the Elizabethans took an interval, aside from any improvised ones which the audience might be inclined to help themselves to when they got bored, needed a change or had somewhere else to go – not to mention the attractive distractions at the Globe itself dreamed up by the more imaginative scholars.[1]

1. The scholarly consensus at the moment on intervals is that there wasn't one in public playhouses such as the Globe and the Theatre, but that there would have been in the more rarefied indoor theatres such as the Blackfriars, in which Shakespeare's company often played after 1608. This however would only have been because the candles which provided the lighting had to be trimmed and replaced. There is evidence that for these purposes musical interludes were introduced – four of them, giving rise to the Shakespearian five-act structure posthumously bestowed on the plays in the 1623 First Folio. The snag here is that *Henry V*,

There are scenes in some of the plays, however, sitting at their halfway point or a little after, whose gentle recapitulations very much suggest the start of a second session. In *Twelfth Night*, Viola-as-Cesario and Feste have a little rally of wit, nothing to do with the plot, as if they were a stand-up act in front of the cloth, waiting for the audience to re-settle –

> VIOLA: Save thee friend, and thy music. Dost thou live by thy tabor?
> FESTE: No, sir, I live by the church

– before pulling themselves together and getting on with the story:

> My lady is within, sir. I will conster to them whence you come ...

As Oberon and Puck meet at the start of Act Three Scene Two of *A Midsummer Night's Dream* there is something of the same feeling, as if the play's engine needed revving up again.

It must be said that there is much to be gained in an ideal world from not having any breaks in Shakespeare, not for music, even Mendelssohn, nor to change the set. For one thing, it honours his brilliant use of counterpoint. The first line of a new scene invariably comments on the last of the dying one; and Oberon's speculation about Titania here, coming directly on her abduction of Bottom, could make for a fine laugh. However, this encounter between Puck and him sits just where in modern practice we are likely to have taken a break – there isn't another opportunity for about twenty minutes.[2] And there is something unusual in the dialogue: it is very rare for Shakespeare to repeat his information without embellishment as he does here, and it suggests there is some need for it. Oberon bluntly reminds us of the plot –

> I wonder if Titania be awaked.
> Then what it was that next came in her eye
> Which she must dote on in extremity

– whereupon Puck describes to him at some length what we have already seen for ourselves.

As a result, the actors need to work specially hard to find something new to express. Here are the data. What has happened over the

which was written well before the move to private theatres (it may have opened the Globe in 1599), has five Chorus speeches and an epilogue, suggesting that even at that stage Shakespeare was thinking in terms of five quasi-classical 'Acts'.

2. An earlier interval, after Hermia rushes off to find Lysander, makes for a short first half; a later one, after Puck puts the lovers to sleep, for a very lengthy one.

ass's head is a surprise, an unusual case of the servant taking over from the master and getting away with it. Oberon's division of labour was clear: Puck was to do the secondary thing, reunite the vaguely described Athenian youth with Helena. Oberon would take care of the main business, medicating Titania so that she would be ready to want anything she set her eyes on – which in Shakespeare's charming view of the forest, was as likely to be lynx, leopard, boar or bear as squirrel or rabbit.[3] So his reactions to the news that Puck has exceeded his brief can be various and colourful – astonishment at his initiative, a desire to interrupt, momentary offence and unexpected delight. Finally, even though he might have preferred Titania to fall for some hateful and aggressive beast rather than an amiable amateur actor, ass's head or not, he pays an unprecedented tribute to his servant's virtuosity:

This falls out better than I could devise.

Puck's big speech, whether a break precedes it or not, is quite daunting: the actor knows that there are few theatrical dividends in an audience watching a character creased up with mirth over something they have already enjoyed and moved on from. Not only that, but we have seen him pleased with his practical jokes before, on his very first appearance. The wittiness of his account of disrupting the rehearsal is no more than average; much will depend on his pleasure at it, including ecstatic physical demonstrations. Suiting an ass's bray to his words is almost inevitable; for Bottom to be parodied in other ways, especially if he has an accent, is likely too; his colleagues' flight through the undergrowth may be mocked because of its working-class clumsiness. It certainly is interesting that Puck continues so patronising as well as mischievous. He now knows – somehow – that the preparations were for

Great Theseus' nuptial day

and that these 'Mechanicals'[4] normally

---

3. There is always something fanciful, or at least unEnglish, about Shakespeare's wildlife. If this were the Forest of Arden in *As You Like It* there would be talk of the lioness who waits (that being 'the royal disposition of that beast') for Oliver to awaken before attacking him – only to be beaten back, somewhat improbably, by Orlando. Or, if it were *Venus and Adonis*, of the equally considerate lion who 'walk'd along behind some hedge' in order not to frighten Adonis.

4. I doubt if I shall keep to my own noble intention not to use this phrase, which is certainly convenient. My comfort is, Shakespeare is not so innocent either: in the working papers that formed the basis of the early Quartos of the play, he at one point refers to them as 'the rabble'.

. . . work for bread upon Athenian stalls . . .

He sounds like an unabashed little Tory grandee.

All in all, he has been, as he knows, extremely lucky. Coming upon a perfectly serious gathering in the forest, he decided partly to turn Bottom into the animal he reminded him of, much as he might snatch a stool from beneath a country gossip. In the way of the practical joker he probably wasn't looking beyond the trick's immediate impact; although the point could be argued, it seems unlikely that he was imagining that Titania's eye would be caught, near her 'cradle' though he and Bottom were. For him too, things fell out better than he could have devised.

In the middle of his speech sits something easily overlooked but indispensable to the actor. Describing the fright and flight of Quince and his friends, Puck finds idiosyncratic images:

> When they him spy –
> As wild geese that the creeping fowler eye,
> Or russet-pated choughs, many in sort,
> Rising and cawing at the gun's report,
> Sever themselves and madly sweep the sky,
> So at his sight away his fellows fly . . .

The picture of these birds[5] escaping the hunter and scattering heavenwards is as vivid as a piece of film – you can feel the weather and hear the sounds, and Puck, breathing the Warwickshire air, loses himself in it for the moment. He was traditionally believed to stamp his feet if he was upset with a house he had visited, and now he tells how, like a pagan dancer, he did the same in Oberon's magic grove:

> And at our stamp here o'er and o'er one falls . . .

All this places him exactly where he belongs. Oberon would never use such images; but Puck is the hobgoblin of stable and kitchen who will end the play sweeping the floor.

The human element in Oberon's plan is again treated as an afterthought:

> OBERON: But hast thou yet latchd the Athenian's eyes
>   With the love-juice, as I did bid thee do?
> PUCK: I took him sleeping (that is finish'd too).

For the audience, knowing the result, this is too casual: the plotters'

---

5. 'Russet' was quite a vague term to the Elizabethans, all right for any brown colour or the grey of the 'chough', or jackdaw.

interest is in inverse proportion to the disaster they are causing. They close on a suspended chord which there is no time to resolve:

OBERON: Stand close; this is the same Athenian.
PUCK: This is the woman, but not this the man.

As the lovers start to assemble, it is as if they are engaged in a continuous argument whose sound, for us, is occasionally turned off. Snapped on again, its intensity has not dimmed; but how many variations can be rung on pursuer and pursued? One last combination: Demetrius and Hermia, the most ill-assorted pairing of all, except that this was the proposition that started all the trouble. Demetrius's delusion that he loved Hermia was a mistake committed in broad daylight without the help of purple flowers; it is becoming clear that it was as wild an aberration as anything caused by Puck.

Not only has the play not seen them alone together before, but they haven't even addressed each other apart from in Demetrius's limp couplet in the first scene. It is immediately clear that, as far as possible within the rhythmic limits, they deal in quite different languages and attitudes to love. Her defiance dappled by the anxiety of searching for Lysander, Hermia eloquently works the possibilities of prescribed verse, even, at the outset, letting it break down altogether. She has reached the point of assuming that Demetrius must have literally annihilated her lover:

If thou hast slain Lysander in his sleep,
Being o'er shoes in blood, plunge in the deep,
And kill me too.

It takes her half a line of silence to recover herself. From here on she will find it easy to over-run the ends of her lines, touching in their rhymes as she passes on to some powerful new point. She starts with a statement of simple devotion very like Helena's earlier claim that Demetrius turned night into day for her:

The sun was not so true unto the day
As he to me. Would he have stolen away
From sleeping Hermia?

What she is doing exemplifies one of the difficulties of playing strong emotion in rhyming verse – it is at least as demanding as Titania's passionate iambics earlier. Expressed negatively, it goes like this. If you start a couplet too strongly, or reach an emphatic peak halfway through its first line, it will take quite some effort to wrench the second half of that line into place; and the word that sets up the rhyme, instead of giving a jab of gas to what follows, may barely get established. The second line then becomes a rearguard action, against failing breath, to hoist both sense and rhyme into place; the clinching word may end up with an oddly indeterminate inflexion. Whereupon the whole effortful business has to start all over again. It is not just a matter of breath control but of developing an appetite for expounding the ideas.

Demetrius can't touch Hermia at this sort of composition, and she herself has never quite done it before. Her hunt for Lysander has put her, so to speak, beyond herself, making her chaotically inventive. The harmless Demetrius now looks like Macbeth to her, so deep in blood that he might as well go forward as back. She imagines that he has hunted Lysander while she slept and dragged his carcass into the undergrowth. What else could it have been? The idea that Lysander might have done what he has – 'stolen away' – is as feasible to her as that night and day should have become madly confused:

> I'll believe as soon
> This whole earth may be bored, and that the moon
> May through the centre creep, and so displease
> Her brother's [the sun's] noon-tide with th' Antipodes . . .

In fact these men are a long way from real violence: their belligerence is all verbal. When Lysander fell for Helena and threatened to kill the 'vile name' of his rival, his chest-beating was a ridiculous by-product of intoxication; now, Hermia's offer to pay the ultimate price is probably sincere, but made to the equally innocuous Demetrius.

Demetrius has still not got into his stride, if indeed he has one. He perhaps thought that his presence and a few routine compliments should be enough to secure Hermia; but now that he is accused of murder he sees that he must come up with something, along the lines of being himself killed, by her cruelty. His next idea is to construct a courtly image, bringing in Venus – his first shot at a metaphor. It isn't really his style, being the sort of thing with which the over-educated Helena outwitted him a while back, but he has a go:

> So should the murdered look, and so should I,
> Pierced through the heart with your stern cruelty.
> Yet you, the murderer, look as bright, as clear,
> As yonder Venus in her glimmering sphere.

This is serviceable, but hardly enough to impress a girl able to coin a lyric about the course of true love never running smooth. Now she feels she is being mocked as much by Demetrius's pretentiousness as his colourlessness. She must feel more at home when, exhausted by the literary effort and preferring to see himself as a love-warrior, he falls back into the blunt violence he used with Helena:

> I had rather give his carcass to my hounds.

This rudeness is, as it happens, a response to a gentler tactic from her – she even called him 'good Demetrius'. So she storms at him. It confirms everything she imagined: he is no better than the horrible snake she felt slithering over her breast as she slept:

> An adder did it! For with doubler tongue
> Than thine, thou serpent, never adder stung.

Demetrius can no more retaliate in style than he can fly:

> I am not guilty of Lysander's blood,
> Nor is he dead, for aught that I can tell.

Not only that, but he then has the bad taste to proposition her like some low-grade Angelo. Enraged by her fury – so unfeminine to him – he spitefully retaliates when she asks, in despair, for reassurance:

> HERMIA: I pray thee tell me then that he is well.
> DEMETRIUS: And if I could, what should I get therefor?

This 'get' is ugly, the word of a man more at home with sleazy male bargaining than with a real woman. However, Hermia is up to him, out-rhyming and out-running him again:

> A privilege never to see me more.

It has been a rout. Demetrius's failure, both in evasion and pursuit, induces abject melancholia once Hermia has left him alone:

> Here therefore for a while I will remain.
> So sorrow's heaviness doth the heavier grow
> For debt that bankrupt sleep doth sorrow owe,
> Which now in some slight measure it will pay,
> If for his tender here I make some stay.

You would think he had undergone some great trial. His speech's air of legalistic tangle – bargains, the balancing of the books, deposits – is typical of someone out of his depth in this unstructured world, and much different from Lysander with his gauds, conceits and love-songs. But it is also, obviously, obscure. The idea that sorrow's heaviness grows because of some debt that sleep owes it is impenetrable on the page even with a reader's leisure, let alone when it falls once only on an audience's ear: it could be cut. No wonder both the Quarto and the Folio make the stage direction that follows sound like an instruction – 'Lye down [and sleep]' – as if we had had quite enough of Demetrius for the moment.

This is a place where a man can change allegiances in a moment, drop off as if suddenly anaesthetised and wake up as sharply. Lysander roused himself from sleep to complete Helena's couplet, and Demetrius can now be imagined dropping sharply through a trap door after his final 'stay', as if adding a full stop. The pause that follows will be long enough for Oberon to sense the audience's laughter swelling, and then to catch it before it bursts:

> What hast thou done?

Puck is, as it were, sneaking away, examining his fingernails and whistling – anything not to catch his master's eye. His triumph over the ass's head has completely evaporated. He has, in general, two reactions to being held to have failed; defensive, and – later, after more vexations – defiant. Now, as the incompetent servant, he is only able to throw up a verbal smokescreen: he seems to be imitating someone else's diction, Helena's perhaps, to give himself the advantage of obscurity:

> Then fate o'errules that, one man holding troth,
> A million fail, confounding oath on oath.

Oberon ignores this, as perhaps beneath contempt, and returns to business by improving a little on his earlier, perfunctory brief. This time, he at least gives Puck the name of the woman he is to find and a quick description of her dejected appearance:

> All fancy-sick she is and pale of cheer,
> With sighs of love that costs the fresh blood dear.
> By some illusion see thou bring her here.

Puck might like more guidance about this 'illusion', but he needs to be seen to be getting on with it, and boasts of another virtuoso flight:

> I go, I go – look how I go –
> Swifter than arrow from the Tartar's bow.

He is back in a moment – the moment used by Oberon to anoint Demetrius's eyes – having had to do very little. It is extremely exciting. The first person he saw was indeed Helena; not only that, but he has a bonus victim in tow, Lysander, keeping his promise to

be 'her knight'. The word he uses adverbially for the possible consequences, 'preposterous', means, in its original sense, back to front;
even if we are taking them half-seriously, they are the sort of things
that make Puck's cup run over.

What follows is as if a match had been set to a box of fireworks –
two hundred lines in which the relationships of all four young people
come near to being destroyed, to the delight of the audience. It is
ferociously difficult, not least because it touches on what many
actors at the age of these lovers find hardest about Shakespeare and
are least prepared for – how to ensure that form and content feed
and do not oppress each other. Tempestuous as the emotions are, the
formal needs of the long scene are importunate: every line has to be
brightly delivered, the notes on the stave cleanly hit, and the rhymes
heard without being laboured. It is what Shakespeare has been
working up to from the start for these four, an experiment in how far
charged emotion can be expressed in a contrived manner.

Part of his showmanship lies in the impression of speed – of composition, which in turn cries out for speed of delivery on the stage.
As with certain paintings done in a passion, it is hard to imagine
Shakespeare going over and over this passage, revising and rephras-
ing. Inspired fluency was certainly typical of him in these years.
Shortly before the *Dream* he had published *The Rape of Lucrece* (at
1900 lines, not much shorter than the *Dream* would be):[6] it too gives
the impression of being done at a sitting, almost on a single breath.
At least that was essentially narrative; the lovers' quartet in the play
has to sustain itself while arcing this way and that between bipolar
arguments.

Technically, this is the manner how. Lysander and Helena start
the scene with a sonnet – only unusual in that the alternating rhymes
are abandoned at the end of each of their quatrains for a couplet.
Then there is a single hanging line, unrhymed:

LYSANDER: Demetrius loves her, and he loves not you

– apparently rather feeble, since everyone knows that and it's not
poetic. But as well as being a cue for Demetrius to wake up and
contradict, this is like a breath taken before the verse moves fully
into rhyming couplets. There will be twenty of them, and in addition
one half-rhyme ('Hermia . . . Helena'), two triplets by way of showing

---

6. Shakespeare was said by his friends never to have left ink-blots on his lines, so swiftly and
confidently did he write.

off ('sort . . . extort . . . sport' and 'bequeath . . . death . . . breath'), a couple of, so to speak, quartets[7] and one non-rhyming repetition ('dear . . . dear'). It is impeccable. Another gear is smoothly engaged as Helena turns on her old friend in blank verse:

> Injurious Hermia, most ungrateful maid . . .

The emotional reason for this – Helena's deepening sense of betrayal and pain – is obvious. Her new manner is more or less sustained until the men go off to fight, leaving the women to finish the sequence in couplets again – a reminder that the general intention is comic.

So what the ear might come to assume is that rhyme is funny and extrovert; that blank verse deals with deeper feelings; and that mutual verse-making, having once reflected closeness (Lysander and Hermia), can express tougher negotiations too (Lysander and Helena). The surprise is to find that blank verse can be funny, as flexible as jazz and very good for insults, and that rhyme doesn't mean that the feelings aren't strong.

Love enters, once again pursuing its fleeing prey. But where Demetrius was combative and clumsy with Hermia, Lysander is truly plaintive, believing himself heartbroken. When he first woke, his new chemistry was firing him up, but now he has settled into desperate sincerity, even mawkishness, less the gallant knight than a man of constant sorrow:

> Why should you think that I should woo in scorn?
> Scorn and derision never come in tears . . .

Even Helena didn't cry over Demetrius like this: and from her point of view, it must be a tremendous act – the last thing it is. For us it is a welcome comic modulation in the way these men and women confront each other: Lysander's helplessness is so convincing that you could forget it is entirely pharmaceutical. Naturally with Helena there's no negotiation. She has reached the position of the Nurse in *Romeo and Juliet* that there is

> No faith, no honesty in men. All perjur'd,
> All forsworn, all naught, all dissemblers

– but her reaction to the void male conscience is more metaphorical:

> Your vows to her and me, put in two scales,
> Will even weigh, and both as light as tales.

7. These two double couplets (four rhyming lines) come almost at the start and precisely at the end of the passage as if they were bookends – the later one forming an excellent springboard back into iambic pentameters.

The battle is, of course, being fought with a technical weapon: the control of an ironic sonnet. Helena's rhyme here is an attempt to close it down before it is complete, but Lysander feels a metrical obligation to finish it and forces the argument forward:

> I had no judgment when to her I swore.

However, Helena can rhyme anything she is given:

> Nor none in my mind, now you give her o'er.

Throughout this initial duet Shakespeare's technique is very audible, as if it were an overture: in contrast to Demetrius's and Hermia's more experimental diction earlier, the statement of theme is quite formal. The argument is so precise that the pattern could, as a rehearsal exercise, be dismantled and the points made tit-for-tat, corresponding lines intercut with each other. Thus Helena's first couplet is an effective answer to Lysander's first, and so is her second, even more so, to his second:

> LYSANDER: Look, when I vow, I weep, and vows so born
>   In their nativity all truth appears . . .
> HELENA: These vows are Hermia's. Will you give her o'er?
>   Weigh oath with oath and you will nothing weigh.

When the text is then reassembled, every point has been answered and each blow returned, but not at the moment of impact. This technical self-consciousness is a canny judgment: the long development Shakespeare has in mind must go in stages, and at this point excitement needs to be limited. Lysander's attempt to start a new measure –

> Demetrius loves her, and he loves not you

– is a dirty move: since Demetrius is after Hermia, Helena, short of a lover as ever, should attend to him. But then Demetrius wakes, bolt upright on cue: the story twists, and the duet becomes a trio.

If Love-in-Idleness has made Lysander a lachrymose version of his romantic self, it has turned the uptight Demetrius into loverman. He proceeds to stalk Helena with style and sexiness, in a language he could never have achieved before:

> To what, my love, shall I compare thine eyne?
> Crystal is muddy! O, how ripe in show
> Thy lips – those kissing cherries – tempting grow!

Just as terror taught Hermia a new way with words, Demetrius has discovered how to jolt a smooth rhythm with stabs of hyperbole. The whitest mountain range in Turkey (Taurus) becomes its opposite, and he breathlessly elliptical:

> That pure congealed white – high Taurus' snow,
> Fanned with the eastern wind – turns to a crow
> When thou hold'st up thy hand . . .

Barely able to control himself, he hurls himself at her:

> O, let me kiss
> This princess of pure white, this seal of bliss!

The effortless heat is hilarious: to Demetrius, this is now the normal way of talking, no labour involved. Perhaps this is how he loved Helena before the play began: for him alone of the four, intoxication is proving corrective, his eyes opening to what was always there. Helena's reaction will suggest whether or not she recognises him from the old days.

As she did when Lysander advanced on her, she abandons affectation: her denunciation of both men would be unanswerable if it were not deluded:

> Can you not hate me, as I know you do,
> But you must join in souls to mock me too . . .
> A trim exploit, a manly enterprise
> To conjure tears up in a poor maid's eyes
> With your derision.

It really is too bad, this compound mockery of the disheartened. It makes her, not for the first time, repetitive; and since her earlier complaint –

> Wherefore was I to this keen mockery born?

– is still echoing in our ears, the actress will want to find something new. It seems to be in Helena's nature not to stop once she's started, and this is seventeen lines of much the same thing. Unless cut a little, they present the scene's first real staging problem: what are the men to do? Try to interrupt? Wordlessly make up to her? Dote on her for her furious passion? Her task is not to allow them space to say anything, even if it leaves her short of breath; theirs is to stay active but not distract too much. It is difficult for her to find the new tones, and difficult for them to express the mounting physical energy they will feel.

However, the moral force being discharged does have the effect of turning them against each other, likewise outraged, as if that was what the general atmosphere required. In the moments before she arrives, they toss the unwanted Hermia to and fro like a hot potato, hoping Helena will approve of their honest ardour:

> LYSANDER: . . . And here, with all good will, with all my heart
>   In Hermia's love I yield you up my part . . .
> DEMETRIUS: Lysander, keep thy Hermia; I will none;
>   If e'er I loved her, all that love is gone.

The outrageous shuffle is done as a matter of life, death and justice. Honour and generosity have become Napoleonic resolve in both men: dumping Hermia is a moral duty. She is now more unwanted than Helena ever was.

This second movement – the trio – has been three times as long as the duet, but still it is brisk, having only a limited stretch of ground to cover. Apart from some of Helena's long speech, it has also been bright and brilliant; but there have been signs of a deeper feeling to enrich its sparkle. One woman is hurt, another vulnerably absent, and both men are unconsciously satirising the inconstancy of their gender, unmanageable when accompanied by such self-righteousness.

At last Hermia, in every mind's eye but not expected, comes into sight, fresh from another bout of trailing through the undergrowth. With her solitary approaching figure – much as when Helena approached the sleeping Lysander – comes something else: comic dread. For once the audience is ahead of the characters, and the better for it: laughter is suspended for a cruel moment, like a pause between two waves. Suddenly Hermia heard Lysander – not dead after all! – just a thicket or two away, though obviously she didn't catch what he was saying, and she is running to him without seeing the pit opening at her feet. She is so relieved when she arrives that she can straightaway indulge in a little rally about her ears having become 'more quick of apprehension' than her eyes in this bosky place; so relieved that Demetrius can be forgiven his trespasses and Lysander lightly interrogated for having abandoned her:

> But why unkindly didst thou leave me so?

Presumably it was for some harmless reason of his own. Lysander is unambiguous in reply, but she is remarkably slow to catch on, as in fact anybody might be:

> LYSANDER: Why should he stay whom love doth press to go?
> HERMIA: What love could press Lysander from my side?

LYSANDER: Lysander's love, that would not let him bide:
  Fair Helena . . .

We hold our breath as she struggles to keep up with him. She is
odious, he insists:

  Why seek'st thou me? Could not this make thee know
  The hate I bear thee made me leave thee so?

'Hate' is a word Lysander uses. He flung it twice at her sleeping
figure when he awoke to his new life; the word is like a fist, not
belonging in a joke. Now he is angry: how can she be so stupid as
not to understand his reasoning? Blankly, she only manages:

  You speak not as you think. It cannot be.

It is not even what he says, but how he looks at her, that terrible
otherness. She feels as if she must have gone to sleep for a day, not
noticed how the world was changing, only to wake and be rebuked
for it. Lysander has been filled up with new genes: he looks and
sounds exactly the same, perfectly understands his surroundings,
but, as much as Bottom in his ass's head, he is translated.

As if such a waking nightmare weren't enough, Helena, rather than
appealing for her support, now turns on her as well. She assumes
that Hermia is acting all this out as part of a three-sided conspiracy,
hatched in odd moments while she was busy soliloquising:

  Lo, she is one of this confederacy.
  Now I perceive they have conjoined all three
  To fashion this false sport in spite of me.

It is obviously their punishment on her for being plain; but even for
someone so uncertain about her looks, her size, her capacity to make
and keep friends, this elaborate conviction is going some. Where has
she got the idea? On the face of it there was nothing insincere in
Hermia's reaction to her new situation; but then everything can be
turned preposterously back to front once an idea takes hold of you
as it has of Helena. Was it perhaps a little suspicious that Hermia
seemed so slow to get Lysander's point? If he was really rejecting
her, was it not somewhat complacent of her to ask him simply:

  What love could press Lysander from my side?

Helena herself would have been a great deal more outspoken. Above
all, there was the collaborative verse, the two love-fascists rhyming
away together: it was their way of excluding her.

The first thing she needs to do is break the rhyming pattern:

> Injurious Hermia, most ungrateful maid,
> Have you conspired, have you with these contrived
> To bait me with this foul derision?

As usual, she will look for a tune, find it wanting, then speak furiously from the heart. She puts her best rhetorical foot forward, the power of her iambics silencing everyone:

> Is all the counsel that we two have shared –
> The sisters' vows, the hours that we have spent
> When we have chid the hasty-footed time
> For parting us – O is all forgot?
> All schooldays' friendship, childhood innocence?

However, these five lines, sketched in her most glowing colours, are all she can sustain before she tips into sentiment. The picture becomes nostalgically fanciful, as if the girls were in a *fête galante* by Watteau or Fragonard, with something of its implicit eroticism: two comely women sitting like 'artificial gods', embroidering samplers, 'warbling'[8] in perfect harmony. They also somehow resembled the figures in a heraldic coat of arms (a difficult one for us):

> Due but to one and crowned with one crest . . .

Then, abandoning the upper air, she becomes herself, thundering that her friend is the kind of Jezebel who will put securing a man before the holy bonds of female friendship:

> And will you rend our ancient love asunder,
> And join *with men* in scorning your poor friend?

In the end her argument is tribal, as if wearing the same school blazer conferred a Masonic bond. They have done their needlework together! Exchanged secrets! Done all the things that allow women to sustain friendships for life as men rarely do!

> It is not friendly, 'tis not maidenly;
> Our sex as well as I must chide you for it . . .

Is this how Hermia remembers the old days? She did speak, in the first scene, about primrose beds where she and her 'playfellow'

---

8. This word, used again by Titania at the end to get the fairies singing, didn't sound as silly as it does now; 'ancient' in the next quotation was an honourable thing, not a decrepit one. But rather than trying to get the audience to listen with four-hundred-year-old ears, we might as well enjoy our quaint version of them.

> were wont to lie
> Emptying our bosoms of their counsel sweet

– but that was nothing compared to this. And from Hermia's point of view, Helena is suggesting something astounding: that at the moment of her greatest hurt she was really egging Lysander on as a big joke. It is as if she were the decadent Marquise in *Les Liaisons Dangereuses* who hires her lover to ruin another girl. She is also being credited with the power to persuade Demetrius to co-operate in the trick: it is outrageous. Hermia may well feel manipulated by Helena, suffocated by inappropriate loyalty. Although it is enough to make her completely furious, all she says is

> I am amazed at your passionate words.
> I scorn you not, it seems that you scorn me.

Her real fire is reserved for later.

As much as Helena's speech itself, it is Hermia's reactions to it, and to some extent the men's, that will keep the action afloat in performance. For Lysander and Demetrius, the question has urgently arisen again – what, without the benefit of words, to play? Admiration for Helena's word-picture? A little impatience with her verbosity? Barely controllable desire (probably accentuated by the unwitting sexiness of the 'double cherry' and 'lovely berries' the girls once resembled)? And it is about to get more difficult, as Helena spells out what she means for not one but two further speeches. Her first tirade, artificial but heartfelt and with a fine kick in its tail, would certainly have been enough: it is all much less vivid on second hearing. This time, for the audience to get ahead is bad; and therefore the actors, a little at a loss but knowing they must keep things going, may take to chasing each other around the stage to help out.

The fact is that from the moment of

> Have you not set Lysander, as in scorn,
> To follow me and praise my eyes and face?

the text needs editing, so blatant is the drop in energy. At some point the four lovers will need to accept that if the play is going to be cut, it is on them that the axe will most regularly fall, and if they are intelligent actors they will be grateful for it. It is almost impossible to imagine cutting the Mechanicals, or Oberon's superb flights, or, (if I am being convincing) Theseus's Court either. But the lovers are cast in a trickier convention: their self-conscious diction is challenging but it can outstay its welcome, particularly when it is pitched, as here, into the unforgiving rhythms of farce. It will also become evident to Helena that her part is likely to suffer the most.[9]

This is not to say that there are not good things in her recapitulations. For one thing, there is some elegance:

> What though I be not so in grace as you
> So hung upon with love, so fortunate . . .

Her view that Demetrius's flattery is all the worse for the fact that he

> even but now did spurn me with his foot

is a nice transference too, since it was her suggestion that he kick her like a dog. And she becomes so irritated by Hermia's great performance of failing to get her point that her nostalgia deteriorates swiftly into playground spitefulness. She feels that tongues are being stuck out at her behind her back, so that she can't afford to take her eyes off anyone:

> Ay, do, persever. Counterfeit sad looks,
> Make mouths upon me when I turn my back,
> Wink each at other, hold the sweet jest up.

Finally comes a nice piece of self-blame:

> But fare ye well. 'Tis partly my own fault
> Which death or absence soon shall remedy.

Why, apart from telling tales at the start, would so much be her fault? This happens to Helena quite often – unlucky in love, she comes to feel unworthy of it and turns against herself.

Hermia's reticence, of course, is not deceitfulness but part of a pattern, and soon she will be unleashed for a terrific pay-off. Put her occasional lines thus far together, and they do suggest either dimwittedness or a dogged refusal to see the truth. Even now that the scene's motor is accelerating, she innocently marks time –

> Sweet, do not scorn her so

– or continues her struggle to keep pace:

---

9. However, she does start with the longest line-count. Without quite knowing how it is still with me, I have an ancient book called *Shakespeare and the Young Actor* by Guy Boas, Headmaster of the Sloane School in Chelsea for two decades from the 1930s and a passionate believer in Shakespeare for schoolboys. It closes with an invaluable measuring of every part in the canon – the lovers being all in verse, this one is provable as prose is not. Helena, as the third part in this play, has 224 lines, Lysander 170, Hermia 159 and Demetrius 132.

. . . Lysander, whereto tends all this . . . Why are you grown so
rude? . . . Do you not jest?

The bridge between Helena's Dip and Hermia's Surge is scrappy
and quarrelsome; nothing new in the plot but the impression, even
though the verse holds, that everyone is talking at once. The jagged
farce rhythms intensify and the rhyme becomes mechanistic:

DEMETRIUS: I say I love thee more than he can do.
LYSANDER: If thou say so, withdraw, and prove it too.

Half-lines and interruptions flurry around the baffled Hermia, made
the better by a splay of marvellous insults spat at her by Lysander:

Hang off, thou cat, thou burr! Vile thing, let loose . . .
. . . Out, tawny Tartar, out;
Out, loathed medicine! O hated potion, hence!

Shakespeare's invective is sometimes as great as his poetry:
Lysander's rattles with frustration as Hermia grabs hold of him and
he tries to do battle with Demetrius. Goaded by him for not being
more violent with her, he uses that word yet again:

Although I *hate* her, I'll not harm her so.

Its brutality steadies everyone's pace so that Hermia's and Lysander's
problem can be restated:

HERMIA: What? Can you do me greater harm than hate? . . .
    Am not I Hermia? Are not you Lysander? . . .
    Since night you loved me, yet since night you left me . . .
LYSANDER: Therefore be out of hope, of question, doubt
    Be certain. Nothing truer. 'Tis no jest
    That I do hate thee and love Helena.

At yet another use of the conclusive word, the scales drop from
Hermia's eyes – or perhaps rise to blind them – and she wonderfully
finds her tongue. Perhaps slowly rather than suddenly, she turns to
Helena:

O me, you juggler, you canker-blossom,
You thief of love! What, have you come by night
And stolen my love's heart from him?

Suddenly her memory has flown back to that fateful arrival in the
forest: going to sleep just then obviously let Helena into her
paradise. And since there is nothing like a counter-accusation of bad
faith to increase hostilities, Helena's gloves immediately come off

too, and the final movement of the sequence begins. It will be a mixture of superb rhetoric between the two women and occasional appeals to the impotent men; and, like all good quarrels, it often seems to end before flaring up again like kindling in a fire.

Helena sees that Hermia's compliment should be returned in full:

> . . . will you tear
> Impatient answers from my gentle tongue?
> Fie, fie, you counterfeit, you puppet, you!

It came so easily, the insult waiting ready-formed at the back of that gentle tongue. There is a sharp intake of breath at its deadly fluency. Hermia – slowly, don't rush it – rolls up her sleeves:

> Puppet? Why so; ay, that way goes the game . . .

Perhaps this friendship – many friendships? – has been a form of truce to appease adolescent jealousy, a decision for love as easier than war. Perhaps Helena always thought the one ridiculously embarrassing thing about Hermia was her smallness; perhaps Hermia once confided in someone else that her tall friend reminded her of a great pole being jigged around by morris dancers.

Now that they are let loose, the women's style, by contrast to the muscle-flexing of the men, is seen to be a fine and filigreed thing, wound with the sharpest thread. Their skill lies in the use of small spiteful words as much as great similes. Hermia is in no doubt about what Helena's main ploy has been –

> And with her personage, her tall personage,
> Her height, forsooth, she hath prevailed with him

– as if men were only interested in giant girls; the improbability is delivered with absolute comic confidence. For herself, she knows she has the power of a bobcat when faced with one of these huge thieves:

> How low am I, thou painted maypole? Speak,
> How low am I? – I am not yet so low
> But that my nails can reach unto thine eyes . . .

Helena's first reaction to this is to play low status. Emphasising great personal meekness, she looks to the men for protection: after all, they are both supposed to be in love with her. She is normally so good-natured, so lacking in 'shrewishness' and not 'curst', that they should defend her –

> I am a right maid for my cowardice.
> Let her not strike me

– but her helplessness is not quite what it seems. She can't resist another flick:

> You perhaps may think
> Because she is something lower than myself
> That I can match her.
> HERMIA: Lower! Hark again!

Then she plays the first string again, using a dozen lines to appeal to Hermia's sense of fair play:

> I evermore did love you, Hermia,
> Did ever keep your counsels . . .

Well, not quite: there was one glaring exception –

> Save that in love unto Demetrius
> I told him of your stealth unto this wood

– and that was where the trouble began. She pretends that the whole experience has been a matter of being 'chid' and threatened by Demetrius: her hard-luck story omits the fact that both Demetrius and Lysander are now besotted with her. Finally she seems to be on her way, quite saintly in her humility:

> HELENA: And now, so you will let me quiet go,
> To Athens will I bear my folly back
> And follow you no further. Let me go.
> You see how simple and how fond I am.
> HERMIA: Why, get you gone; who is't that hinders you?
> HELENA: A foolish heart that I leave here behind . . .

But don't be fooled:

> HELENA: O, when she is angry she is keen and shrewd.
> She was a vixen when she went to school,
> And though she be but little she is fierce.

This one was unprovoked. Although her batteries seem to discharge more quickly than Hermia's, Helena is clearly just as much of a fighter, even if her methods are a little more complicated and her invective less vivid.

For the third time, meanwhile, the men have faced their old problem: gagged emotion. What to do this time? Clear the area like seconds in a boxing-ring? Feebly reassure Helena? At last they come back into focus a little –

> LYSANDER: Be not afraid; she shall not harm thee, Helena.
> DEMETRIUS: No, sir. She shall not, though you take her part

– and as Hermia flies at Helena, Lysander, ever more picturesque than Demetrius, manages:

> Get you gone, you dwarf,
> You minimus of hindering knot-grass made,
> You bead, you acorn.

The men continue to believe they can settle the whole problem by agreeing to have a battle, like Tweedledum and Tweedledee: Helena, once the wallflower, will be fought for like some medieval princess:

> LYSANDER: Now follow if thou dar'st, to try whose right,
>   Of thine or mine, is most in Helena.
> DEMETRIUS: Follow? Nay, I'll go with thee, cheek by jowl.

This is already comic: there is little reason to think the men are particularly warlike, or that the outcome is likely to re-unite Hermia and Helena. Never mind: while the champions march away, tall in their own eyes, the women scatter in a flurry, Hermia threatening nails and teeth and Helena candidly relying on her legs. Hermia's curtain line returns her pretty much to where she came in:

> I am amazed, and know not what to say.

The banality forbids us to think that there is anything heroic about any of this.

Indeed there isn't: this brilliant episode has delivered the extremes of romantic tragedy in the farcical register of Feydeau. It has been remarkable, if a little too long and not without the odd dropped stitch. Though every company's experience will be different, certain things are obvious; its prodigious energy in particular, and the virtuoso technique that is called for. It also needs staging, big-time. Such a scene is where the theatre and life threaten to part company a little: left to themselves, many actors arguing will do something true enough to life – pursue the enemy, stand nose to nose and shout at them. But in a play, to insist on a few extra feet of space between the combatants, a physical restraint across which contentious points have to fly, can freshen up an argument no end: and it's certainly much better than playing tag all over the stage. Also, over and over in the scene, positions of relative strength have to be found and then generously relinquished for weaker. If Hermia is to interrupt effectively, she probably needs to find a place between the others and play to both left and right of her, rather than trying to get three people on the far side of the stage to look across at her; then she has to give Helena the same position, angry as she is. The men have to become very clear when they can intervene strongly and when, rather than distracting with half-moves, it is better to hold a discreetly charged position. A cunning director may not impose too much of this on the first day, since the cast needs to breathe free air and invent; but things will eventually come to such a chaotic point that some firm choreography will be much appreciated in the end.

By the opening night the physical disciplines will most likely be second nature and much enjoyed. This sort of thing is not the ultimate test of the four actors, but it is invigorating: ice-skating rather than emotional therapy, but still ice-skating with a heart. I said earlier that they would have to be good enough for Strindberg: but they will also need to be instinctively comic. Young Touchstones and Merry Wives may be better cast, in fact, than tomorrow's Hamlets and Violas.

On top of all the other technical demands, a taste for physical clowning helps: amidst all the tension and excitement, these young verse athletes may become gymnasts as well. The smallness of Hermia and the tallness of her friend are of course an open invitation, and it is surprising that quite a number of productions make relatively little of it. But I have seen Hermias on Helena's back, on Lysander's too, flying horizontally in the air, suiting the action to Lysander's words by behaving like a cat, or being picked up and leaned against a wall. Some Helenas seem able to carry the men one under each arm. The men can become locked together in their aggression or supine in adoration. Once invented, all such gags have to be slickly orchestrated – not only for safety and clean visual line, but to ensure that what is being said rather than done stays at the front of the mix. With luck, the physical jokes will be remembered by the audience like a series of snapshots: they came out of nowhere and disappeared as sharply, quick as the surrounding language. In short, the argument calls for visual as well as verbal elegance. Quite hard; and if you can get through it without something painful happening to Lysander's crotch, you're a better man than I am.

I would like to say that the pause after the lovers leave will be heavily expectant, as the audience speculates on how Oberon and Puck, sole begetters of all this chaos, can begin to redeem it. But the fact is that they may want to celebrate what they have seen with applause before being reminded of the bigger picture. Judging when the moment is right once more, Oberon again turns on Puck, accusing him in one line of carelessness and in a second of sabotage:

> This is thy negligence; still thou mistak'st,
> Or else commit'st thy knaveries wilfully.

To all intents, they are exactly where they were two hundred and fifty lines ago. Their measure of frustration is highly interpretable. Is Oberon humorous or furious, Puck calm or bitterly aggrieved? One clue of a familiar kind: Oberon's annoyance earlier at the trouble between Demetrius and Hermia stayed within the decorous limits of rhyme, but this is coming through in passionate blank verse. Puck, equally engaged, joins him in it for a moment but quickly retreats into his defiant jingle:

> Believe me, king of shadows, I mistook.
> Did not you tell me I should know the man
> By the Athenian garments he had on?
> And so far blameless proves my enterprise
> That I have 'nointed an Athenian's eyes.

He is right, of course: he did exactly what he was told, as far as he was told it. He goes further. However distressing this is for Oberon, Puck continues to like its preposterousness:

> And so far am I glad it so did sort
> As this their jangling I esteem a sport.

Deadlock, and a real distinction of character: Puck, though in some ways closer to us, doesn't have what might paradoxically be called Oberon's human dimension. He felt a little for the neglected Hermia, but that was a form of prejudice: he lacks Oberon's overall sympathy for all parties, and, for him, the more cruel it all is the better. This may be his great moment of rebellion against his master's pieties and the inadequacy of his instructions; he has reached a limit of sorts and can no longer be blamed and blamed again. The speech, in other words, may come out quite violent.

They are left staring at each other: Puck, affronted, has nothing more to say, and Oberon will have to fix not only the usual problems but their relationship. He either ignores the defiance or absorbs it; his one concession is to start rhyming again. He has a new plan, a third and surely last attempt to put things right with his mighty magic. For a start, he will make night fall: or rather, since it is already night, he will make Puck call up a deeper darkness, a miasma from one of the four rivers of Hell in fact, to cover the upper world:

> The starry welkin cover thou anon
> With drooping fog as black as Acheron.

Moving inside and above it, Puck, credited with powers at least as great as encircling the earth in forty minutes, must discharge another wonder. Since in Oberon's view it really is possible that the men have become mad enough to fight, they must be led this way and that in the foggy gloom, Puck ventriloquising their voices so that they are always at cross purposes, until, exhausted by chasing and emotion, they drop. Then, since he is the outstanding problem, Lysander's vision is to be corrected with an antidote – a new herb from Oberon's collection that obeys the curative balance of nature as a dock-leaf a nettle, one

> Whose liquor hath this virtuous property
> To take from thence all error with his might.

He will take the same medicine to Titania and release her from bondage – but only after he has used her benighted condition to wrangle the little Indian boy away from her. Oberon's intention that

> . . . all things shall be peace

is thus highly subjective. Titania will be subdued for good; and as for the humans, he goes on the splendid male assumption that if Lysander only falls again for Hermia and leaves Demetrius with the one he always wanted, it will be all right with the girls, who by now might have a right to some explanations. He has everything to gain from his plan; Puck, as is the way with servants, not much.

In narrative terms, this is no more than an evident threading of the play's final reel. The hint of closure on both human and fairy stories is even underlined by a light metrical signal, though we will not recognise it yet. The lines of Oberon's couplet

> When they next wake, all this derision
> Shall seem a dream and fruitless vision

really have (unless you make the pedantically trisyllabic choice of 'deris-i-on' and 'vis-i-on', which I don't recommend) only four beats, and so edge towards the effect achieved in the play's Epilogue, when Puck will suggest in this shortened metre that the evening's performance has had the same negligible effect on the audience.

However, something else has been cooking away under Oberon's speech, at a different temperature. The clue is one of Shakespeare's great tricks, the monosyllable:

> And back to Athens shall the lovers wend
> With league whose date till death shall never end.

Oberon's wish for their future lives, once they are woken and dispatched on their way, is surprisingly whole-hearted, its promise of infinity a sign of yearning. This is a new emotion into which the actor can gratefully sway. Such a thing is, of course, not Puck's way; but Shakespeare can take his sensibility as well and touch something new into it – apprehension. Once he seemed to see the geese rising and heard the jackdaws cawing at the report of a country gun; now he is alert to a deep reason for hurry:

> For night's swift dragons cut the clouds full fast,
> And yonder shines Aurora's harbinger,
> At whose approach ghosts wandering here and there
> Troop home to churchyards . . .

This heavenly verse for a heavenly chase could have come from Oberon, if Oberon were ever to feel fear: hovering between rhyme and blank verse, it is certainly the most poetic thing Puck has done. The first of his kind to sense daybreak, he is as frightened of it as if he were one of the damned souls himself, scuttling back underground as light rushes towards them:

> . . . lest day should look their shames upon
> They wilfully themselves exile from light
> And must for aye consort with black-browed night.

He sees it as sharply as a vision of hell. Like a human father dispelling fear – not of the dark but of daylight – Oberon is there for him, superb and confident. He is gamekeeper in his own preserve, a forester treading the groves with Puck beside him: to finish their business before day breaks will be an easy matter now that he has poured this glorious reassurance into him:

> But we are spirits of another sort.
> I with the morning's love have oft made sport
> And like a forester the groves may tread
> Even till the eastern gate all fiery red
> Opening on Neptune with fair blessed beams
> Turns into yellow gold his salt green streams.

The images are blinding, like the first day of the world, as vivid and radiant as even Shakespeare ever gets.

Although Oberon will continue to call on Puck and give orders, this is the last time he will truly speak to him in the play; and Puck now seems to become as independent as his equivalent figure in *The Tempest*, the liberated slave-spirit Ariel. He will only address Oberon once more, to remind him of the need for haste. Their fascinating relationship has in the end been undefinable – master-and-servant, sorcerer-and-apprentice hardly come close to it. In what way did Oberon need Puck, apart from to run errands, and what were Puck's feelings about his protector? To Puck, 'your servant', Oberon was always, simply

My lord . . . captain of our fairy band . . . my fairy lord . . .

– until, ambiguously, when they were both in error, he became 'king of shadows'. Oberon's habit was to call Puck to his side more fulsomely:

My gentle Puck, come hither . . . Welcome, wanderer . . . How now, mad spirit . . . Welcome, good Robin . . .

Finally, their falling-out, if that is what it was, was expressed metrically, each echoing the other's diction; and their reconciliation, if that was needed, was achieved through a mutual flight of poetry as astonishing as any sight of them, forever linked and moving through the sky, would have been.

Now Puck has new work and a new strength. He calls himself 'goblin' at last, the remorseless lord of misrule whose traditional 'Ho-ho-ho!' and stamping dance frightened the Mechanicals. He seems to swell in front of our eyes into an ancient figure of dreams:

Up and down, up and down,
I will lead them up and down
I am feared in field and town . . .

In fact he has to preside over a particularly difficult spasm in the play: the lovers are never going to be as funny as they were in their long scene together, and what needs to be achieved is mainly mechanistic. To give it force, a visual effect is wanted to suggest that the familiar forest is sinking back into a darkness as deep as the one that enveloped Hansel and Gretel, and that the unknown terrors Hermia once sensed around her may at last spill onto the stage. And, of course, some inspired physical invention for Puck in what will be his last piece of conjuring tonight.

Much of his energy will have to go into traffic-control. The Folio says he keeps 'shifting places' to confuse the lovers, which he certainly can; but equally he might hold his ground as if he were presiding from the crown of a roundabout. It is simple enough, in a technological age, for him to seem to throw his voice this way and that, perhaps even generating (as he did in Reinhardt's film) the fog of Acheron from his mouth. He certainly needs to exude power, not physical effort.

The Elizabethan theatre had four main entrances; as Lysander and Demetrius come blundering in we may feel we need more. Lysander is first; Puck-as-Demetrius convinces him his enemy is close at hand, and tempts him off to 'plainer ground'. The real Demetrius then arrives in the same place, having heard Lysander's voice; but by now Lysander is gone, and seems to be calling him to a new rendezvous – blaming him, indeed, for not being there already. Demetrius chases off to the new place. The stage is momentarily empty, whereupon Lysander returns, presumably by a slightly different route, feeling he has been led by Demetrius in a great circle into a 'dark, uneven way', though in truth he is back where he started. In fact, not much ground has been covered, but Puck's simple expedients have made it seem more. In this forest one can become tired and confused, recognise no landmarks, and collapse at a moment of great anger. So Lysander drops out of the game, hoping he can sustain his righteous violence when he wakes:

> Come, thou gentle day,
> For if but once thou show me thy grey light
> I'll find Demetrius and revenge this spite.

He thus misses Puck impersonating him in perhaps two more places; Demetrius describes the same baffled circle till he too is back where he started and the two of them, convinced of each other's cowardice, sleep, relatively, side by side.

The arrival of the women, exhausted by nature not fairy interference, is an altogether more eloquent matter. Puck abandons his devices and simply watches, while the verse shifts elegantly into split-sonnet form, punctuated by his jigging commentary. While the men seem indistinguishable by now, the women, though implicitly akin by virtue of speaking in the same form, remain sharply differentiated. As she prepares to let sleep obliterate her loneliness, Helena is typically figurative –

> O weary night . . . shine comforts from the east . . .

– while Hermia, more homely and more truly poetic, feels 'bedabbled' with the dew and torn to ribbons by the undergrowth again. It

would not be her style to apostrophise 'O long and tedious night' as
Helena does, any more perhaps than it would be Helena's simply to
say

> I can no further crawl, no further go;
> My legs can keep no pace with my desires.

Both, however, are emotionally wide open: Helena sees that, ugly
and defeated bear that she is, she must get away from people who
'detest' her 'poor company', and in fact that she must get away from
herself for a few hours. Then Hermia ends, most touchingly, with a
small bedtime prayer, a Christian intercession in an increasingly
pagan place, for the lover who has caused her so much trouble:

> Heavens shield Lysander, if they mean a fray.

It is hard to imagine either man offering either woman the same
blessing. Puck, with his usual bias, is impressed, and wants peace for
them –

> Cupid is a knavish lad
> Thus to make poor females mad.

– but his job is to wind all four together with his charm, the
equivalent of Oberon's benediction over the nobility later on; for this
purpose, even Lysander becomes 'gentle lover' again. As he spins
their cat's cradle, Puck moves between two- and four-stressed lines
– with even a hint, when he gets to 'Jack shall have Jill', of a jazzy
shift from common to waltz time. Sounding a little like Lear's Fool,
who will end another great scene of storm by mixing *Child Roland*
with *Jack the Giant-Killer*, he finally folds three country proverbs
together:

> . . . every man should take his own . . .
> Jack shall have Jill,
> Naught shall go ill;
> The man shall have his mare again, and all shall be well.

When the lovers wake, the baffling fog will be no more than harmless ground-mist and their ears will no longer be ringing. Who would
have thought that such a scene, moving from fairy delirium at the
ass's head to high-precision farce, would end with four exhausted
people on the ground, lulled by the equivalent of a nursery rhyme
from an invisible man afraid of the morning?

The only difficulty now is that it feels a little as if the play might
be ending. The lovers have engaged our attention for so long, from

argumentative peaks to comatose valleys, that they have banished most else from our mind. Instinctively the audience senses closure, but the fact is that this is only the end of Act Three, with a good half hour's playing time left, and there is a lot more to get through. This is very typical of Shakespeare: what you might call the Act Four Lag, when for one reason or another the action significantly decelerates, is a feature of many of his greatest works, and is quite critical in the *Dream*. How he will manage to drive all his story-lines towards the finishing line is the big question, and it crucially implicates director and cast. From now on there can be a minimum only of grace-notes and as much urgency as possible; fortunately, the inspiration approaching the stage now will come as an enormous sensual shot in the arm.

SEVEN

Act 4 Scene 1

Puck's Stygian fog lifts to reveal an ass in the arms of a queen, his great breathing mass held in gossamer. Since Jack shall have Jill and naught shall go ill, Titania, more powerful than the seasons, at last has her donkey with the kneadable cheeks and irresistible ears. This is a forest of infinite sites, in every clearing a *tableau vivant* of familiar friends in new configurations, each able to distract us from the last. Hard as it would have seemed to forget Nick Bottom, even he was no match for the lovers' latest adventures, just as the sleeping Titania was obliterated earlier by his rehearsal in the wood.

When she awoke to greet him then, Bottom was alarmed, but now he is in paradise, a creature of finesse, all deftness and detail:

> ... Monsieur Cobweb, good monsieur, get you your weapons in your hand and kill me a red-hipped humble bee on the top of a thistle; and, good Monsieur, bring me the honey bag.

This is Bottom joining the creators, shimmering with invention. His workman's prose, as sensuous as Titania's poetry, is being used not for debunking *double entendre*s or even for plain talk, but to celebrate his appetite for imaginative life. Sexual joy has released a mind tied up in daily constrictions such as the carding of wool and the strategies of rehearsals; his years of wary self-regard are being rewarded with limitless indulgence.

He continues exactly where he left off when, in the first flush of asshood, he courteously introduced himself to Titania's retinue – at such length in fact that he had to have his tongue tied up. We may notice it only subliminally, but he is now breaking one of the play's habits, which is to deliver a rhyming quatrain such as Titania's here and follow it up with a couplet. This is not for Bottom:

TITANIA: Come, sit thee down upon this flowery bed,

> While I thy amiable cheeks do coy,
> And stick musk-roses in thy sleek smooth head
> And kiss thy fair large ears, my gentle joy.
> BOTTOM: Where's Peaseblossom?

Love is showing the weaver the world all new: he can glimpse sinew under his skin, see past the knots in the wood of the trees to the busy world within them. The effect of Titania's affection has been twofold. Partly it has made him a fully-fledged ass, thinking farmyard thoughts, in constant need of scratching and dry hay; but he has also, as a lover should, become the poet of invisible things, a sunlit William Blake. His new contentment fills him with largesse. The fairies – Cobweb, Mustardseed and Peaseblossom – must be dignified with courtly names, the French 'Monsieur' and the Italian 'Cavalery'; they must each have a job to discharge, and be treated affably but with the firmness of an enlightened master. Like Theseus later, he has the ruler's distrust of too much bowing and scraping: in his Court, Mustardseed must 'leave your courtesy' and simply shake him by the hand ('neaf'). Grown intimate with better acquaintance, this approachable prince warns the tiny Cobweb against being drowned in overflowing honey on his mission, but can also imagine the full-sized, human barber's chair he will need for his own great haircut:

> . . . for methinks I am marvellous hairy about the face; and I am
> such a tender ass, if my hair do but tickle me, I must scratch.

Then there is music and food. His favourite instruments remain the tongs and bones, which sound like the spoons played by a music-hall speciality act. Bottom's patriarchal sense of himself extends to Titania as he gently rejects her offer of a fancy menu ('new nuts') in favour of what he knows – oats, dried peas and a bottle of hay – and then asks her to remove her 'people' while he is lulled to sleep by country music.

The fairies are like a luxury fantasy of limitless manservants; Titania a male dream of female accommodation, almost numbingly attentive. There are not even forty lines of the rhapsody between them: it can last no longer than a dream can survive daylight. Their helpless collusion is touching: all they would have to do, if the drug allowed it, would be to look at his lower half to destroy their shared delusion. It is also erotic enough to encourage some directors to make the play's interior explicit, particularly when the fairies go and leave the lovers alone. Titania, all honey so far ('my gentle joy . . .

my sweet love') and fairly silent, now wraps herself around him in a
burst of active imagery:

> So doth the woodbine the sweet honeysuckle
> Gently entwist; the female ivy so
> Enrings the barky fingers of the elm.
> O, how I love thee! How I dote on thee![1]

But just as at their first meeting, there is an odd chastity in it. In the
plays of Shakespeare men and women talk filthily with their own
sex, but when they meet subsume it all in poetry. All the human
straining to break free of oneself and defy decay, the desperate inventiveness and outstripping of limits we associate with sexual expres-
sion is, in his theatre, alchemised into superb musicality. This was
the only way he could do it: despite the extreme suggestiveness of all
the parts being played by boys, or rather because of it, it is unlikely
that there were many displays of physical affection on the
Elizabethan stage. There were of course zealous puritans around to
complain, as they always have done; in any case I fancy the groundlings, like astute critics, would have rejected such a thing as children
do the soppy bits in a film now. A degree of self-censorship was
probably combined with the fact that such a thing just wasn't
needed by the time Shakespeare had filled the gap with language.

Nevertheless, at such moments we realise for a change not how
near Shakespeare is to us, but how far away: we are by now both
much advanced and utterly corrupted. When an actress first stepped
onto the English stage in December 1660[2] everything changed. So
naturally we have become used to rampant Titanias and priapic
Bottoms, and, in *Hamlet*, Gertrudes and Claudiuses caught at it by
their retinue. Antonys and Cleopatras feel they must engage in quite
exotic practices because of their huge erotic reputations – all the
more so since these famous lovers have very few scenes together. But
in the extraordinary meeting of the Queen of the Fairies and King
Donkey, there can be something fine and tantalising in their restraint,
all of what D.H. Lawrence used to call 'the sex business' being
poured into their words.

---

1. Much ink has flowed over the fact that the honeysuckle and woodbine can hardly entwist
each other since they are different names for the same plant – Dr Johnson even proposed that
the woodbine meant the leaves and the honeysuckle the flower. The general agreement is that
for Shakespeare, woodbine equals convolvulus, or bindweed.

2. Generally thought to have been Margaret Hughes as Desdemona in *Othello*.

Bottom's timely 'exposition of sleep' makes him the fifth recumbent figure on the stage. Titania will be a dozing sixth in attendance: the others are all unseen to each other and the latest two invisible to any human passers-by. With Titania's arrival the lovers faded out of focus; soon, with that of Theseus, Bottom will instead. Meanwhile, where can they all go? Best in the staging to start with what you want to achieve for Oberon's impending purposes here, and for Egeus's later, then track backwards to settle where the lovers need to have collapsed in the first place.

Oberon has been watching, always watching. Once he was the invisible witness to Helena's and Demetrius's arrival in the forest, then an observer of the lovers' quartet. Now he comes forward[3] to suggest that, with whatever feelings, he has witnessed Titania's love scene. He is the King, on permanent patrol, but there is something forbidding in his ubiquity, since you never know if his presence is ominous or benevolent. Wherever a visitor goes in this forest, Oberon could be just behind a bush, ready to cast imperious darkness across the moon. Practically speaking, unlike with Demetrius and Helena, I am not sure it is wise to see him watching Bottom and Titania – their strange innocence could be lost if we keep checking what this baleful figure thinks of it.

There is certainly a sense that he has been trailing Titania: what he now describes is something other than what we have been watching. It seems to be an earlier encounter, when he supposedly found her helplessly wandering in the woods

> Seeking sweet favours for this hateful fool

– picking flowers, in other words, to elaborate Bottom's odorous garland. According to Oberon – transferring some of his own feelings to the inanimate – they were distressed by it:

> . . . that same dew which sometime on the buds
> Was wont to swell, like round and orient pearls,
> Stood now within the pretty flowerets' eyes
> Like tears that did their own disgrace bewail.

Beware the men of poetry in Shakespeare – they often peddle the most specious reasoning. There is certainly some prejudice in Oberon's

---

3. It would have been easy enough to have Oberon watching from the upper stage at the Globe. There is in fact a charming series of drawings by the recently lamented C. Walter Hodges, suggesting how this and other critical scenes from the play might have been put on. Our choices now will be different, but Hodges's studies are delightful to look through.

version of things. He was at the time about to exploit Titania's
condition by reproaching her for being infatuated – which is rich,
since it was his doing – and swiftly bargaining the changeling out of
her. It was all a complete success. Titania, her priorities utterly
altered,

> . . . in mild terms begged my patience

– then meekly agreed, even sending one of her own fairies

> To bear him to my bower in fairyland.

Having caught her out, Oberon will now graciously restore her to his
favour. It is difficult to like him for this. The success of his vendetta
at such a pleasurable moment sets us at odds with him. Whatever he
says about the night gone by, it has not been at all a 'vexation' for
Bottom – or for Titania, who for a moment found someone to love.
To Oberon, the sight of them entwined is only 'sweet' because revenge
is so, whereas to us it truly was sweet: entirely funny and charming.
Bottom is not a 'hateful fool' either: Oberon is beginning to come
across as a killjoy on the scale of Malvolio. And this time he seems
to be on his own: 'sweet Robin' is present, but distant and completely silent, rather than, as he once would have done, exulting in
the preposterous 'jangling'. Puck has become a functionary, it seems,
without views of his own; all he will contribute, once Titania and his
master are reconciled, is a new warning of the approach of daybreak,
in more muted terms than before.

Since, in Shakespeare, a suspicious mind is as helpful as the ability
to read, there are times when you want to look again. In the course
of his speech Oberon used one sympathetic word, a possible complication within himself:

> Her dotage now I do begin to pity . . .

This 'pity', possibly a hypocrisy, could also be quite a complicated
tissue of mortification and second thoughts. His speech is then quite
long, even anxiously reiterative. It also sounds a little fictional. It is
hard to imagine Titania arriving at her enraptured moment with
Bottom just after enduring a meeting with Oberon in which she was
taunted and begged his patience. What 'mild terms' can they have
been that she used? Has she really been so apologetic about her love
for Bottom and then played the scene with him? How much of what
Oberon insists on to Puck are we to believe, and how much does it
mask his own inconvenient feelings?

It is said that there are two tragedies in life: not getting your heart's desire and getting it;[4] the disappointment that accompanies revenge is a perplexing emotion. It is possible that now Oberon has what he wanted, there is a flatness in it; it is really Titania's love he needed back, not his little hostage. The shame that he feels for her may also be his own shame. If so – and it depends, as everywhere else, on how 'human' he is – a rich meaning is moving underneath his lines. If the dew on the flowers resembled tears of embarrassment – the picture is more tender than is strictly needed – he might only have been able to invent such an image if he knew how they felt.

Certainly we need to feel he has some inclusive purpose if we are to regain enthusiasm for his powers. And indeed it does seem to be there, sweetening his mood – he will now reinstate Titania, swiftly restore Bottom to himself, and release the lovers too, so that they can:

> . . . all to Athens back again repair
> And think no more of this night's accidents
> But as the fierce vexation of a dream.

These benedictions over the humans could be the making of him, dispersing what remains of his authoritarianism and spite.

He turns to Titania with his antidote – he calls it 'Dian's bud', which sounds a more solemn thing than 'Cupid's flower':

> Be as thou wast wont to be
> See as thou wast wont to see . . .

It is the familiar chant, but informed with eagerness to regain a lover he has made into a stranger. Vulnerable as she wakes up, Titania falls in easily with his change of heart: he is immediately 'my Oberon', and she must tell him her gross dream of being 'enamoured of an ass'. Poor Bottom, asleep and suddenly detested. She does ask one question:

> How came these things to pass?

– but is unlikely to get a reply: she seems, in the maddening way of the compliant heroine, content to leave it at that. The prevailing four-beat rhythm is in any case good for a question but less so for a lengthy explanation, which is therefore postponed. Oberon is firm on the point:

4. George Bernard Shaw in *Man and Superman*.

> Silence awhile . . .

Rather, he needs quiet music not to disturb the sleepers while he dances ritually with 'my Titania . . . my sweet Queen':

> Sound, music! Come, my Queen, take hands with me . . .

His eight rhyming lines that accompany their movements are designed to shut out argument. Attending to Puck's warning of daylight they will now lie low till the next night –

> We the globe can compass soon
> Swifter than the wandering moon

– when they will, somehow, reprise their dance in Theseus's house. Titania makes only the lightest demand for their journey:

> Come, my lord, and in our flight
> Tell me how it came this night
> That I sleeping here was found
> With these mortals on the ground.

This mysterious moment of dance, to 'still music' struck from the spheres, signals the first of the play's reconciliations and suggests some departures. One of which is that of King Bottom: the wondrous ass's head is relegated, almost unnoticed, to the property basket. This seems likely to be Puck's last action: he has nothing more to do, is ignored by the King and Queen, and seems to be leaving the play. They, but not necessarily he, soar away, their flight tiny against the lightening sky. They have promised to bless the wedding, but only vaguely: we never really expect to see them again.

The fact that Theseus and Hippolyta suddenly stand in their places is a theatrical temptation. When, for the Royal Shakespeare Company in 1970, Peter Brook cast Theseus and Oberon with the same actor, and Hippolyta and Titania too, it was much noted and its meaning speculated on.[5] Seeming novel at that moment, this doubling was very probably done in Shakespeare's time (it is also

5. Brook also doubled Philostrate with Puck and Egeus with Quince. Occasionally, and interestingly, the only doubling is of Hippolyta and Titania, as if the feminine principle united those characters in a way that the male doesn't the men. Aidan McArdle played Philostrate and Puck in the RSC 1999 production, thus becoming, in steep contrast, both Theseus's and Oberon's 'manager of mirth'; it was a central idea that the whole of Theseus's Court, not just its leaders, had the opportunity to explore their sexual ids before resuming their courtly egos at the end (the First Fairy appeared in the Court as a sort of trainee Philostrate). Some of Puck's fear of daylight in Act Three Scene Two thus became terror of having to return to his buttoned-up human self.

recommended in the Commonwealth 'droll' mentioned earlier) when, as now, it presumably combined artistic dividends with good theatre economics. It may well be true that better actors can be secured for Theseus and Hippolyta if they have the more attractive parts as well – although I hope I am proving that Theseus needs no apology. In Brook's case, the doubling was done without changes of costume, so that there was no delay and the actors suggested the transformation in their manner: in fact throughout this legendary production theatre illusion was abandoned for highly visible expertise with nothing up its sleeve. But, in any other context, what does the double mean? It requires effort to see Oberon and Titania as the Unconscious of Theseus and Hippolyta, or – despite the play's title – to interpret fairyland as the engaged couple's dream; and the use of the word 'forester' in Oberon's recent description of himself and in Theseus's opening line now makes for a pleasant echo but no more. In most productions, the doubling is pure showmanship: and certainly the effect of darkness turning to morning mist over the fields, scaring Puck away and ushering in the hunters with their braying horns, is spoilt if the actors have to stop to change their clothes. Any kind of interlude invented to cover such a thing will interrupt Shakespeare's considered rhythm as disastrously as Mendelssohn's Wedding March used to do Act Five.

In fact there is a more interesting linkage going on in this scene of three episodes. In the lightest possible way, the behaviour of three kings, one of them temporary, is being compared at a moment that they lose regality. Bottom, magicked into imperial splendour, now snores obliviously; in Oberon's questionable regime, morality continues to be confused by sorcery and self-will, albeit blessed by great utterance; and now a third monarch arrives, Theseus, full of orders, but, in truth, pitifully intent on his latest effort to impress Hippolyta. Whether magnanimous or authoritarian, all three are very much compromised by desire.

Absent so long, Theseus and Hippolyta are obviously still in negotiation, the man eager to settle their bargain with a hunting expedition while the woman continues to bide her time. As Lysander once did with Hermia and Helena, they have been observing the 'rite of May' – the traditional gathering of new forest growth to bring back into the city as a sign of seasonal regeneration; and Theseus, in the morning's 'vanguard', as he somewhat militaristically puts it, wants to use what remains of it to show off his dogs. A pack of these well-matched hunting beasts will stand on a peak with them (Oberon's forest landscape having developed a mountain), and their accidental music will ring round the valley below:

> We will fair Queen, up to the mountain's top
> And mark the musical confusion
> Of hounds and echo in conjunction.

Elizabethan hunters were much concerned with the choral potential of their dogs – theirs is a sport that still retains quite a range of arcane rituals. As a means of impressing Hippolyta, however, it is disastrous, since she seems to be more of an expert than Theseus himself, and her apparently formal reply disguises a superb putdown. You couldn't exactly call it rudeness, but it is discomforting for him that she should reminisce about the day when she went bear-hunting with Hercules and Cadmus. At the 'gallant chiding' of their animals

> The skies, the fountains, every region near
> Seemed all one mutual cry. I never heard
> So musical a discord, such sweet thunder.

This was more than a hunt: it was godlike. The Spartan hounds they used were legendary; Cadmus founded the city of Thebes; Hercules was related to Theseus but had on the whole a better reputation. Do Theseus's ears deceive him, or is he being upstaged again in front of his own entourage – in front, particularly, of Egeus, an uncomfortable ally at all times? What is it with this impermeable woman? He had best make one thing clear to her, there is nothing wrong with *his* pack either – they are from the same stock as Hercules', if not quite as pure-bred:

> My hounds are bred out of the Spartan kind . . .

In his anxiety he makes them sound hideous, over-developed bloodhounds with a hint of the bovine:

> So flew'd, so sanded, and their heads are hung
> With ears that sweep away the morning dew,
> Crook-kneed and dewlapp'd like Thessalian bulls . . .

They may, he concedes, be a little 'slow in pursuit', but they do make a fantastic noise:

> a cry more tuneable
> Was never holla'd to, nor cheered with horn
> In Crete, in Sparta nor in Thessaly.

We may not catch the references, but the loud male heartiness of this – Theseus as noisy as his dogs – compares poorly, as usual, with Hippolyta's verbal elegance, not to mention her easier relations with the deities. And he ends weakly, his bombast evaporating – if she doesn't believe him, she must just wait and see:

> Judge when you hear.

If Theseus is cast in standard heroic mode, this passage simply meanders by in a remote convention. But put it in the hands of an actor with a sense of comedy, unafraid of looking uncertain in a confident costume, and something very entertaining should emerge from Theseus's *braggadocio.*[6] Above all, he and Hippolyta will be held in the same human register as everyone else: manoeuvring and suspicious, they are on as difficult a journey as the young lovers and, I would say, as the King and Queen of Fairies. Under Hippolyta's scrutiny, Theseus continues to show poor metaphorical taste, a tendency to issue unenforceable orders and a desperate need for jollity. Equally, if her ambiguity has been his punishment, surely it will soon be time for Hippolyta, who is beginning to look glacial rather than mature, to let him off a little more lightly.

In the midst of his mortifications, Theseus is generally saved by the bell, and the interruption usually has something to do with Egeus. Now, as Theseus almost trips over a sleeping form, he is reminded of something he may have forgotten, the passion play that interrupted his wooing four days ago. Egeus, in attendance, identifies his daughter first, then her despised lover, then the approved Demetrius and finally the disregarded Helena – who seems so little-known in the Court that her name is always preceded, for purposes of identification, by her parent's. This doesn't necessarily mean that the couples are lying together: it only matters, in Puck's earlier disposing of them, that Egeus can believably recognise them in the order that he does now. And though in a moment Theseus will suggest they are in pairs by making thunderous jokes about coupling wood-birds, it may be more interesting when they wake up to watch them finding their way towards their partners, symmetry as difficult to achieve in their physical ordering as in their experience. As there is quite a lot of text to cover now, it may not be best served by an actor speaking at length from the security of his partner's side.

---

6. Not unlike that of the *miles gloriosus*, the stock figure of a braggart soldier, used in early Roman comedy and quite often by Shakespeare (Pistol in *Henry IV*, Parolles in *All's Well That Ends Well*).

Theseus's response to Egeus's discovery is spectacular. The only reason for young people to get up so early would be to do May Day observance, and they must have chosen this spot because, like Coronation sightseers sleeping on the royal route, they were excited about Theseus's forthcoming wedding:

> hearing our intent
> [They] Came here in grace of our solemnity.

A good ruler has a memory for names and dates. How readily Theseus recalls that this is the day he himself set as Hermia's deadline – or indeed whether he would have recognised the quartet at all without Egeus's help – will suggest how professional he is these days:

> But speak, Egeus; is not this the day
> That Hermia should give answer of her choice?

His sense of humour, it turns out, is equal to his self-importance: he decides that a good plan will be to blast the four into wakefulness with a great peal on hunting horns, like bursting a paper bag at a person's ears:

> *Horns sound; the lovers wake; shout within; the lovers start up.*

Then, their hearts racing, they will have to deal with another joke (reflecting Theseus's preoccupation with feast days) and be alert enough to get the point that a few months have gone by since the fourteenth of February.[7]

> Good morrow, friends; Saint Valentine is past;
> Begin these wood-birds but to couple now?

'Couple' is not the most gracious word he could have used: 'uncoupling' is what his dogs have just done, and its sound also brings a certain carnality into the proceedings. But then Theseus was ever a bit suggestive – see his early speech about the virgin life.

Naturally enough, the lovers are unable to manage very much:

> LYSANDER: Pardon, my lord.

Theseus fills the gap with some leisurely antitheses between concord, hatred and jealousy, but all the recent sleepers can feel is that a dream is curling away from them:

---

7. The origin of this is that birds traditionally chose their partners for life on Valentine's Day, while humans might select them just for the day. There is also a Valentine tradition, oddly echoing this play's upheavals, that a woman had to take as a lover the first man she happened to see; this once led Samuel Pepys's wife to keep her hands over her eyes most of the day because the decorators were in.

> LYSANDER: My lord, I shall reply amazedly,
>   Half sleep, half waking. But as yet, I swear,
>   I cannot truly say how I came here.

We recognise the halting human process of this: waking is bringing no respite, only further anxiety. Lysander's rhythm –

> But as I think – for truly would I speak –
> And now I do bethink me, so it is:
> I came with Hermia hither . . .

– perfectly suggests the partial capture of what has nearly gone. On top of which Lysander is facing, at a vulnerable moment, the full apparatus of the state, albeit off duty: he in particular could be the first lamb at the slaughter.

Shakespeare has not really attended to the state of Theseus's relationship with Egeus here, but the actors, especially Egeus, need to know. They parted company with some unease, with Theseus's promise of 'some private schooling' possibly covering his chagrin when he found that Demetrius had a complicated past. Although it doesn't seem that Egeus's position – chief courtier, favoured businessman, what you will – has been seriously dented, that equivocal memory may still be there. The imminent novelty is that it is the simple honesty of the lovers' account of themselves that will determine Theseus's thinking, rather than old loyalties to class or generation.

Faced with Lysander's respectfulness, Egeus is as truculent as ever:

> Enough, enough – my lord, you have enough!
> I beg the law, the law upon his head.

But this is no longer the way to get Theseus's ear, if it ever was: Egeus sounds like someone from another age. Time is beginning to slow down for the elucidation of miracles; but one false step and all four lovers could be out. Though polite, Lysander has been less effective than he was in the first scene, and his blundering reference to 'the peril of the Athenian law' has now given Egeus a perfect cue to call the heavens down on them. There is little more to be expected from him: the real surprise is Demetrius. So stolid before, he emerges as a spokesman, poised and truly poetic, with the advantage of being able to hold the attention of a conservative audience. Trusted, he can guide them to the heart of the matter:

> I wot not by what power,
> But by some power it is – my love to Hermia,
> Melted as the snow, seems to me now

> As the remembrance of an idle gaud
> Which in my childhood I did dote upon . . .

It is so well done that Hermia could hardly be offended even if she were minded to be. He candidly admits his mistake, one that a young man might make on an impulse, though it wouldn't usually cause such trouble to his friends: now he is returned to health and everything is recoverable. In his lucidity, he rarely ventures beyond words of two syllables, until the open-vowelled emotion in his last line breaks the pattern:

> But as in health come to my natural taste,
> Now I do wish it, love it, long for it,
> And will for evermore be true to it.

Irresistible. The tense delicacy, and above all transparency, affect Theseus so strongly that he immediately overturns the law of Athens:

> Fair lovers, you are fortunately met . . .
> Egeus, I will overbear your will . . .

To Egeus this is the most extreme waywardness, but to us proof that a new side of Theseus has been touched. These lovers on the grass seem right and natural: he likes the look of them, and the romantic in him has to approve. There is a further outburst of regal enthusiasm. Not only can they each marry whom they wish, but they will all be promoted to become part of his own wedding, both the temple ceremony and the reception in the palace:

> Three and three
> We'll hold a feast in great solemnity.

The long-awaited royal marriage is now a triple event, embracing four civilians; and it is Demetrius who has done it. Old Nedar won't believe it. Hunting is cancelled; and as for the father of the other bride, the bluntest dismissal. The whole thing is achieved in ten brisk lines, the situation that caused the play overthrown to create its ending. Even Hippolyta is confidently swept up en passant, without so much as a 'What cheer, my love?':

> Come, Hippolyta.

Maybe, with her too, decisiveness will be more effective than endless, uncomfortable parley.

With the general exit, the suspense becomes as tangible as if one of the lovers had been left alone for a soliloquy. The chemistry of

Theseus's young clients is, of course, a little complex by now. Demetrius has no idea why all this has happened to him – his revulsion from Helena, his infatuation with Hermia or his route home – but at least it could be seen as part of life's old story. The strange fact is that both he and Lysander are even now under the influence of fairy charms, but opposite ones: Lysander has been cured by 'Dian's bud' while Demetrius has been made susceptible to Helena again by Love-in-Idleness. The effect in both cases will be righteous and permanent. Whatever he remembers, Lysander never explains or apologises to Hermia or understands why he might do so; perhaps Demetrius will excuse himself to Helena later. The women, whose memories are as clear as daylight, remain as baffled as before, but at least their numbers have come up. Shakespeare's limited interest in these details – and sense of hurry – is such that he now gives them only a valedictory moment which explains nothing to them. He then dispatches the men into social behaviour at the wedding-party, and the women, like Egeus,[8] into a complete silence for the rest of the play, without an outlet for their complicated feelings.

Meanwhile, in a passage made beautiful by its hesitancies as much as its found language, they do not so much address their partners as pool their uncertainties, so that for the first time we feel a group of three made four: Demetrius, the architect of their problems and now their heroic advocate, is central to it, and in fact it is odd how little Lysander contributes. The point could be made that he has the greatest recovery to make, but his silence is probably circumstantial rather than because he is standing off, introspecting.[9] Demetrius, having saved the day, makes a start:

> These things seem small and undistinguishable,
> Like far-off mountains turned into clouds.[10]

In this flux, the form of things still shifting, what he can see is different on either side of a blink: the world is not quite reliable. It is Hermia – Demetrius's foe at the last count – who catches his drift, and finds a sensuous image for the same thing:

8. Probably. But see later.

9. When I directed the play, I gave him part of Demetrius's speech, just as an attempt to improve on Shakespeare.

10. 'Undistinguishable', the word used earlier by Titania to describe the overgrown mazes, seems to be made up by Shakespeare for this play and never used by him again.

> Methinks I see these things with parted eye,
> When everything seems double.

One eye seeing differently from the other: it is the way we have been watching much of the play.

The two speeches are enough to clear the fumes: let them go. Helena, who like Hermia is separated from the night's events only by a healthful sleep, picks up her half-line with the scene's loveliest thought:

> So methinks;
> And I have found Demetrius, like a jewel,
> Mine own and not mine own.

She barely trusts her good fortune, the miracle of recovering him forever ambiguous: the object of her love cannot belong to her because of its intrinsic beauty, and yet it can, because there it is, in her hand. It is lucky that he has done so well for the team: at last we can accept her estimate of him.

The balancing of these unsteady moments is wonderfully done, and begins to give the play a new, grave significance.[11] Now Demetrius can turn the lights up to full:

> Are you sure
> That we are awake? . . . Do not you think
> The Duke was here, and bid us follow him?

Suddenly it is a simple thing to move off down the road like a group of young people unlikely ever to fall out with each other again:

> Let's follow him,
> And by the way let us recount our dreams.

The actors will have seen that in a sense this is where their stories end – even at their own wedding their identities will fade in the crowd – so if there is to be a scene of reunion, this is it. Put simply, they will want to kiss, perhaps express mute regret (the men), some graciousness (the women), an adjustment to experience (both). However, while Shakespeare is always interested in the effect of life-changing journeys, he can be surprisingly economical about it. The director may feel like a killjoy, but the brevity in the writing is a warning to keep moving.

---

11. As already noted, this is the part of Benjamin Britten's score that is the most moving; the whole scene also compares with such a great operatic quartet as the canonical *Mir ist So Wunderbar* in Beethoven's *Fidelio*, in which deluded romantic love, fear of discovery, paternal blessing and sexual jealousy are woven beautifully together.

The lovers are not the only ones who need to be recovered: Nick Bottom is another hero about to regain twenty-twenty vision. He has still greater extravagances to justify. Appropriately, Shakespeare contextualises his return in the theatre idiom. Perhaps before we even see him stirring, out of the darkness of Titania's bower comes the call of an actor, reassuring his director:

When my cue comes, call me, and I will answer.

As he sits up, the honest face is that of a strangely missed old friend, back from his Bermuda Triangle. Rubbing his eyes, he is as vulnerable as Lysander and the others were, and his bizarre, half-funny dream spills over for a moment or two. It seems at first to have been about plays, not fairies. The cue he means was the one that Flute overran last night at the Duke's Oak:

As true as truest horse that yet would never tire.

But that feels impossibly long ago to us. Shakespeare astutely replaces it with a reminder of the title in hand –

Most fair Pyramus . . .

– and then confirms our bearings with the names of other players, ringing out through this less and less enchanted glade:

Peter Quince! Flute the bellows-mender! Snout the tinker! Starveling!

Unlike the lovers, who found their way back slowly, Bottom has snapped swiftly into the mode in which we left him, but is now gradually assailed by doubt. As far as he is concerned, he went behind a tree to see a noise that he had heard, and now he is back, ready to continue the rehearsal. This feels like his second shot at it: once before, he got to this point and found himself in a troublesome solitude – and now he is in it again. It seems he keeps falling asleep at this party and waking to find the room empty. It is another practical joke; but whereas last time his so-called friends returned with an elaborate show of horror, now they have simply

stolen hence and left me asleep.

Imagine repeating such an unfunny trick: why this campaign forever to unsettle his confidence? He stirs uneasily. Then his memory starts sifting, setting a proper distance between the jumbled events. Before, it was moonlight; now the sun has risen – time enough for him to have been filled with

A most rare vision.

A vision, in fact,

> . . . past the wit of man to say what dream it was

– neither pleasant nor unpleasant exactly, but utterly puzzling. With the delicacy of the lovers – and the same tendency to monosyllables – he tries to catch it for us as it slips away:

> Methought I was – there is no man can tell what. Methought I was – and methought I had – but man is but a patched fool if he will offer to say what methought I had.

His way of confiding is warm, intimate and generous, as if he were beckoning us to come and sit very close to him. But somehow he cannot bring himself to say it, not even whether the dream was good or bad, or even a mixture, as such things are: he keeps reaching the point and backing away, in disbelief, or pleasure, or shame, leaving one clue to it in his phrasing:

> Man is but an ass if he go about to expound this dream.

Repeatedly coming back to the point, he can add nothing. This dream had 'no bottom' both in the sense that it was profoundly hard to understand and because it was a form of nonsense, a vision, like Prospero's, whose fabric was baseless. Its only proper place is in a work of art:

> I will get Peter Quince to write a ballad of this dream

– and in fact (coming to his showman's senses) he will perform it as a ballad before the Duke 'at the latter end of a play', surely the forthcoming *Pyramus and Thisbe*. An excellent scheme: not to tell us now, but to sing a song about a man transformed into an ass who slept with the Queen of the Fairies just as Thisbe dies – it should nicely upstage Flute's efforts.

The irresistible speech is laced with characteristic jokes: attempting to give his experience a Biblical tinge – 'the eye of man hath not heard . . . '[12] – Bottom falls into a quintuplet of transferred epithets. It mixes fun and superstitious fear, an inability to account for things but an equal inability to let them rest. And it is preferably accompanied in performance by only the most tentative miming of imaginary ears and snout, not to mention what else 'methought' he had. Easy does it: Bottom is essentially a chaste man, friendly and confidential,

12. 1 Corinthians 2: 9.

so remembering what he was endowed with is both a delight and an embarrassment, like that of a shy man forced to boast publicly of his conquests. And none of it has a lasting effect on his general temper: he is about to continue exactly as before. As he goes whistling down the road after the others, a scene full of apprehensive re-orderings closes with an absolute lack of doubt.

Things are moving rapidly. In two hundred lines (less than ten minutes) a remarkable parenthesis, opened and closed by Bottom, has moved us from the height of fantasy to the workaday world. Six people have woken up, with more or less difficulty. The enchanted wood is to be abandoned as briskly as the ass's head, the fairies apparently finished with. Every principal character apart from Peter Quince has been on, yet the flow has been steady and the changes unforced. And starting from a point within it is an equally rapid arc: only seventy lines will have separated Theseus's abandonment of his hunting expedition and his reappearance married.

Like the protagonists, we leave this moonlit place with mixed feelings. It was marvellous, but a person could also be turned into a beast with great ears and other hugenesses; a sympathetic young man could become a human beast prepared to murder the woman he was to marry; the unlucky in love were further mocked, serpents crept into the hearts of men and across the dreams of unguarded women. The figures who created these confusions were magnetic, but equivocal in the extreme. Nothing of it will be mentioned again by the victims, but they will no more forget it than they would an aeroplane crash they have survived together. It was full of ambushes, a kaleidoscope of nocturnal colours, only minimally instructive; now it is mid-morning, the sun is climbing in the sky and it is time to go home.

EIGHT

Act 4 Scene 2

The sun is not so high where Quince lives, however: it feels more like an interminable, hopeless wet morning. It is as if the night has been disturbed by a great accident or emergency, or by a bad dream which refuses to evaporate. Quince remembers that his rehearsals broke up in horrified confusion; now, in his workshop perhaps, his becalmed team hope to pick up the pieces. He asks Starveling, probably not for the first time in the hour, whether there is any sign of Bottom. But the weaver is not back at his loom – or even doing his voice exercises – so they must fear the worst. To Starveling, the supernatural event they witnessed means he has been not just translated but 'transported' – as indeed he has, in more ways than one.

This being a scene in which the audience knows more than the characters, the vigil is briefly done: its main benefit lies in unwitting jokes like this of Starveling's, which make us think warmly of Bottom's adventure. It has a slightly ritual feel, almost as if it were in verse: the first six speeches, shared between Quince, Starveling and Flute, take shape like some much-repeated call and response:

> QUINCE: Have you sent to Bottom's house? Is he come home yet?
> STARVELING: He cannot be heard of. Out of doubt he is trans-
> ported . . .

This is followed by question and answer again for Flute and Quince, then agreement between them, before Flute objects to Quince's word 'paramour' and breaks the rhythm. Even in what seems the easiest prose there can be authorial cunning: the effect here is to stretch out the sense of time a little without taking up too much of it.

The dynamic of any group that has lost its star prevails. These are now disappointed and leaderless men, with a certain mob logic; not only have they mislaid Bottom, but Quince, instead of rallying them, is as plaintive as the rest. In the absence of command, a small mutiny breaks out, and their characters seem to change a little. Above all, Flute finds his voice. He has said virtually nothing in his own person till now, apart from briefly objecting to playing a woman on the grounds of burgeoning testosterone; he was so overcome in rehearsal that he contributed nothing to the stylistic discussions and then rattled off his part cues and all. Now he almost runs the scene, cutting through the small talk. He points out that without Athens' best actor the show is dead in the water:

If he come not, then the play is marred. It goes not forward

– though, with a tiny interrogative, he still hopes to be disproved:

. . . Doth it?

So reluctant to get started, he is now the most stricken, his disappointment stoked by hero-worship of Bottom. He cannot tolerate Quince's vocabulary on the subject of the great man:

QUINCE: . . . he is a very paramour for a sweet voice.
FLUTE: You must say 'paragon'. A paramour is – God bless us –
a thing of naught.

This furious and unnecessary prudishness, as if Quince had used a very bad word rather than quite a courtly one, comes from his suspicion that Bottom's honour is in some way being slurred. The whole thing is now Quince's fault; the idea of the play, the cross-gender casting, the humiliation of being corrected for reading his script wrong, and above all the lost opportunity to share a stage with one of the greats. And now the director is just dithering mournfully about. For his part, Quince must be wishing he hadn't bothered with this boy.

Beneath all their depression might be lurking a little sense of not having done as well as they might have. Faced with something which could have been a trick of the light, or even a practical joke by Bottom himself, they simply ran away and left him. The wood suddenly seemed alive with animals and random obstructions, as threatening as such dark places can be when you get a fright – especially if you were none too sure about coming in the first place. Could they have been a little braver, a little more comradely? They all ran to their respective homes and pulled the blankets over their heads.

In another character surprise, it is the deferential Snug, rather than the voluble Snout, who brings the news of Theseus's wedding and ventures his opinion on their loss. The first part of the scene barely specified time or place, but calendar logic returns with his arrival – the wedding has been and gone and the day is moving rapidly forward. The lion-in-waiting also brings a touch of economics with him to leaven all the melancholy disappointment: if things had gone forward they would all have been 'made men'.

This makes Flute still madder. It occurs to him that Bottom would so have impressed the Duke that he would have won an annuity of sixpence a day for life – he couldn't have 'scaped' it. One would hope there would have been something for the rest of them as well, but Flute seems so generously carried away that he is thinking only of his hero. It's an interesting detail about how things seem to work. If you do a good show, you get sponsorship, perhaps for good, just as Shakespeare hoped to secure as much as a thousand pounds from the Earl of Southampton by, with great ado, dedicating his narrative poems to him.[1] Sixpence a day was certainly a good deal, at the top edge of the average daily salary of a late Elizabethan artisan, so that the actor could either have retired or doubled his money by continuing to work. The thought becomes an obsessive mantra for Flute – he intones it four times in four sentences, before miserably underlining the reality:

> . . . or nothing.

This talk of real consequences gives a tough warp to the working men's charming wish to succeed as actors – they need a lucky break, and the play could have meant real advancement.

It couldn't be a better cue. Perhaps he has been there behind them for a little while, having slipped through the door to wait for the best moment; perhaps his call comes faintly from a distance like a song, silencing them all. Either way, Flute's definitive description –

> O sweet bully Bottom!

– has done the office of an announcement. It is answered by the hail-fellow, actorish, somewhat nautical, and above all jubilant greeting:

> Where are these lads? Where are these hearts?

As he ran, Bottom was no doubt continuing the battle to expunge the awkwardnesses of his dream while treasuring the good parts.

---

1. A miscalculation in his case, since the young Earl came into his majority crippled by debt and the writers all dropped him like a hot potato; Shakespeare possibly transmuted him from a fruitless patron into the fair young man of the Sonnets.

Whether or not he will be able to speak of it, he is, above all, excited by the thought of breathing the warm familiar air of his friends, and has quite forgotten their cruel abandonments. Like a flood, tearful delirium follows. At the same moment, the status quo snaps sharply back into place: only Quince and Bottom speak from now on, even Flute sinking back into his old open-mouthed attitude. Quince's tongue is especially loosened:

> O most courageous day!

It sounds like a verbal slip, excitement overriding language, but needn't be; it is as eloquent an invention as Miranda's 'brave new world' in *The Tempest*. As Bottom overrides his partner, something is still battling away inside him: he will tell them, he won't, yes he will, but then he doesn't:

> Masters, I am to discourse wonders; but ask me not what. For if I tell you, I am no true Athenian. I will tell you everything right as it fell out . . . Not a word of me. All that I will tell you is – that the Duke hath dined.

This is like his shyness with us; he is not coy, but instinctively keeping his precious midsummer night's dream to himself. It makes for a wonderful indecision, that of a comical Hamlet, right up to the significant pause near the end. And then the subject closes for good. Whatever it was, it's gone.

All Bottom's interest now is in the common good. The day has accelerated, and there is no time for anything very much. What there is would surely be best spent rehearsing, but Bottom seems indifferent to that: it has proved a perilous business in the past. It will be enough if everyone has a quick look at the script and hopes for the best, having gathered some costumes together (and, in Starveling's case, some quite complicated props for Moonshine). Strings must be found to attach false beards around their heads – only for him, most probably (Thisbe? Wall?) – and in a deep theatrical malapropism, he recommends new ribbons for their pumps, which would make rather balletic footwear for *Pyramus and Thisbe*. Pumps were like what they are now, dancing shoes, but used for comedy then instead of the traditional thick-soled buskins of tragedy: perhaps Bottom still thinks of the performance as a very good and merry piece of work. With a marvellous disregard for the time available, Snug must allow his nails to grow long enough for a lion's claws – a business hardly more difficult in his case than getting his lines learned; and as a company they must be careful (as actors are to this day) not to eat a meal with garlic and onions in the few minutes left, since

> we are to utter sweet breath, and I do not doubt but to hear them say, it is a sweet comedy.

As Shakespearian time-scales go, all this has not been too bad. Theseus said at the start that the new moon would rise in four days and then the wedding would take place while Hermia agreed to her father's terms. The period of grace has shrunk, as time will in plays, to the two nights that, strictly speaking, she and Lysander have been on the run: the first a decoy when they lay low in Athens to disarm suspicion, and the second their time in the wood. This morning Theseus and Hippolyta went hunting and found them, whereupon Theseus realised that Hermia's day of decision had arrived. This scene with the actors back in Athens is happening a short time later, to allow Bottom to bustle the single mile home to them. Snug, and then Bottom, have emphasised urgency. Shakespearian 'double time' – here, the insertion of unnoticed signals whereby two 'stage' nights appear to expand to four – is his usual way of maintaining narrative energy while suggesting a longer span of experience within it.

In rehearsal, we must sometimes ask ourselves naturalistic questions to which there is no reply as if we still needed to have the answers ready. Noting the literal impossibilities, we politely keep them to ourselves: it is best that we know where Shakespeare is executing his sleights of hand, so that we can take care that the audience misses them. Here he has taken a large risk with credulity. Bottom has announced that 'our play is preferred' even though Theseus will only make his choice early in the next scene: strictly, there has been no time for even a provisional thumbs-up for *Pyramus and Thisbe*, or for Bottom to hear about it. The real reason is that Shakespeare can't waste time with trivia at this end of the play, but the actor playing Bottom has to know what he thinks he means. So, let us say that he is carried away and gambling on success; or perhaps he detoured by the palace on his way back from the forest to pick up the news that they have made it, in some inscrutable way, onto a short-list. And let's believe it too: as always, the acting will be richer for its sense of conviction. We have to be equally sure how long his friends have been waiting for him, and at what time of day – if for no other reason than that people behave in one way in the mornings and another in the evenings, and likewise if they have been waiting for two hours rather than eight.

The most verbose character on the stage finally issues a sober order:

No more words.

Like 'Hold or cut bowstrings' when they first met, it is a moment of stillness, six divers gathering themselves for the final plunge. They have, in a just world, little to fear. Restored to their proper internal structure and without too much time to be nervous, they will surely look all right when they arrive at the palace, breathless, shabby and hopeful, a little down at heel compared to their rivals. The flurry of familiarities, the sunny vernacular, the overflow of fellowship among the 'most dear actors' all suggest that none of them need to go into any mysterious woods again. On the day of solemnities and merriment promised in the play's first lines, the rapt, hilarious and sacred business of preparing to act a play begins.

NINE

Act 5 Scene 1

Something has changed at the palace:

> 'Tis strange, my Theseus, that these lovers speak of.

The possessive endearment comes in a voice quite different from the one that blunted Theseus's frantic wooing and outboasted him in the hunt. It is, in fact, Hippolyta's first kind word; becoming married today has seemingly had the same effect as a successful wedding night.

Marriage has loosened Theseus's tongue as well, or let him find it properly at last. For one thing, he contradicts her quite calmly:

> More strange than true. I never may believe
> These antique fables, nor these fairy toys.
> Lovers and madmen have such seething brains,
> Such shaping fantasies, that apprehend
> More than cool reason ever comprehends.

As, fresh from the temple and a good dinner, he then presumes to explain the nature of such things – the only speech in his part that anyone remembers – it is clear that his turbulent character has gained some unblustering confidence. He was never short of opinions, but they didn't have quite this assurance, this overall reach. He is, for once, not talking about himself, or barely, and lucidity has taken over from the old huff-and-puff: he will be much better on the lunatic, the lover and the poet than he was on withered dowagers and dewlapped hounds.

These philosophical speeches in Shakespeare have become so anthologised in the mind that it can be difficult to read them for what they are. Often they seem to exceed their context – Jaques' 'Ages of Man' in *As You Like It* is an obvious example – and to be a little more than the occasion calls for. Also, you might have expected

Theseus to count himself a member of at least one of the human types he is disparaging. Certainly we have to assess why he is doing it, rather than simply bathing in his eloquence: his aim, after all, is to discredit the experience of four people with whom we have travelled a long way.

His speech puts together some surprising ideas: to bring the amorous and the literary, obvious enough bedfellows, into line with the inhabitants of Bedlam prison for the insane, objects of horrified fascination to the Elizabethans, is certainly provocative. There is both suaveness and a guarded intelligence in it, the moderate empathy of a ruler who can allow himself to enthuse up to a point; he knows that it takes all sorts, even if he cannot in the end approve a world in which a bush or a bear can be taken for something other than itself. On the other hand, to compare all lovers to madmen because some of them see beauty in the face of a mere gypsy is an inauspicious position for a man to take on his wedding night.

Through it all, of course, runs the usual conservative streak: there is more style than generosity here, and a residual taste for showing off. According to Theseus, anything that smacks of the picturesque (the 'antique'), or of the over-active brain in general, is to be wary of: the proper position towards the unknown is sceptical going on dismissive.[1] So he is still showing less intuitive wisdom than Hippolyta. Never mind the glib soundbites, she might reply – the lovers have had an irreducible experience, thick with imagination; their minds have been 'transfigured so together', so the continuing story of their life might well turn

> . . . to something of great constancy . . .

It is a brilliant choice of a noun, linking constancy in love to consistent meaning in life. Her ability to touch in a nuance is still well beyond her partner's.

Clearly the lovers have talked about their adventures in the wood as fully as Theseus invited them to do – if only so that Shakespeare could illustrate the developing relationship between him and his

---

1. It seems that Shakespeare added the section on the lover as an afterthought, perhaps on the eve of the printing of the first Quarto of 1600: the lines are mislineated in that edition as if inserted in a hurry. It is odd – you would think the lover the most important of the three in the context: no one has been talking about madness or poetry. This Quarto was probably taken from Shakespeare's working papers rather than from the acting company's version (which would have remained their copyright).

bride. However, despite his mention of 'fairy toys', it seems unlikely that fairies have been discussed, any more than they were by Bottom as he considered his dream. The fact is that the lovers know nothing about fairies, only that they have been through some odd experience, now scudding away like a cloud that was once a mountain. In the theatre, however, we will somehow assume that both they and Theseus now know everything that we know, magic potions, fogs of Acheron, hobgoblins and all.

Unable to reconcile male packaging with female associativeness, Theseus and Hippolyta have to leave it at that while the subjects of their small dispute join them. Their exchange may have been private, or attended by supportive courtiers, as their opening scene could have been. The newly confident married man may have wanted to entertain his retinue by acting out the characters he was inventing, just as Jaques might in the 'Ages of Man'. That's a matter of taste, though at some point in the play it will have been helpful to see this couple *tête-à-tête* and unaware of an audience.

At least this time they haven't left each other feeling cold and excluded. In retrospect, it was important that Hippolyta initiated the argument with her endearment, because the disagreement hanging in the air now seems to be less that of two unhappy people than of married adults. As for its subject, whether the lovers' experience has any real meaning, the decision, fortunately for the play, is left open: while Theseus has been busy denying the essence of what we will continue to watch, Hippolyta's apprehension of it keeps it alive.

An exchange of pleasantries between the Duke and his protégés, a small rhetorical flight required by the occasion, dies, as such things will, of its own too much: Theseus wishes them superlative joy three times in two and a half lines, and they can hardly match that. What next? After his brief outing as an intellectual, something of his emphatic restlessness reappears, and he even seems to forget that he has just got married. To summon Philostrate, his 'usual manager of mirth', to his side to discuss entertainments

> To wear away this long age of three hours
> Between our after-supper and bedtime

could perhaps be a measure of ardour – the day waning as slowly as the old moon did – but 'supper' and 'bedtime' sound more homely than passionate, the vocabulary of the long married rather than the bridegroom. Theseus could presumably curtail the wait if he wanted, but he seems keener on alleviating the boredom of a 'lazy time' than on getting Hippolyta to bed. Masques, dances, revels, plays

> To ease the anguish of a torturing hour

– where are they? This determined mirthfulness and fear of having nothing to do could make him a tiring husband.

There is quite a textual puddle next, and some evidence of rewriting. As an alert actor of Egeus may well point out to his director, in the First Folio, put together after his death by Shakespeare's colleagues, there is a variation from the earlier Quartos. Philostrate's speeches are assigned to Egeus, while the reading of the play-titles on offer to Theseus is given, for no evident reason, to Lysander. Since the Folio is likely to have been the first version to be drawn from the playing script, this curious change would presumably be in the light of performance, and therefore has some conviction. The featured cast could in a certain small sense be reduced by it, Philostrate becoming no more than a mute supernumerary. But it doesn't help much – he still exists, named in the first scene – and it raises quite large issues about the interpretation of Egeus, especially his measure of co-operation when events have so soundly defeated him. It seems hard, confounded by Hermia and Lysander and overruled by Theseus, for him to be in charge of the entertainments for his recalcitrant daughter's wedding.

On the other hand, without this complication, Egeus's silence, if he is there at all, is almost unbearably loaded, though that itself gives him something to act, in good humour or ill. From the moment that Theseus disabled the patriarchal laws of the land in Hermia's favour, Egeus has been dispossessed, struck dumb. He could have made a proud and disgusted exit at the end of the hunting scene, potentially an exile or a radicalised critic of the regime. Or he could be here now, doing his best, a reconciled guest at the wedding rather than a ghost at it. If so, he needs an attitude: in the absence of lines, it should be discreetly handled, since Shakespeare's characters generally define themselves by speaking rather than refusing to. He could, later on, dance with his daughter, reluctantly or not; chat with or cold-shoulder Lysander. In fact, the *Dream* shows its youth among Shakespeare comedies in that no one is pointedly left out of the final reconciliations – pointedly in the sense of it being mentioned. On the whole, that was a later development: in Shakespeare's maturity, characters such as Don Pedro in *Much Ado* and Jaques stand avowedly aside from the final community, temperamentally separate and more or less poignant. But in the early 1590s, we are encouraged swiftly to forget such disharmonies as that Doctor Pinch has been burned half to death in *The Comedy of Errors*; or that Proteus has survived his own threat to rape Silvia to enjoy the happy ending of *The Two Gentlemen of Verona*. Whether or not the Folio's hint is taken up, this seems likely to be what Shakespeare is after with Egeus, his view being that as the play doesn't need the character any more, his attitude is neither here not there. The fact is though that we are not so tolerant of a part being simply discarded like the ass's head.

Whoever is in charge of the entertainments – and there is quite a good part for Philostrate if the Folio is ignored – it is certainly an attractive idea to divide the long speech describing them between him and Theseus, as a sort of feed and payoff. For Philostrate to make the hopeful suggestions and for Theseus to confound them has obvious comic possibilities. What is on offer seems to have been officially vetted, perhaps after an inspection of rehearsals. But nothing seems quite right to Theseus, at least not the proposals from the mainstream. 'The Battle with the Centaurs' – quite apart from being dauntingly sung falsetto to a harp accompaniment – is essentially a hymn to Hercules, a bigger star than Theseus and one whom Hippolyta has already used to keep him in his place; and the violence it relates took place at a wedding feast, so this re-enactment is not well timed. Equally shocking for the occasion is Ovid's account of Orpheus being torn apart by the Thracian women in their 'bacchanals'; Theseus turns it down, but not without mentioning the glorious moment when it was performed for him when he

> . . . from Thebes came last a conqueror.

Most revealing of all is his swift refusal of the lament of the Nine Muses for

> the death
> Of learning, late deceased in beggary.

His instinct to see this as 'some satire keen and critical' by which he could be embarrassed is extremely sharp. It might be hard for us to see how it could give offence, but the Duke of Athens can hardly countenance a link between scholarship and social disinheritance.

So Theseus's attitude to the short-list starts with vanity and ends with impatience; the latter at the idea of some kind of agitprop company whom Philostrate should have sent packing on sight. So far, so not so good. As a result perhaps, the decision he is about to make is autocratically wayward, and it causes Philostrate the kind of public discomfiture that Olivia subjects Malvolio to when she stands up for Feste in the early stages of *Twelfth Night*. The fact that Philostrate feels the need to emphasise the proletarian nature of the next company on his list, Quince's, suggests that the others tendering for the job are acceptably courtly; and it seems to him that a 'tedious brief scene' of 'very tragical mirth' performed by working men could be as embarrassing as letting in a boisterous set of clowns who believe in audience-harassment. He is horrified by Theseus's unexpected interest in them, and goes to great and unwitty lengths to put him off, revealing himself in the process as a patronising lickspittle. To him our actors are no more than

> Hard-handed men that work in Athens here,
> Which never laboured in their minds till now
> And now have toiled their unbreathed memories . . .

For a moment you see another reason for Philostrate to be doubled with Puck – the same scorn of the working class.[2]

We on the other hand approve Theseus's tolerance, however devilish it seems to Philostrate:

> And we will hear it.

The most unexpected things change the direction of a man's thinking, and Theseus seems suddenly to dislike the surrounding snobbishness. Hearing the actors described as brainless plebeians, he has resolved to take a chance, since

> . . . never anything can be amiss
> When simpleness and duty tender it.

To Hippolyta, this fit of semi-socialism may seem no more than a trick of the royal trade, like remembering the name of the chimney-sweep or putting on a construction-worker's hat. She certainly suspects his motives:

> I love not to see wretchedness o'ercharg'd
> And duty in his service perishing.

2. Though he makes great play of having been reduced to helpless mirth at the rehearsal of *Pyramus and Thisbe*, we know Philostrate hasn't seen it, unless Shakespeare, forgetting his story, imagines for the moment that he has. On the other hand, how has it got onto the short list without being looked at by someone, just as all Elizabethan plays were vetted by the Queen's Master of Revels? Enough.

She is right in one way: on the whole, a tone-deaf plumber shouldn't be allowed to sing opera to the King. But Theseus is righter. His determination to distinguish honest labour from presumption – not to mistake the manner for the man, in fact – has the smack of wisdom, albeit with a slight sense of patronage:

> HIPPOLYTA: He says they can do nothing in this kind.
> THESEUS: The kinder we, to give them thanks for nothing.

The way he explains himself is perhaps the most impressive thing he does in the play: he sounds like a professional sharing his day-to-day experience of government. Strategic nurturing is part of the job; kindness and forbearance are learned virtues, and they should accompany an astute distrust of flattery.[3] His plan this evening is the opposite of mockery, unless you regard it as the deepest mockery of all – a poker-faced appreciation that will gratify the performers while cementing the ruling class's confidence in its ability to dissemble:

> Our sport shall be to take what they mistake.
> And what poor duty cannot do, noble respect
> Takes it in might, not merit.

After all, no one knows how to behave with you when you are the Duke. Years of facing nervous supplicants liable to

> . . . shiver and look pale,
> Make periods in the midst of sentences,
> Throttle their practised accent in their fears

has taught Theseus to pick a welcome out of a shambles and develop a nose for 'audacious eloquence'. It is the same acumen that helped him spot political satire inside one of the evening's proposed plays.

The probable gentleness of 'Trust me, sweet' – perhaps Hippolyta is about to contradict – is his equivalent of her 'my Theseus'. It delicately overbears her, but allows us to leave them on fairly equal terms, well enough settled for the play's purposes. Indeed, in Theseus's last words –

> Love therefore, and tongue-tied simplicity,
> In least speak most, to my capacity

– is just a hint that they themselves, used to relying on their defensive wits, might come to appreciate the quieter harmonies of everyday

---

3. Queen Elizabeth I was famous for this: there are a number of recorded instances of her reassuring nervous commoners as they ground to a halt while making formal addresses to her. No doubt she was purchasing loyalty for life with a small flattering lie. This overt tribute to her from Shakespeare perhaps doesn't quite qualify as 'tongue-tied simplicity'.

life. Whatever you think of his politics, Theseus's ease and eloquence has become as attractive to Hippolyta as her imaginative sympathy to us. She warms to him, and they settle to watch the play.

He was certainly right about the nerves: Peter Quince, introducing Pyramus and Thisbe, is about to make notable periods in the midst of sentences – while Flute, muttering anxiously to himself backstage and half-listening for Thisbe's cue, may very likely shiver and look pale. Stepping out on his own and suspecting nothing, this is Quince's great moment, one of those splendid authorial prologues that Ben Jonson[4] and Christopher Marlowe (but Shakespeare only with great sophistication) used as a means of warming up their audience. In the end he has written his not in the 'eight and eight' or 'eight and six' argued over with Bottom, but, near enough, in decasyllables, with an echo of the truncated sonnet form much used by the lovers. In content too, it is not what Bottom advised, since it doesn't refer to him at all but wisely ingratiates itself generally, almost exactly answering Theseus's expectations: this effort will be easy for him to indulge, and he will feel good about himself. Quince's courtesy is impeccable: he uses the same charming word 'gentles' as the Chorus does habitually in *Henry V*, and he emphasises the actors' humility and harmlessness. The unexceptionable sentiments are even quite well put, and graced with a modest antithesis:

> To show our simple skill,
> That is the true beginning of our end.

So what goes wrong, causing the spoken speech to decline from coherence into a ruinous mess? Presumably Quince's sense of occasion, his overexcitement about the glittering prizes ahead, and the shock of seeing attentive upper-class faces looking closely at him after rehearsing to the blank walls of his room. They reduce a perfectly adequate composition to obscurity and then to the hilarious opposite of its meaning:

> Consider then, we come but in despite.
> We do not come, as minding to content you,
> Our true intent is. All for your delight
> We are not here. That you should here repent you
> The actors are at hand . . . [5]

---

4. Jonson, ever the show-off, writes introductions to *The Alchemist* and *Volpone* as acrostics, the initial letters of their lines vertically spelling the name of the play; presumably this was for reading rather than performance. When the theatres re-opened with the Restoration in 1660, such speeches would be put into the mouths of that great erotic novelty, the star actress.

Really it's a matter of breathing, and the catastrophic effect of stage fright on that mechanism. All verse-speaking needs to be supported by the steady bellows of regular, controlled air, but nerves make you pant and grab. On the very first line – a harrowing moment – Quince stops at the end instead of continuing on. After that he keeps running out of breath half way through a line – the third, seventh and eighth – which obliges him to take a pause that sounds like a full stop. Feeling catastrophe gathering, he becomes preoccupied and stops concentrating on the meaning of his words – anxiously shrinks away from them, in fact – so that the speech, no longer belonging to him, wobbles anonymously into insult. You can hear the same muddle sometimes at weddings, when people unused to reciting are faced with material that they haven't really practised enough, and from whose meaning they are distracted by momentousness. Nerves prevent them using the part of the reading eye that looks ahead, scanning the next three or four lines and preparing to accommodate them; before long there is little left but a locking of the jaw and freezing of the eye.

Quince is rewarded with the opposite of understanding – an antiphonal salvo of mockery. Theseus, Lysander and Hippolyta compete for the most elegant putdown, to their great satisfaction and our mirthlessness, and each contribution is as hard to understand as Quince's mangled lines. There is a laboured pun on punctuation –

> This fellow doth not stand upon points

– some piety –

> A good moral, my lord; it is not enough to speak, but to speak
> true

– with jokes about horseriding and children's failure to master musical instruments thrown in. Even Theseus, who promised 'noble respect', contributes twice, his good intentions apparently abandoned. It is hard to imagine a blunter form of getting the bird: it is as if a row of six ill-trained critics were there, not taking notes but loudly discussing what they are going to write. Our real-life audience,

---

5. This part of the speech should go, rather nicely:

> Consider then we come – but in despite
> We do not come – as minding to content you;
> Our true intent is all for your delight;
> We are not here that you should here repent you;
> The actors are at hand . . .

like the Mechanicals, will have to start coping with what issues from these well-bred mouths, accepting that this is a form of theatre in which spectators answer back to draw attention to themselves.

At least Theseus declares that the enterprise is not quite doomed; he briskly moves matters on:

> Who is next?

The First Folio, again substituting theatre practice for Shakespeare's drafts, pleasantly brings on the rest of the actors by introducing 'Tawyer', who was in fact a musician in Shakespeare's company, to blow a trumpet fanfare to announce *Pyramus and Thisbe*. At this point Quince, pleased no doubt to have company, begins to recover his form. Just as his Prologue was, originally, satisfactory, there is nothing wrong at all with his 'show' in which, in the manner of the time if at more than usual length, each character is introduced and their story explained so that there shall be no unwelcome shocks later. It is a little laborious, that's all, especially if, as seems likely, each of them steps forward on cue and perhaps suits an action to Quince's words. This time, if there is a weakness in the writing, it is in the clinching of the somewhat erratic rhymes. Whenever he found a thought falling short of a full line, Quince seems to have scratched his head for parenthetical padding to drag it to its metrical destiny:

> This man is Pyramus, if you would know;
> This beauteous lady Thisbe is, certain . . .
>   . . . if you will know,
> By moonshine did these lovers think no scorn
> To meet at Ninus' tomb, there, there to woo.
> This grisly beast, which Lion hight by name,
> The trusty Thisbe, coming first by night
> Did scare away, or rather did affright . . .

The contentious things the actors discussed earlier – the lion, the chink in the wall and the moonlight – are honourably dealt with, and the really provocative matter of Pyramus killing himself is invested with a resounding alliteration, as if it were absorbing the violence of the event:

> Whereat with blade – with bloody, blameful blade –
> He bravely broached his boiling bloody breast.

Alliteration again does the work for Thisbe's suicide, which is also blessed with a homely description of the night that conceals it:

And Thisbe, tarrying in mulberry shade,
His dagger drew, and died.

The audience is, relatively, stilled by this improved performance; no more hooliganism for the moment, just a note of interest from Theseus and some unfunny ingratiation from Demetrius:

THESEUS: I wonder if the lion be to speak.
DEMETRIUS: No wonder, my lord – one lion may, when many asses do.

Perhaps Bottom hears that final 'asses', perhaps not.

The crowning performance of *Pyramus and Thisbe* which now starts properly is – together with the show of *The Nine Worthies* presented to a similarly disrespectful group of courtiers in *Love's Labour's Lost* – the most extensive experiment Shakespeare made in presenting a play to a stage audience, apart from the more deadly business of *The Murder of Gonzago* in *Hamlet*.[6] The efforts of Nick Bottom, Peter Quince and their friends hardly have that sort of effect on *A Midsummer Night's Dream*, but the device toys with theatrical identity in a similar way, layering it double. Also involved is a form of licence: the audience's desire that all will end well when they sit down to watch the *Dream* is wonderfully relaxed by their being allowed to enjoy one disaster after another in *Pyramus and Thisbe*.

If indeed it is disastrous. Put simply: whose side is the real audience to take, and when; and how laughable or otherwise is the show to them as opposed to the Court? What is it about these two hundred lines, with their interruptions, stallings, and occasional riffs of conviction, that has marked them down as one of Shakespeare's comic triumphs? Why, in the hands of a master-dramatist, is the sight of theatre going wrong so appealing, and how wrong is it going here?

The script of *Pyramus and Thisbe*, as we already know, is middling, not terrible: its gentle absurdities are not, with momentary exceptions, the stuff of belly-laughs. The tremulous quaintness of the writing suggests that elements of a style several decades old have been

6. He wasn't quite the first to do it, though he certainly developed the idea in a remarkable way. Thomas Kyd's *The Spanish Tragedy* (1589, and therefore fresh in the mind) has its hero Hieronimo staging a play written in four different languages at the climax of the revenge action. In it is the memorable stage direction 'Hieronimo knocks up the curtain'. Massinger's *The Roman Actor* (1626) will use plays-within-a-play still more elaborately: an actor is seduced on the stage by the Emperor's mistress, and then killed by the jealous Emperor during the course of his next performance.

unearthed – as was, more or less, the case: the main object of Shake-speare's satire was the same Arthur Golding[7] whose 1567 translation of Ovid had provided him with much of the suggestive material for the play. Some of the rhymes are naive, and some of the linguistic effects, particularly Bottom's, are pastiche; but some of it could equally be Shakespeare on an only slightly off day. Thisbe's and Pyramus's dialogue bears some relation to Hermia's and Lysander's in the first scene of the *Dream,* and the whole story has echoes not only of *Romeo and Juliet* but of the four lovers' recent experiences in the wood.

As far as the acting goes, Quince has suffered the cost of hasty preparation and, perhaps, personal shyness; and both Bottom and Flute will make a typical mistake, originated by Flute and rapidly becoming gospel – 'Ninny's tomb'. For the rest, the quality of per-formance is an open question: it may even be reasonably good. Apart from Quince's mistakes, no technical hitches are specified by the text, only a running accompaniment of unhelpful interruptions from the audience; there are a couple of unplanned departures from the script by Bottom, innocently keen to explain the mysteries of his craft, and a wonderfully shaming retort to the barrackers by the modest Starveling.

So it would be possible to play this as a perfectly clean show, the more remarkable considering Bottom's 'translation' in the midst of its only rehearsal. But it wouldn't be very satisfactory to end such an evening with a dour lesson in the heartlessness of audiences and the dignity of amateur dramatic societies. It is fairly clear from the fore-going scenes, with their observation of Shakespeare's own profession at work, that the result is not to be a solemn affair.

In our own rehearsals, meanwhile, it will be best to let the stew cook gently. Knockabout is easy to invent, but comic business devised by a cast anxious to do justice to a famously entertaining scene risks making the Mechanicals seem much stupider than they are; and in any case, determination to get laughs generally has the opposite effect. So the trick will be to let things develop while staying true to life, concentrating on what might individually become of these well-intentioned men under stress. Is such-and-such a joke truly charac-teristic of Snug, or of Quince, Snout or Starveling, extending what

---

7. He is taking particular revenge on Golding's laborious fourteen-syllable lines, and his tendency, like Quince's, to use repetitions of 'did' to work up the portent and pad out the metre.

we have already seen of them? Since much of *Pyramus and Thisbe* is a succession of 'turns', each actor may become anxious that he is not as funny as his predecessor; but he doesn't need to be, or in the same way – for Snout to be earnest or Starveling black-affronted is as valuable as Bottom tripping over his sword. In fact any group of experienced actors will know where the best jokes lie: everyone has been under-rehearsed, unsure of script and audience, at some point in their lives. The performer's comfort is that once he has risked humiliation by stepping onto the stage, his willingness to abandon hope may win him a special form of respect in the end.

For the enterprise is always fragile; and it is a mysterious fact that, by stumbling at the start, Quince lets a particular joker out of the pack. Or you might call it the Cock-up Virus. One mistake – a lost prop, a catastrophic 'dry', a paralysing scenic hitch – tends to multiply itself, according to some deadly law that nobody understands. Infected, the inanimate becomes alive and inimical; things jump out of two left hands. Once glimpsed, the serious-minded panic that results may embarrass a polite audience; but in a play-within-a-play the licensed hilarity is as fitting a climax as multiple deaths are to the tragedy of *Hamlet*.

With the arrival of Snout the tinker to present a wall, we can see that the company's honourable principles are already overrunning their ability to deliver. The distracting argument that arose over verse forms between Quince and Bottom has allowed a real tactical error to slip through. Had Snout spoken in prose, or some easy form of blank verse, he would have avoided the insidious comedy that comes from his insistence on rhyme: it is odd to talk of a wall, a hole and a chink in couplets. This is almost the only time that *Pyramus and Thisbe* uses this self-conscious form. Oddly enough (and perhaps because he is no longer referring to building materials),[8] Snout's final effort –

> And this the cranny is, right and sinister,
> Through which the fearful lovers are to whisper

– is quite an honourable half-rhyme. The stage tradition that has grown up – that Snout should hesitate over its sophistication and perhaps

---

8. Post-Brecht and post-Brook, we might say that it would have been better for him simply to come on in a basic costume and say who he is. An Elizabethan wall, as evidenced by the reconstructed Globe Theatre in Southwark, would have been compounded from sand, goat's hair, lime and river-reeds.

say 'whinisper' – has become so hoary that most self-respecting directors will want to avoid it on principle.

What Snout says to explain his appearance is correct enough, though it does seem aimed at the slightly backward. His patient eagerness to establish the ground-rules is a measure of seriousness, even if it may have been a mistake to draw attention to the excellence of his costume:

> This loam, this roughcast, and this stone doth show
> That I am that same wall; the truth is so.

How can he be wearing all three convincingly, especially given the speed with which everything has been thrown together? Is this a big square costume with bricks painted on it, worn like a sandwich board, or a bedraggled tabard daubed in dust, or even a three-dimensional structure like a small house? The problem could defeat a more sophisticated designer than Quince has available, and it certainly relies rather heavily on the goodwill of the audience, which may not be available.

And how has he come to this point, standing here like a tortoise with too big a shell? He was the quiet one at the original meeting at Quince's house; in the forest he was Bottom's ally, judiciously concerned to disarm the fears of the ladies about bloodshed and wild beasts. Finally, it was he who said that the one thing you could never do was 'bring in a wall', and with the logic of such things, here he is doing it – with a speech, as it turns out. How happy is he about this? Well, not too unhappy, I would suggest, and in any case, in control: a display of reluctance or temper is unlikely to help at this point. As a trouper and a decent colleague, there is no reason to think he isn't doing his best.

As with the dumb show, Snout's acceptable performance provokes no mockery. When Theseus adjudges

> Would you desire lime and hair to speak better?

perhaps he means not only that it is unusual to hear a wall speak so elegantly, but that he cannot imagine anyone discharging the job better. And Demetrius's

> It is the wittiest partition that ever I heard discourse, my lord

is pure praise if you don't look too closely at it.

Things are not going too badly. But the stylistic uncertainty, the wobble between highfaluting and folksy, doesn't bode well for such specialities as Moon and Lion. And Snout's Wall was really yet another prologue, a further postponement of the defining moment when a protagonist must shift things into high romantic gear.

The fellow coming on now (perhaps in one of his highly coloured selection of beards) looks like the man to do it. The audience leans forward: this could be the star of this shaky business. Unfortunately Bottom will make it shakier; we may have been better off with the unassuming Wall, who had no affectation about him. Bottom's bombastic fusillade as Pyramus –

O grim-looked night, O night with hue so black . . .

– extends to a ridiculous point a very small piece of information: that it is night, that Thisbe may not have arrived, and that there's a wall to look through. It is constructed of familiar literary tropes, none of them despised by Shakespeare himself: a repeated personification ('Night' and 'Wall') to headline two different parentheses; the single exclamatory 'O' used to tremendous repeated effect in Othello's final passion and the Nurse's lament for Juliet; and the blind attack, for purposes of pathos, on lifeless objects nearby. Here the wall is cursed for deceiving Bottom; in *Richard III* Queen Elizabeth asks the stones of the Tower of London ('Rude ragged nurse, old sullen playfellow') to protect her doomed children.

Obviously the conventions are degraded here because they express so little about either the nature of night or why Thisbe might have let Pyramus down. The fact that the writer half-understands them, and that Bottom takes such relish in rolling the cadences off his tongue, seriously threatens the play's chances: in both cases we sense vacancy behind the posturing. And there is no likelihood, now that his big moment has arrived, that Bottom will be moving through this repetitive litany with anything other than a self-satisfied, comically maddening deliberation. Not only is he acutely aware of what he considers his technique, but he has a weather eye on his audience in a way that his colleagues, locked in bewilderment and alarm, do not. So much so that it only takes the briefest interruption from Theseus, standing up for the abused Snout –

The wall, methinks, being sensible, should curse again

– to bring him down to the front of the stage to buttonhole the heckler.[9] But only kindly, as if Theseus were an ignoramus: Bottom has

9. You can look at the audience asides during the 'plays' in Morecambe and Wise's classic TV shows to see how well this joke has lasted.

to point out that in this context an imperative like 'should' has lost its moral sense for a dramaturgical one:

> No, in truth sir, he should not. 'Deceiving me' is Thisbe's cue.

'Sir' is not quite respectful enough for the occasion, but forgiven because of Bottom's kindness in taking a non-initiate by the hand and guiding him through the entertainment:

> You shall see – it will fall pat as I told you. Yonder she comes.

Wall, meanwhile, has been roughly treated. He was wooed by Bottom into showing him his 'chink' – the tiny gesture from a probably large figure of loam and roughcast would be funny even it weren't also haunted by a not-quite-specific vulgarity. And now he has been cursed for his pains, and possibly roughed up a little as well.

It can happen in the theatre that the best-equipped actor wrecks the show. A smattering of ability may be worse than none at all, and audiences can be more irritated by a mannered central performance than a competent supporting one. It looks as if this may be happening here, in which case all, from Quince's point of view, will soon be lost. Flute's arrival as Thisbe, for all that he is cross-dressed, momentarily stabilises things. He starts, perhaps tentatively, with an unassuming quatrain, even quite pretty, and respectful to the abused Wall:

> My cherry lips have often kiss'd thy stones,
> Thy stones with lime and hair knit up in thee.

He will have his work cut out though: the show is still hovering over a chasm opened up by Quince's agonies and Bottom's grandiloquence. Now it drops a few hundred feet more through the air because of a catastrophic malapropism from Bottom – one which Quince himself committed in the rehearsal:

> I see a voice.

He compounds it:

> Now will I to the chink
> To spy an I can hear my Thisbe's face.

'Chink' is becoming an unfortunate motif, and Bottom's mistakes are not over: 'Ninny's tomb' is just round the corner. Some of them will pass us by: pairing 'Limander' with Helen of Troy is a complicated error, mixing the stories of Alexander (another name for the Trojan Paris) and the very unfaithful Helen on the one hand, and that of Hero and Leander on the other; Shafalus and Procrus should, as it happens, be Cephalus and Procris. Whether it is Bottom the actor, Bottom the text-editor, or Quince the possible script-writer who has got this wrong is not clear: all are unreliable. The rest is just clumsy: Pyramus's greeting to his lover –

> Think what thou wilt

– sounds a little rude, and his belly-flop from classical invocation into

> O kiss me through the hole of this vile wall

is an anti-climax that would not have been committed by Hermia and Lysander, who are now watching their own rhetorical style parodied.

With the lover's tryst and Wall's courteous departure –

> Thus have I, Wall, my part discharged so;
> And being done, thus Wall away doth go

– it is as if Part One had ended. The stage is empty; and the interval comments from Theseus and Demetrius are quite harmless. In fact they are gibe-free: a routine comment from Theseus and a mild joke from Demetrius along the lines that walls have ears. Cutting across them comes Hippolyta, sharp and unambiguous:

> This is the silliest stuff that ever I heard.

It epitomises the censorious intelligence she stores behind her stylish manners; the hapless actors, who may be within earshot, have become the target for her residual resentment. Theseus's reply to her is startling – it sounds highly ambiguous, but impressive in some way or other:

> The best in this kind are but shadows; and the worst are no
> worse, if imagination amend them.

It is difficult to know what he means. If comparing actors to shadows is meant as a generous thought, it follows that the best acting is indefinable: that even the slightly talented, as long as they are imaginative enough to 'amend' themselves, share in its numinousness. But if the comment is critical, it means that even Laurence Olivier is a thing of no substance.

Much depends on whether the current relationship between Theseus and Hippolyta is better served by Theseus moderating her sharpness or by his dismissing the actor's profession as briskly as he did the lover and the poet. His potential for perceptiveness and its opposite as usual allows for contrary readings: and his character remains an open question. I incline to the sceptical, obviously, but I also wish I liked him better: it would be comforting to see him as the voice of reason, calm and parental. But I find his insights provisional and his wisdom disappointing, and the fact is I don't trust him – do you?

If Hippolyta was sharp before, she is now plain rude:

> It must be your imagination, then, and not theirs.

Even if this is gently delivered it does no favours to the actors waiting to continue: Hippolyta is proving quite a surprise, her distaste fast hardening into snobbishness. By her side, Theseus now seems the more generous, if somewhat elusive:

> If we imagine no worse of them than they of themselves, they
> may pass for excellent men.

Another calculated ambiguity: is it that the puffed-up actors think they are excellent, or are they indeed excellent because of their humility? If they really have no high opinion of themselves, then the least their audience can do is not have a lower.

Whatever its colouring, it would be a pity to let this exchange slip by. In fact, the danger in all of the Court's reactions is that everyone seems to be displaying much the same dismissive attitude: their comments lie flatly side by side, single epigrams without much interplay apart from appreciation of each other's wit. It is becoming quite hard to trace individual character, especially among the lovers: it might as well be Lysander or Demetrius delivering any given taunt. In the second half of the scene, as their reactions get less and less pleasant, any sense that they provide a reliable barometer of the quality of the performance fades away. Potential patrons to the tune of sixpence a day or not, the deplorable behaviour of the upper classes at the theatre is being ruthlessly observed: among the male spectators there is a strong sense of the rugger club, as if some hapless performer had offered a poetry reading to such a gathering. They are certainly undeserving of Quince's 'gentles'. But then I would think that, wouldn't I, as would Shakespeare and his company: this, after all, is what we believe in.

In fact, most productions will be on the lookout for some moment when the tide turns in the actors' favour and their innocently

vigorous performance begins to work. For instance we may find that
Bottom rises to the occasion far better than expected, and begin to
feel that some hint of the theatre's power may reside even in these
rather chancy vessels. Duke Theseus seems ready to extend further
benefit of the doubt:

> Here come two noble beasts in: a man and a lion.

Part Two is beginning. Instead of following Aristotle's doctrine that
effective tragedy depends above all on action, Snug and Starveling
return to scene-setting and the poetry again becomes unassuming.
Snug, in his improbably ferocious part, has borrowed from Bottom
the idea of identifying himself by name and trade:

> Then know that I as Snug the joiner am . . .

His speech has been written for him with little allowance for his
tentative personality, for it is exceptionally boastful: the ladies will
'quake and tremble' at his version of the lion's 'wildest rage'.
However he gets into a pickle as he tries, in the prevailing style, to
put the distinction between actor and part beyond doubt. As Snug
he is a true lion, but, in a tangle of double negatives, in no way its
mother –

> A lion fell, nor else no lion's dam

– a comfort since, if he really were here as a lion, he, Snug, would
be at great risk:

> 'twere pity on my life.

He may find himself puzzled by his own argument and end irreso-
lutely, as unlike a lion in tone as appearance.

Nevertheless, like Snout, he is approved for his thoughtful
explication:

> THESEUS: A very gentle beast, and of a good conscience.
> DEMETRIUS: The best at a beast, my lord, that e'er I saw.

Unfortunately, this pun of 'best' and 'beast' is enough to set them all
off. Demetrius, Lysander and Theseus catch a special Shakespearian
sickness from each other which we have to assume played well with
their audience but is quite irritating for us. And they just can't stop.
According to Lysander, breaking a longish silence, Snug's lion is
more like a fox, that is, wily rather than brave, to which Theseus
adds the goose who was thought to be stupid, which in turn

provokes more obscurities as to whether the fox 'carries' it. A director would need to be a true purist to allow all this listless joking to survive, and a great optimist to think much of it will travel. However, it does build up a solid obstacle for the nervous Starveling, waiting and not sure when to begin.

The treatment dealt out to him when he does is one you wouldn't wish on the dog that accompanies him. It is as if the pack was instinctively picking on its weakest victim. The skinny tailor – unprotesting about his original casting as Thisbe's mother, nervous about Pyramus's suicide and afraid of the very idea of a lion – finds himself dealing not only with his lantern, thorn-bush and possibly real dog, but with the flat discourtesy of Hippolyta. She even complains that he is outstaying his welcome –

I am aweary of this moon. Would he would change

– when in fact her husband and his friends have barely allowed Starveling to get started. They have interrupted both his attempts with a fusillade of hoary jokes about horns (cuckolds) and his own spare appearance:

THESEUS: He is no crescent, and his horns are invisible within the circumference . . . the man should be put into the lantern. How is it else the man i' th' moon?

A quiet man, but methodical as his trade requires, the tailor reckons his best way is to go back to the beginning each time:

This lanthorn doth the horned moon present . . .

Just once he is allowed a second line of what might have been an interesting speech –

Myself the man i' th' moon do seem to be

– but that's it. Theseus, checking Hippolyta, allows him a brief moment of attention – 'we must stay the time' – and Lysander encourages him to start, as he has already twice tried to do: it is too late.

I have the feeling that Starveling is a gentleman – in fact I fancy him as a widower, joining the local drama group for companionship. In a way he combines two characters who participated in the equivalent show in *Love's Labour's Lost*: the country curate Sir Nathaniel, 'a foolish mild man' overcome by nerves and barracking, and the schoolmaster Holofernes, who at a certain point can take no more and roundly reproaches his audience. It is of course possible to play the rout of Moonshine as a pitiful business, and Starveling's reaction as either plaintive or petulant: but the alternative is a burst of moral courage. Seen like that, his rejoinder is superb, Holofernes speaking through the mouth of Nathaniel:

> All that I have to say is to tell you that the lanthorn is the moon,
> I the man i' th' moon . . .

This after all is the very basis of theatre; but Starveling can sustain little more and relapses, his props suddenly becoming a comfort blanket:

> . . . this thorn bush my thorn bush, and this dog my dog.

The special beauty of it, apart from the charm of using the antique word 'lanthorn' (lanterns were made of horn and it puns with 'thorn'), is the little jolt of anxiety Shakespeare gives to a man who has surely never spoken like this before. He could simply have said 'All I have to tell you is . . . ', but the extra phrase betrays the effort that is going into his dignified speech.

It is as well that Starveling's pale frame was not dressed in the finery of Thisbe's mother as originally threatened to face this particular crowd: that torment is Flute's as Thisbe herself. Ever anxious about his masculinity, briefly drawn into the passions and loyalties of the profession, he is again facing a murderous audience, with Demetrius on a particularly witless riff. His job for the moment is to announce a change of location; from what sounded when Pyramus and Thisbe met like the adjacent houses of their families, to 'Ninny's tomb' (imagine Quince's reaction once more).

Flute is immediately chased away by Snug, giving a controversial performance as Lion: it is 'well roared' according to Demetrius, but 'well moused' to Theseus, as if it were no more impressive than a cat playing with a tiny victim. The actual chase – a joiner pursuing a bellows-mender in drag – is unlikely to be impressive. Only a little scurry is seen, accompanied by the transfer – never easy – of stage blood from Lion's mouth to Thisbe's mantle, even though Thisbe has not been hurt. The most dignified figure on the stage at the moment may be Moonshine, shedding his beams – so much so that even Hippolyta warms to him a little:

> Truly, the moon shines with a good grace.

Pyramus then returns, trying not to see Thisbe's mantle too soon. Once again, Bottom is longer on exclamation than content. Four lines are given over to celebrating the brightness of the moon which enables him

> . . . to take of truest Thisbe sight

– and they give him a further opportunity to hang himself. When the turning point – the sight of Thisbe's bloodstained dress – comes, he suddenly moves into the 'eight and six' Quince originally wanted to use for the Prologue. The 'eight' in fact includes an internal rhyme which turns it into two 'fours', and for a moment the tragic material turns into a jingle:

> But stay, O spite!
> But mark, poor knight,
> What dreadful dole is here . . .

At first blush, the rhyme seems a miscalculation, but there is something surprisingly good about this balladeering style. Apart from containing a homely reference to the tufts of material professionally familiar to Bottom –

> Cut thread and thrum

– its naive music and clattering alliterations manage to express an emotion strong enough to turn even Hippolyta around:

> Beshrew my heart, but I pity the man.

In a slyly effective strategy, Bottom now returns, as a change of pace, to Quince's decasyllables:

> O wherefore, nature, didst thou lions frame . . .

It is worth noticing such a small felicity because there are also, of course, plenty of opportunities for the actor to mock Bottom's lament. After 'O dainty duck', some have gone for 'O dear' as if it were the familiar commonplace rather than a description of Thisbe; and the rhyme of 'good' and 'blood' is comical nowadays. But the fact that both jokes are probably anachronistic[10] suggests that nothing particularly silly is intended. Seen impartially, *Pyramus and Thisbe* is developing a new and graver mode now that its innocent figures think they are in the presence of death.

Shakespeare's satire is, in fact, quite subtle. In a way the literary pastiche is the least of it; so too is the acting style, since there is no

---

10. Best guesses about Elizabethan pronunciation have 'good' and 'blood' rhyming, just as, in another Shakespearian commonplace, 'prove' and 'love' would have been.

particular evidence that he was parodying the manner of any rival troupe. The real novelty is the idea of working men, as opposed to the kind of university wits that Bottom may have ousted for the evening, doing performances for aristocrats: it just didn't happen at this time, or much at all since the Mystery plays of the Middle Ages.[11] What an exceptional trick it would be if this company, so despised by Philostrate and so harassed by its audience, was about to become unsettling.

The Mechanicals' blindness to what would be an appropriate choice of play for their engagement this evening is a theatrical benefit: at their moment of union, the three pairs of newly-weds are being invited to consider the tragic loss of a lover. It should be as unwelcome as a joke about a corpse in the mouth of a best man. What does it make them feel? Whatever, the Mechanicals are wonderfully impervious, and Bottom again moves into his eight and six. There is nothing much wrong with it, apart from a typical slip ('Tongue, lose thy light'), a forced rhyme between 'pap' and 'hop', and a return to verbosity in 'dead . . . die . . . die . . . die' when he stabs himself. But peeking out of it all is a genuinely good line, rough but graceful –

> My soul is in the sky

– which prefigures some similarly striking imagery in Thisbe's death speech. A heft of feeling can be sensed behind the innocent lines, and it may yet galvanise the performance: you never know what can be done with a so-so script if the underlying situation is affecting.

Especially as the Court now plumbs new depths. Bottom's heroism has already provoked Theseus into a comment as feeble as anything by Demetrius –

> This passion, and the death of a dear friend, would go near to make a man look sad

– and now all the men quibble impenetrably between 'die', 'ace' and 'ass' like public schoolboys embarrassed by a show of emotion. It's pathetic, of course, and begs to be cut, except that it confirms the state of play, the facetious Court now dropping well behind the actors

11. The first English comedy in prose, George Gascoigne's *Supposes*, dates from 1566, when Shakespeare was two, but later he used the play as part of the plot of *The Taming of the Shrew*. This novel form may also have given him the idea of putting on this demotic style of entertainment at Theseus's Court.

in our affections. Hippolyta has in a sense to call them to order with a practical criticism:

> How chance Moonshine is gone before Thisbe comes back and finds her lover?

She at least is still paying attention to the play, observing possible errors: if Starveling has anticipated his exit (in his upset, perhaps) he has removed illumination from the scene. However her sympathy is very limited: for her as well, there is less and less to be said for this event. Somewhat erratically, having been moved by Bottom, she now hopes that Thisbe will not speak as lengthily as 'such a Pyramus':

> I hope she will be brief.

The odd process whereby evident mistakes develop an unlikely grace deepens with Thisbe's death scene: Shakespeare seems to be suggesting that a tendency to muddle language up is a guarantee of honesty in such a world. Once again, the absurdity is obvious if you want it – the jingliness of the eight and six (without a quatrain to qualify it this time), the simple rhymes, and a confusion of natural colours which renders the manly hero's lips, nose and cheeks lily-white, cherry-red and cowslip-yellow, and his eyes a vegetable green. But this is Pyramus's sweetheart, after all, blind with love and straining this way and that to do justice to his beauty. By insisting that he is this pastel-coloured masterpiece, she is transported into the Warwickshire air breathed by the Mechanicals and Puck, and her lament is curiously affecting. Where Bottom wanted the three Fates to 'cut thread and thrum', Thisbe calls on them to lay their milk-white hands in the blood they have spilt by taking their 'shears' to Pyramus's 'thread of silk'. It's surprising William Blake didn't spot this image and paint it: its odd poetry is certainly not the silliest stuff that I for one have ever heard.

Nobody confronting death on the stage can be entirely funny; even the crudest manner commands respect. It may be that, at last, both we and the onstage audience can share the actors' mortal apprehensions; and since cheap music is famously potent, their naive tunes may serve better than some organ whose bellows Flute repairs. Bottom, though inclined towards that sound, earned a modicum of respect when his grand music began to crack into pieces; Flute, confronting a 'real' body and acting in a simpler way, seems to silence the enemy altogether.

Flute even survives the risky business of running on one's own sword, often an embarrassment in the theatre (the breathless gasp) – even though Bottom, taken up with himself, may have been careless where he has discarded it. This second death, its three valedictory words replacing Pyramus's six rattling 'die's, has real dignity:

> And farewell friends,
> Thus Thisbe ends,
> Adieu, adieu, adieu.

The stillness that follows these words is evident – when Theseus and Demetrius comment, it is to summarise the result of the tragedy, not to judge the acting:

> THESEUS: Moonshine and Lion are left to bury the dead.
> DEMETRIUS: Ay, and Wall, too.

From them, such restraint amounts to applause.

In fact it is very interesting how lightly Flute, even though dressed as a woman, has got off throughout. He attracted no special fire in his duologue with Pyramus at the wall; and he was positively praised for his flight from Lion. Only Snout, in fact, was treated with so much forbearance. The only reference to Flute's appearance was very brief, from Demetrius:

> A mote will turn the balance, which Pyramus, which Thisbe is the better – he for a man, God warrant us; she for a woman, God bless us.[12]

In fact none of the actors' costumes, which one would think readily mockable – Flute's perhaps some out-of-date dress of his mother's, Snout's unwieldy assemblage, the nursery tawniness of Snug – have been commented on.

This is part of the point. You never know what will go well in the theatre – as any actor will testify who has rejected a script that seems to have no quality, only to find it transformed by whoever finally took the part. The ability to make a word travel, or a sincere emotion to carry, even a smell to seem to be shared, is an unliterary activity, to do only with the human tissue of the actor. Sometimes the clothes don't matter; and the incongruities of life are as interesting as philosophical justness. Since few people speak wonderfully under stress,

---

12. 'God bless us' seems to have been a commonplace, the Elizabethan equivalent of 'God help us'. The line was cut in the First Folio: a law of 1606 had forbidden taking the Lord's name in vain on the stage.

words may fall short of feelings, a banal image be chosen, a silence express more than a speech. All good theatre writing allows the human breath – broken, particular, incongruous – to pass through it, and it may not look like much on the page.

And I don't quite see the point of this long final scene unless it carries some of that meaning within it; unless, in fact, it demonstrates in some way the stubbornness of theatrical effect. One of the further ironies of which, at the risk of denying my livelihood, is that there are times when the professionals (let alone semi-pros like Bottom) aren't the best. One of the most moving versions of *Twelfth Night* I ever saw was a school production, utterly inadequate from a technical point of view, but whose sincerity – particularly from the girls in their plaited wigs and musty old dresses – took the audience straight to the melancholy, hopeful heart of the play. The closer the amateur comes to professional skill, the more irritating the shortfall: so Bottom may have been the least impressive this evening. Certainly the company's established star will have to keep an eye on his talented leading lady from now on.

On the other hand he is irresistible. Leaping up now to put an end, as it might be, to Flute's round of applause, he falls back on his old habit of tutoring his audience, pointing out that Demetrius has the plot wrong, 'I assure you'. Denying that Wall is still available for the burials, he goes on to suggest an afterlife for the story, involving a reconciliation. In what may be a sly reference to the Montagues and Capulets he has just been writing about, Shakespeare makes Bottom claim that

> The wall is down that parted their fathers.

Though the meetings of Pyramus and Thisbe did seem a little clandestine, this is the first hint we have heard of parental opposition to their love, and it is barely touched on in the sources. In any case, by recovering so quickly from death, Bottom has insisted that the interesting business is now done: he would have had little patience with the hundred and forty lines of discussion and reconciliation that follow the deaths of Romeo and Juliet.

All in all, it seems to him that his company has had a great success. Now, anything goes: there is even a spoken epilogue in his mind and an Italian country dance – a Bergomask – which presumably needs no rehearsing. Theseus responds to this idea opaquely, to say the least. He assumes that the epilogue would be an apology for

the play – which it might not be – and then seems to look forward
to the extinction of the actors:

> No epilogue, I pray you; for your play needs no excuse. Never
> excuse; for when the players are all dead, there need none to be
> blamed.

What is Bottom to make of that? Theseus hurries on, with a joke: if
only the author had played Pyramus himself and hanged himself in
Thisbe's garter, it would have been 'a fine tragedy'. Oh yes, and so
it was of course, and 'very notably discharged'. This, by the way, is
the man who said a quarter of an hour ago that he was going to show
special kindness to his entertainers.

The actors gaze blankly at their patron, trying to see the best in
it. There seems to be no offer of sixpence a day, or anything like it.
Not even Bottom knows what to say. It is remarkable how rude
people can be. Even professional actors sometimes have to listen to
some wiseacre who thinks it his duty to give them his candid
criticisms after the show, when all they want is a drink. Theseus, who
benevolently chose this company against all advice, couldn't resist
making fun of them; he will remember his wedding evening as one
in which he had a good laugh at his subjects. Perhaps this is to
overstate, but there is little escaping the unpleasant edge in it, the
snigger beneath the word-games. We are about to leave this deeply
divided character on an equivocal note: would not the older
Shakespeare have arranged for him to earn the blessing he is about
to receive from Oberon by showing a better side?

In a way of course Theseus's bathos is another theatrical gift: it
keeps the play alive. And the Bergomask is allowed, an opportunity
for various interpretative tilts. Perhaps the Court patiently watch; or
perhaps the Mechanicals' honest endeavour has earned them a
certain equality, so that Hippolyta dances with Bottom, say. There is
no stage direction in the early editions of the play indicating when
the Mechanicals should leave. Later commentators assume it is after
this dance, before Theseus goes into verse to disparage them openly:

> This palpable gross play hath well beguil'd
> The heavy gait of night.

Surely, they say, Theseus wouldn't be so impolite about them if they
were still there. I wonder. But instead of having the actors simply
make themselves scarce without a word, why not make them stay to
endure this further offhand criticism? Alternatively, they could go

before Theseus speaks, but with goodwill, breathless with the dance and with much wordless well-wishing.[13]

Either way, Theseus is making his view clear, even though he softens it a little with an antithesis:

> I fear we shall outsleep the coming morn
> As much as we this night have overwatch'd.

This is either a light social comment, or his opinion that, for a temperate person, none of this was worth staying up so late for. It is greeted with an appreciative chuckle, no doubt. He warns his obliging friends that his marriage to Hippolyta will be noted for the next fortnight

> In nightly revels and new jollity.

A four-day holiday for his subjects at the start of the play; two weeks of street parties at the end. Everyone's fun is firmly scheduled, from the unabashed mouth of the person to be celebrated. By contrast, the wedding night he has looked forward to for so long sounds to be a heavy and wintry one. It is ushered in by the midnight bell tolling with an 'iron tongue': for all its heady scents, it has a 'heavy gait'. One small felicity:

> Lovers, to bed; 'tis almost fairy time.

Since Theseus doesn't believe in 'fairy toys' this has to be a joke, like hoping his guests won't let the bugs bite their toes; such things have no place in his coercive, rational world. Well, that's all he knows. This reminder of the huge alternative we know about puts us at an advantage: we can see further. If he only knew it, his security, his wife's fidelity, even the good looks of his children are about to be guaranteed by forces he doesn't even acknowledge to exist.

Altogether, he is closing the play's human business with a benediction so drained and opaque that it can only be provisional. We regret the departure of the Mechanicals, and are sorry to be left with two noble couples in which the women are completely silent and a third which, for all its progress, seems to be chronically disputatious. This is no more than half-closure for us. Cold night air

---

13. The predispositions of directors are written all over this moment. In some productions the police have moved the Mechanicals on as soon as they have finished dancing; in others the actors have refused Theseus's patronage – even in as romantic a version as Max Reinhardt's film it was the Court that sneaked away, so that the Mechanicals found they were dancing on their own.

needs to clear the fumes left by its inhabitants before this house can begin to be truly warm and safe.

So, as if from deep in its heart, comes Puck, perhaps carrying a domestic broom. He will sweep Theseus's limited blessing aside to make space for the deeper peace of Oberon and Titania, and he is more ambiguous than ever before. On the one hand he looks like nothing more than the traditional Robin Goodfellow, auxiliary housekeeper to country wives. But his words have the effect of flinging open shutters and doors so that night comes tumbling in. At the beginning of today he could see dragons racing along the edge of darkness with daylight on their tails; now that night has returned, the same dragons are drawing blackness back across half the earth like a screen.

Although it is midsummer, his images could hardly be more wild and wintry:

> Now the hungry lion roars,
> And the wolf behowls the moon . . .
> Whilst the screech-owl, screeching loud,
> Puts the wretch that lies in woe
> In remembrance of a shroud.

The language we have been humouring in *Pyramus and Thisbe* is immediately forgotten – this is the real, living thing. In place of eyes as green as leeks and an ineffective lion, true predators are at the window, imprecating and tormented: the wolf's 'behowl' is a word used by Shakespeare here and nowhere else. The vitality of the language is remarkable – the swift sense of wilderness, the bold repetition of the onomatopoeic 'screech'. So vivid, in fact, that the actor may want to colour the words rather than let them conjure, opening up the vowels of 'roar', 'behowl' and 'screech' as if mimicking the animals. It's a mistake – the imagery will do its own work if the actor's voice is offered to it unassertively.

Puck's terrors may not have left him, but now he is master enough of them to turn their force on us. He is careful to weave homelier sights and sounds into his discords – embers crackling in the fire, the ploughman sleeping off his labours and perhaps his ale. But these barely stir beneath an unforgiving darkness and a cold moon: a few steps away, graves are creaking open once more, and suicides rising from floods and crossways. The words smother the Mechanicals' fun like a blanket over a fire. But Puck is only posting a warning, and his tone swings abruptly on a completely unexpected word – 'frolic': he switches into couplets and his voice becomes warm. The fairies, Hecate's out-riders, are instantly delightful and tiny, and

> not a mouse
> Shall disturb this hallowed house.
> I am sent with broom before
> To sweep the dust behind the door.

There is nothing to fear after all: having seemed to raise the dead, the light four-beat rhythms settle the nerves. The Puck is indeed Robin Goodfellow, his besom routinely sweeping in return for bread and milk.

Prepared for in this way, Oberon's arrival with Titania and their fairies is a beautiful and heartstopping moment. They are obviously returning the compliment paid long ago when Demetrius and Helena arrived in Oberon's forest. Those they are about to bless are oblivious, sunk at last in a healthy sleep, and the head of the household will presumably continue not to believe in them anyway. We, the theatre audience, receive these visitors on their behalf, their arrival satisfying our own need for reassurance. The 'house' now means both Theseus's palace and the homes we ourselves have left empty, as well as being professional parlance for the theatre building itself.

If Puck brought in the terrors of the night but carried a broom, Oberon can strike ringing poetry from the gently breathing household. The glow of the fire is now augmented by fairy light, described by an adjective, 'glimmering', that keeps coming to Shakespeare in this play, but which he used in no other work:

> Through the house give glimmering light
> By the dead and drowsy fire . . .

But Oberon too is a countryman: just as if they were outside, the fairies must

> Hop as light as bird from briar

– and before scattering through the house they must dance 'trippingly' and sing a 'ditty'. The words have become a little unfortunate, but we have to take them seriously. There is an archaism too: to 'rehearse . . . by rote' actually means repeating accurately from memory, not preparing. It is a tricky moment: now that everything is detailed and intimate, any generalisation in choreography or musical setting could be destructive – the judgment is at least as nice as it was for Titania's lullaby earlier. Several editors propose both song and dance before Oberon speaks again, but an interlude delaying the text is unlikely to be congenial; some discreet underscoring of it is surely best.[14]

With his beautiful blessing, Oberon completes his journey: from vengefulness to lonely success to this determination that the lovers shall find their way home. Now he is all theirs. Childless in any sense we understand, he guarantees them; these humans, unlike Titania and himself, shall

> Ever true in loving be

and the children of all three unions will be protected from wayward 'nature'. The blemish of 'mole, harelip', 'scar' and 'mark prodigious' might seem a detail more human than we would expect from Oberon, but it in fact is much to the point: such things have always been thought to be the work of malevolent fairies. But he is a spirit of another sort. He is specially benevolent to Theseus in his 'best bride-bed', visiting him and Hippolyta as one royal to another – he and Titania will personally preside over the human patrons who caused them such mutual rancour earlier. Oberon seems able in fact to offer complete protection to our world without leaving his own:

> With this field-dew consecrate
> Every fairy take his gait
> And each several chamber bless
> Through this palace with sweet peace . . .

The visitors scatter through the house's walls and wainscoting for their night's work, fireflies covering everything with light.

Shakespeare's endings can be long-drawn-out affairs. Sometimes the cause is not in the ending itself but its preparation – that Act Four Lag, lying in wait for the unwary director in the form of endless parley before the big battle (several History plays), the mirthless repetition of jokes that were good and sufficient the first time (Aguecheek in *Twelfth Night*, Autolycus in *The Winter's Tale*), the treading of narrative water to allow the leading actor to have a rest (*Hamlet, Macbeth*). In other cases – *Measure for Measure, Cymbeline* – the closing twenty minutes themselves need watching, their denouements are so intricate. The sheer prodigality of what Shakespeare

---

14. The Folio prints Oberon's speech 'Now until the break of day' as 'The Song' but doesn't attribute it to a singer; the earlier Quarto gives him the speech but doesn't suggest he should sing it.

has proposed to himself for *A Midsummer Night's Dream* makes it particularly difficult to close all the files properly. In acting terms, it is largely a matter of picking up the cues and avoiding attractive dying falls like the plague; behind which lies the powerful principle of teamwork. With the best will in the world, the actors of Theseus, Puck and Oberon, completing their own parts in turn, may feel it is up to them to bring the play in and sink into that deadly last-moment cadence. But they must push forward, Theseus a bit brisker than he thought necessary (they are going to bed), Puck a little more upbeat as he sweeps the floor (he has work to do), and Oberon's instruction played not as the end of something but as the start of a long night's housekeeping.

It calls for astute direction too. Between Theseus's departure and Puck's extraordinary arrival, it is perfectly possible to leave the stage empty as long as it is, so to speak, still breathing; but it is more audacious to have him revealed by the general exit in the same warm spot that the humans are leaving. Then, as he finishes and begins to sweep, we need to hear Oberon's voice as soon as possible, especially as he is at the head of a line of fairy traffic which will take time to arrive.

The same holds for Puck's return at the very end to fulfil a familiar convention of Shakespearian comedy, the actor taking leave of the audience on behalf of his colleagues. In fact this was the first time Shakespeare had used it – if you discount *Love's Labour's Lost*, which ends with a song and a single line in part addressed to the audience by Don Armado. Occasionally Shakespeare contented himself with a closing dance, but in the *Dream* that has been and gone. So Puck comes forward, as Feste and Rosalind will later, taking off his mask to reveal the working actor – sort of. In fact he is only uncovering another mask, just as one of his names conceals a second. Interestingly, he never quite comes out of character, despite expressing routine hopes that the audience has had a good evening and that the word-of-mouth will be good. Where Rosalind and Feste will operate in a no-man's-land between character and actor, referring openly to 'this play' and 'our play', Puck continues to speak of shadows, visions and dreams. He compulsively names himself ('honest Puck . . . else the Puck a liar call') before ending as the Robin who will make amends, not simply for the inadequacies of his profession but for everything unruly beyond our sight.

His language cunningly combines his fairy provenance with theatrical vocabulary. The 'serpent's tongue' he hopes to escape belongs in the world of spotted snakes but also refers to bad report in the theatre. He describes himself and his colleagues – human as well as fairy – as 'shadows', a word he has already applied to Oberon ('king of shadows'), and which is in any case the standard description of an actor, used by Theseus during *Pyramus and Thisbe*. Throughout he talks of 'mending', of making 'amends', as if some damage had been done, or as if we needed reassurance that we are now safe. There is always a bargain to be struck with Puck, and often a playful flick of danger. If you leave him milk he will help with your housework; if you applaud him now he won't disguise himself as a threefoot stool or make you spill your nightcap. If we have disliked the evening we can imagine it was all a dream as we 'slumbered here', to be cured by daylight. But really, it did happen and it could again. We cross ourselves in order not to tempt fate and excuse our blasphemies with little rituals of absolution; likewise it's as well to appease Robin, the reason for those odd little misfortunes, the slips and slithers and bad luck that recur during the working day. And indeed we never do know what guards us in the night. Once we might have knelt and said our prayers; later on we forestall darkness with goodwill towards those we love and fear to lose before morning, wishing them Good Night, Sleep Well, Get Some Rest. Puck may even have a final theatrical trick up his sleeve, like killing the lights or creating a last sound effect, to prove the terms are still his. Certainly the figure taking his leave is not quite the chummy actor, more the ambiguous and powerful substance around which the actor is wrapped like the transparent shadow he is.

CONCLUSION

Regent's Park, 2003

My invitation to direct *A Midsummer Night's Dream* in 2003 at the
Open Air Theatre in Regent's Park, the most beautiful of natural
settings, came during a foul London dusk the previous October,
while I was playing a paedophile judge for a few episodes of a long-
running TV series. We were starting a long night of filming on a
houseboat on the Thames, in which various abysmal fictional deals
were to be struck; I listened to the new proposition on a mobile
phone, swaying gently on a gangway, peering into a channel of water
between boat and shore as scummy as the transactions on board.
Turning hairpin bends from one world to another is a feature of our
profession. I have never lost the habit of being immediately quick-
ened by any respectable new offer of work; for another thing I hadn't
been involved in preparing a Shakespeare for several years, and had
forgotten how he immediately sets the blood racing. I have been
known to sleep not at all when Shakespeare is proposed; since on
this occasion I was about to be awake anyway, the night-shoot ahead
– the longest way I know of spending eight hours – looked much the
better for letting such a play edge into my mind's eye.

The good old *Dream*. Known so long, and so obviously wonderful
we hardly need to say it; so famously good that somehow it can be
hard to take seriously. So many challenging productions, so many
swoonings at its exquisite fairy poetry, so many gales of laughter.
Why is it then that I can't remember whether it is Hermia or Helena
who loves Lysander, whether Quince is a carpenter or a lady's tailor
– and what is all the business about the little Indian boy? Perhaps
because, as if by some oversight, I've never been in it, even though
I've played in *Love's Labour's Lost* and *Measure for Measure* twice
each and *Troilus and Cressida* three times – what kind of way is that
to spend a life? Surely though, I must have seen the *Dream* ad

infinitum. Not so. Have I perhaps let it pass every time it has come up, unless I have had a friend in it, or unless the new version had some startling reputation for originality? To go to a traditional production would be like putting down some interesting book in order to learn to read all over again. As dawn rose over the Thames, I realised I felt about as close to *A Midsummer Night's Dream* as I did to the mindset of my deviant judge.

It is usual enough, when about to do a classic, to trawl through your memories, partly in the hope of not finding anything too intimidating. As in many things, long-term recall can be sharper than short-term. I probably saw more Shakespeares as an early teenager in the late 1950s than I ever have since. In 1957, I was in the Old Vic audience when, boosting a minor tradition of pro-fessional comics appearing as Bottom, Frankie Howerd played him as part of the company's Five Year Plan to present the whole of Shakespeare. This was at his own instigation I believe, at a time of re-evaluation, as it's called, of his solo career. For the record, it was a triumph for Howerd, not least because of the critics' surprise at his instinctive gift for playing in a team – not, obviously, a stand-up's habit – even if it was surely a pity to hide that face of his inside an ass's. The main thing I remember of his performance is the plume on his Pyramus helmet always ending up in his mouth. I also recall Coral Browne as Helena looking over her shoulder to see whom Lysander really meant to embrace as he approached her; but then my attention was often limited in those days to bits of acting that I could then go and practise at home. I also remember Derek Godfrey's extraordinary diaphanous blue-green costume as Oberon, which made him as iridescent as a humming bird, and the very beautiful woodland setting designed around him by James Bailey.

I then saw Peter Hall's Stratford version in 1959. This was set in a Tudor country house, surely in Warwickshire, only adapted up to a point to suggest the forest, and it had Vanessa Redgrave as Helena and Charles Laughton as a gentle bully Bottom. Unlike Frankie Howerd, he sported ass's ears and hooves only, his exposed face doing the rest. Albert Finney was Lysander and Ian Holm Puck; Lila de Nobili's costume designs were above all suggestive of Nicholas Hilliard's miniatures of Elizabethan courtiers. I duly witnessed Peter Brook's in 1970, planted like a great tree in the play's history and im-possible to ignore, even if I secretly still dreamed of Derek Godfrey's shiny blue wings. I have mental snapshots of Richard Griffiths's delicate Bottom in John Barton's RSC production of 1977, and of Mike Gwilym as Oberon and Juliet Stevenson as Titania in Ron Daniels' in 1981, set backstage in a Victorian theatre and using puppets as fairies. However, it may be that none of these made the impression, to plunge back still further, of the summer of 1955 – a salad year of theatre infatuation when I was taken to the same Open Air Theatre in Regent's Park which I was contemplating now. If I had but known, it had just reopened after a dark year imposed by financial hardship – a perennial problem which had never become so bad as to force a closure before. The legendary Robert Atkins, actor-manager of the company since 1933, was a little deaf by now, but he played Bottom all the same, as he always had, with magnificent *droit de seigneur*, since the inauguration. It is not that I remember the details, apart from the ass's head of course, more that it fed me what I depended on – the cocktail of sound, meaning and physical presence that intoxicated me whenever I sat in a theatre. Dazzled as I was by Shakespeare's clamour and insinuation, I may have also grasped, amidst the poplar, sycamore and hazel which still frame the stage at Regent's Park, that the experience was acutely vulnerable to adventitious short-circuits such as the weather.

Despite a remarkable record of survival on a very small element of public subsidy followed by none at all, in a climate liable to enforce daily cancellation, the Open Air Theatre has, during my working life, enjoyed the status of a minor institution. Minor only because it has sometimes been treated within the industry with a certain dismissiveness – recently, I'm glad to say, less and less so. In the 1930s, as many as 3,000 people a night might turn out to sit in deckchairs to watch Anna Neagle, Jack Hawkins and Vivien Leigh on the greensward; now, much redesigned and at a capacity of 1,200, the theatre is generally full of an unusually classless audience, often brought together by the need to entertain their children, who may encounter Shakespeare for the first time here. The more cynical professional view is that the best that can be hoped for from an acoustic riddled by low-flying aircraft, wind and rain, the susurrus of trees and the trumpeting of the elephants in London Zoo, is a kind of village-green cheerfulness. Actors can be reluctant to submit themselves to this onslaught, which may also include a certain give and take with an audience which is allowed to bring its refreshments in as well. In recent years though, superior productions of quite rare Shakespeares and an annual musical have drawn full houses and the attention of the first-string national critics. The arrival of the Globe Theatre on Bankside, whose painstaking reconstruction aims at the physical sensation of its Elizabethan namesake, provides genuinely friendly competition. The two companies have made doing these plays in the open air, come wind and weather, more attractive not only to actors, but to designers willing to accept as the matrix for their thinking either the permanence of an Elizabethan playhouse or, in Regent's Park, an unalterable forest glade. In fact, a good night in the Park is not only magical in itself but brings you as close to the spirit of the original event as you can get – not because it resembles Shakespeare's theatre but because it creates something of the same state of mind, the same communal wish, shared risks and hardy interplay between actors and audience.

As the oily water continued to slap against the house-boat like the dreams of my abominable judge, I could see how hard it was going to be to pull off the proposition from a practical point of view. After the TV, I was going to be touring as Ibsen's John Gabriel Borkman until the very Saturday before *Dream* rehearsals needed to begin. Then, by a neat coincidence, I was due to fly to Moscow a couple of days after its opening to rehearse, in Chekhov's house, Peter Stein's production of *The Seagull*, work on which would then continue on the director's estate in Umbria and be completed at the Edinburgh Festival. So at both ends of the job was a sort of full stop: I certainly wouldn't be able to stay close to the production after it opened, and as for the pre-rehearsal period, many of the auditions and design meetings – the whole range of activities for which directors are little rewarded but which take up as much energy as rehearsals – would have to be held on Sundays between my touring dates or on weekday mornings in various regional rendezvous.

That of course could all be fixed; more troublesome was this feeling that I might not have a personal response to the play – in fact, something died a little whenever I thought of it during the subsequent days. I could see that it was a lovely and dazzling thing, and that its fantastication was a designer's temptation (though not in the Park). I knew that ballet and song seemed to loom even when the text doesn't call for them; that over the years many small children had peopled its fairy world; that other children love to watch much of it and that we are allowed to become like them when we do. On the other hand, the demanding age in which I have grown up finds something not quite right about all this, so that one is now expected, clutching Freud's *Interpretation of Dreams*, to dig deeper for images of subconscious anxiety. Young hooligans have replaced pretty children as fairies, and rough magic has jostled sleight of hand out of the way. The range of choice I faced felt quite inhibiting.

So – back to the head of the river. London's theatres were closed by plague in 1592 and stayed shut for nearly two years. At the outbreak, Shakespeare was twenty-eight, and had probably been in London only two or three years. He had *Titus Andronicus*, the three Parts of *Henry VI*, and possibly *Richard III* as well, behind him – some, in the conjectural world of Shakespeare premieres, would say *The Two Gentlemen of Verona* and *The Taming of the Shrew* as well. Though it is quite difficult to measure the success of individual plays, fairly clearly he was tipped for the top, if not quite at it. In the pestilential silence that now fell, he adapted himself. Showing an instinct for social mobility, he shifted his attention to the literary world, whose intrigues may, then as now, have been a little finer-spun than those of the theatre and rather more precious in tone. Taking his cue from Christopher Marlowe, whose brilliantly erotic *Hero and Leander* he may have read in manuscript, he wrote two narrative poems of his own, and somewhat grovellingly dedicated them to the Earl of Southampton, an apparently Maecenas-like patron whom he may also have admired sexually – the unattainable Adonis in *Venus and Adonis* is in some particulars a portrait of him. This poem was printed in 1593 by – a homely touch – an old Stratford schoolfriend, and *The Rape of Lucrece* followed in 1594. Both were phenomenally successful, and a new audience embraced Shakespeare even more enthusiastically than the old; but by the end of 1594 he was back in the sawdust, as a founding member, actor of moderate achievement, shareholder in and essential playwright of the Lord Chamberlain's Men, whose star actor was Richard Burbage. Now, like Molière and Chekhov ahead of him, he was creating parts for actors he knew, who performed them in a Shoreditch playhouse simply known as The Theatre (built by Burbage's father), alternating with occasional appearances at Court; when the lease there expired, the actors dismantled their building, moved it plank by plank across the river at London Bridge, and swiftly reconstructed it as the Globe. Their new home opened its doors in 1599, probably with *Henry V*, in which the figure of Chorus famously – and a little disingenuously – kept apologising for its deficiencies.

A *Midsummer Night's Dream* belongs after the re-opening of the theatres but before the move to the Globe, along with *The Merchant of Venice*, *Romeo and Juliet* and *Much Ado About Nothing*. Certainly it was known by 1598, when it appears in a list of Shakespeare's works to date in *Palladis Tamia*, a treatise written by an early literary train-spotter, Francis Meres; the best guess is that it was two or three years old by then. As is the way with Shakespeare plays built around a marriage, there has been a farrago of efforts to place its first performance in some noble household on the occasion of a wedding, possibly in the presence of Queen Elizabeth – Shakespeare's company providing the entertainment *du jour* as the less capable Bottom and his friends do for Theseus. A somewhat similar conjecture is attached to *Twelfth Night*, which, it has been suggested, owes its appearance to the call for entertainments on that day during the visit of a certain Duke Orsino to the Queen; but it must be said that neither Orsino in that play nor Theseus in this is a particularly savoury picture of an Italian nobleman or an English bridegroom. There is no real lead to be found here; what is sure is that the *Dream* soon became part of the company's repertoire in the public theatres, since by the time a 'booke called A mydsomer nightes dreame' was published in Quarto in 1600, it had been '. . . sundry times acted'.

In this edition, the characters' names and their entrance and exit cues are not standardised, randomly varying between Titania and Queen, Puck and Robin, and Bottom and Pyramus. There are some pleasantly personal touches, like separate entrances for Flute and Thisbe, as if Shakespeare had forgotten that they were the same person, and one for Helena in the first scene long before she is called for, as if the four lovers were an inseparable unit in the author's mind and so might as well all come on together. A very similar Quarto appeared in 1619, three years after Shakespeare's death; and finally the play features in the First Folio assembled by John Heminges and Henry Condell, Shakespeare's devoted fellow-actors, in 1623. There are a few oddities in the language, caused no doubt by erratic assembly, but they are not nearly as numerous as in other plays: the text is fairly 'clean'.

A comparison with the literary works immediately preceding the play is in some ways more revealing than one with the pre-Plague *Titus* or *Henry VI*, say. Shakespeare seems to have come through this period with a literary self-consciousness which immediately spilled into the *Dream* and its contemporaries – *The Comedy of Errors*, *Love's Labour's Lost* and *Richard II*. All of them suggest a lyric writer consciously using poetic conventions liked by his audience, but once in a while impudently exploding with light and revealing them for the limited things they were. Shakespeare could turn a rhyming couplet with the best of them; but no other Elizabethan poet would have had a heroine describe herself as being as ugly as a bear or make a fantastical Spanish grandee refer to his mustachio as his 'excrement'. In *Venus and Adonis*, in a wonderful sketch of the shock of bereavement, the goddess of love sees her beloved dead on the ground: her sight grows 'treble', then 'double', his limbs multiplied by her skittering optic nerve. Then her eyes retreat into 'the deep dark caverns of her head' like a snail whose tender horns have been hurt. It is pleasing to notice that Hermia in the *Dream* also sees her troublesome experiences with 'parted eye', and that in Berowne's great speech on love in *Love's Labour's Lost* the horns of the 'cockled snail' stand for its extreme sensitivity.

All Shakespeares are attended by a tower of critical Babel, but in the case of the *Dream* its volume is fairly low. In any case, if practitioners affect to scorn theatrical precedent, they have even less use for literary criticism. There is one exception on both counts: the great Harley Granville Barker, who apart from being a fine actor and director and a superb playwright who has suffered unfairly by comparison with George Bernard Shaw, published fourteen Prefaces to Shakespeare's plays between 1927 and 1946. They are a most unusual achievement, appropriately scholarly and entirely practical, if a little tainted with snobbery and – oddly, in view of his championship of that new thing, ensemble acting – a sometimes patronising attitude to the less important characters. Barker is the commentator that the profession genuflects to as readily as to his subject. I turn to his Preface to the *Dream*: if nothing else his production of the play was part of his ground-breaking seasons of Shakespeare at the Savoy Theatre in London between 1912 and 1914. To an audience that over the previous thirty years had seen battery-powered fireflies attached to a huge corps de ballet of fairies, Theseus's wedding-ship sailing through the forest into Athens,[1] real rabbits following trails of feed around the stage[2] and a battle between a wasp and a spider,[3] he

1. Augustin Daly's 1895 New York production, on tour in England.
2. Beerbohm Tree, 1900 and 1911.
3. Frank Benson, 1889.

offered a radical change of diet. Swiftly drawn coloured curtains effected the rapid changes of location Shakespeare imagined, Oberon and Puck were once more cast with men, the gold-painted fairies resembled Asian deities rather than muslin wraiths, and the lovers' clothes suggested eastern Europe while Bottom stayed firmly in Warwickshire. Most interestingly, Puck blatantly dimmed the stage lights to create the fog that confuses Lysander and Demetrius. Barker also served notice on Mendelssohn in favour of English melodies orchestrated by the great collector Cecil Sharp, founder of the English Folk Dance Society. His extreme innovations were a reaction not only to Victorian kitsch but to the bare-stage puritanism of William Poel that had briefly succeeded it, and his values are a tap-root for many modern productions. In particular he demanded – it seems obvious now – the swiftest possible delivery of the fullest possible text.

So in this Preface Barker will surely have something to say. Or rather Prefaces – he wrote one in 1914 and another in 1924. Although his own production was reasonably fresh in his mind at both times, his accounts land with a slight sense of anti-climax. The second and longer is still brief, not much over 15,000 words,[4] and it seems to shrug the play off a little. During the gap between the two he had changed his mind about Theseus: in the first Preface he declares there is nothing much in him and nothing at all in Hippolyta, but by 1924 he is calling Theseus a romantic hero with a large helping of humour and wisdom.

We also learn that in this play Shakespeare is more of a poet than a dramatist; that there is little light and shade in the verse, which 'flows like a river in sunlight'; and that there is no complexity of plot or development of character. Also that the 'daintily ridiculous' Titania is a spoiled darling when she is happy, but destroys the natural world around her when she is not: Barker finds little 'excuse' for her speech about the dreadful weather in Act Two Scene One beyond its beauty. He is not charitable to Hermia and Helena either: I have noticed this slight streak of misogyny before. The fact is that these important essays occasionally show a tight-lipped primness absent from Barker's wonderful dramas, perhaps because he was already, to all intents and purposes, retired from practice. Really it is time the world had a better series of books on individual Shakespeare plays.

4. There are briefer – *The Winter's Tale* rates 2,500 and *Twelfth Night* comes in at barely 3,000.

For a start, I was pretty sure that he was wrong about Theseus – both times. During my thoughtful weeks I chanced to go and see Joel Zwick's delightful 2002 movie *My Big Fat Greek Wedding*, about the trouble caused to a Chicago Greek family when its ugly duckling daughter, turning rapidly beautiful, chooses to marry an American. The crucial role is that of her father Gus, proprietor of 'Dancing Zorba's' restaurant, who is so determined to keep Greek identity alive in his adopted community that he is fond of challenging anyone who will listen to find a single important English word that has other than a Greek origin. Even 'baptism' and 'kimono' pass his test. He is thus a comic version of the domineering parent of many movies, while his determination that everything Greek is better than anything else is reminiscent of Chekhov's one-act play *The Wedding*, in which Kharlampy Dymba, a Greek confectioner, makes much the same point to the wedding guests:

> ZHIGALOV: Tell me, are there tigers in Greece?
> DYMBA: Yes, is tigers.
> ZHIGALOV: And lions?
> DYMBA: Is lions too. In Russia is nothing, in Greece is every-thing. In Greece is my father, my uncle, my brothers. Here is nothing, isn't it?
> ZHIGALOV: I see. And are there whales in Greece?
> DYMBA: In Greece is every damn thing.

Gus is finally reconciled to his new son-in-law when he realises that his surname, Miller, is close to the Greek word for apple, while his own is reminiscent of that for orange, so that, for all their differences, 'we are all fruit in the end'. Gus's sense of being directly descended from Pericles and Socrates, together with his great warmhearted-ness, happens to match that of some of my own Greek acquain-tances – pride, tenderness, the need to share. So why not set the *Dream* not in the ancient Greece of cotton dresses and knobbly knees but in a modern Athens, where Theseus could suggest those qualities but also an opposite potential – that, as it did under the Generals in the late 1960s, military force could swiftly rewrite history, appro-priate culture and up-end liberal values. The forest where he hunts would become the hilly expanses of Macedonia; Lysander and Demetrius the self-conscious Greek poet and the Athenian equiva-lent of a Thatcher child. The Mechanicals, meeting in the town square to plan their show, could be dressed in the working clothes of the 1940s and 1950s – heavy brown and black flannel, berets and boots, Quince in a sober three-piece suit – with a judicious dose of warm colour here and there.

I took to Paul Farnsworth, my designer, not only this idea but a list of the flowers the play mentions: cowslips, Love-in-Idleness, wild thyme, violet, woodbine, musk-rose, eglantine (sweet briar) and oxlips, as well as the orbs, acorn-cups and dewdrops. The play's animal life is dominated by the king of beasts, but it has another scale as well – snakes, bats, newts, blindworms, spiders, spinners, beetles, bees, glow-worms, painted butterflies. Then, the fruit: apricot, dewberry, grape, fig, mulberry. We looked (in Nick Knight's book *Flora*) at microscopic images of leaves and blossoms to find the extraordinary range of primary colours almost never seen by the naked eye, in the hope that we could make them the palette for the costumes of the fairy world, and at one point thought of rendering the humans' clothes in more manufactured versions of the same tones.[5]

The stubborn reality of Regent's Park liberates in some ways but in others holds you to a conventional line. It seemed to me that there could be a staging problem in its relative spaciousness – long entrances down grassy banks on either side, through the auditorium and from the depths of the trees – so that it might be very difficult to create surprises. A fairy can hardly materialise suddenly in such a wide open space, or Puck be instantly there even though you haven't seen him enter. So we planned to augment nature with some constructed bushes which would close down the playing area and concentrate the action, hoping they would be well enough made not to suffer next to the real thing – as indeed they were. We made a circular clearing at stage centre such as you sometimes see in the wilder kind of wood, as if some small open air auditorium had been abandoned, and marked its outline with apparently random pieces of broken masonry.

We then planned a small acting level above upstage centre, partly to avoid the crush of sleeping bodies on the now reduced area below – Titania could rest up there – and behind that stood a great upright golden disc. The effect of a double circle – above and below – had something both theatrical and ancient Greek about it: the disc suggested both sun and moon, and, because of its uneven surface,

---

5. The fairies' costumes were painted by Silvana Sacco, who did similar work for *Lord of the Rings*; she blended and enhanced the colours to give them a beautiful organic feel.

took the light as interestingly as the moon does to the naked eye. On the stage floor we made three great wooden uprights like columns: once the action moved away from Theseus to the forest they collapsed like fallen trees. Lying amidst the rubble they said something of the chaos Titania laments in the natural world.

This was all very well, but as our subtle view of the fairy costumes would eventually prove, the one certain fact about working in the Park is that you can't get too damned clever. You also quite quickly learn some arcane but absolute local knowledge. Any production of the *Dream* has to take its interval in the same place, after Act Three Scene One, since at any other feasible point some supposedly sleeping actor will be condemned to lie on the ground throughout it, exposed to the audience. This practicality means that if, as a guest director, you refer in rehearsal to some line or moment in the middle of Act Three Scene One, someone who has worked there before may well answer, 'Oh yes, just about 8.45 p.m.' The virtue is that some barely perceptible lighting can be added to Bottom's transformation just as the sun goes down. By the time the audience then come back from the interval, this artificial light has taken over completely. Adding to their impression that the wine here is good, a ravishing new world seems to have developed in their absence – an enchanted concentration of light with an indefinite mass of vegetation whispering and swaying behind it.

The question of the rain is another obvious singularity. For a time there used to be a large tent to which cast and audience could repair and continue if the weather turned, but in 1960 it blew over. It is sometimes said, with some truth, that if the company manager stands on the picnic lawn and the rain runs off his nose in a continuous stream, as opposed to merely dripping, the show is cancelled. This decision is never taken until the performance time of 8 p.m. exactly, since as everyone knows things can change in a moment – conversely, there have been cruel examples of shows being cancelled at that point and an audience leaving as the sun came out, too late.

There are less obvious things to consider. If you use musical instruments played live, as I intended to, they have to be backed up with a recorded version that can be used in a level of rain which would allow the performance to continue but damage the instruments. If the ground is wet, consideration has to be given, fairy charms or not, to some form of sheeting on which the lovers and Titania can lie during their long slumber; and certainly, in an atmosphere bad for the chest and larynx, some voices (depending on their timbre as much as their strength), can, however well produced, be vulnerable to damage, so the understudies have to be ready at all times.

Like the RSC and other repertoire theatres, casting at Regent's Park is a complicated committee affair: with very rare exceptions, each actor has to be in a minimum of two of the season's three productions, so the three directors have to agree, taking and giving a bit. I was matched with *The Two Gentlemen of Verona* and *High Society*, which brought some dividends – good Cole Porter singers from the musical for the *Dream*'s fairies, strong women's parts to offer in each of the Shakespeares. I fought for some actors and compromised on others, and before long forgot which were which; an ensemble company like this protects its weaknesses and maximises its strengths, while the salary budget stays within bounds so that the theatre stays open. The rehearsal period for the two Shakespeares, opening the season together, would be short, but it is remarkable how the same actors, once on terms with each other, can work on a quite different second play – or a third or a seventh – more quickly than separate casts could.

With some cunning, I managed to secure a Snug on guitar, a bazouki-playing Flute, Quince for the dulcimer, and Bottom on wind instruments, and so was able with conscience to ask Terry Davies, one of the great theatre composers, for a mixture of eastern European styles – recorded pan pipes for Puck, sinuous quarter-tone movements for Oberon's and Titania's dance, a Fairy lullaby with a jittery subtext under its smooth surface. The climax was a rousing Greek Bergomask which Scarlett Mackmin brilliantly choreographed and which I still hear with pleasure.

We rehearsed the two shows for five weeks, which necessitated twelve-hour days twice a week, and Saturdays as well. This schedule was, as it must be, mounted on a rigorous structure of priorities whereby one production has first call on its actors on any given day – the overall aggregate obviously being equal. The non-prioritised show has to make do with whoever's left over, and timings have to be observed with military precision, as actors are often nipping off from one rehearsal room to another at an appointed moment – for the directors therefore, no overrunning and much co-operation. When I asked for a full company call for the *Dream* after a week, for good enough reasons, it meant that *The Two Gents* could do nothing at all that morning: the idea was treated tolerantly, like a novice's aberration, but I didn't do it again.

Coming in, the audience found the Mechanicals slowly erecting a curtained stage for Theseus's wedding entertainments, which, had they known it, they would end up occupying – two uprights defining it with a red embroidered cloth hung between them. They worked in a slow, deliberate way, as if slightly becalmed – no sudden movements to make the audience think the play was beginning. Snout was particularly sceptical about the engineering; Flute and Snug tuned their instruments. As Theseus and Hippolyta drifted on with brandies to sit uncomfortably opposite each other, their attitudes indicated that the story was starting and the Mechanicals faded into the background. When Philostrate was sent off to choose entertainments, they set upon him – discreetly, as the main scene was continuing. The nature of Theseus's court was pointed up when Egeus burst violently in: Theseus's first reaction was to reach for his gun, but only so that the audience could note it fleetingly, not so emphatically that he became a gangster.

The square-jawed Demetrius aligned himself with Theseus and Egeus while the more rock 'n' roll Lysander lounged as much as he dared to without giving offence. The former group laughed openly at Theseus's idea of a girl wasting herself in spinsterhood, then remembered that Hippolyta was there so that they were – never mind little Hermia – in mixed company. It turns out that there is a great need for pace when Theseus leaves this scene, which is hard for Lysander and Hermia, whose main job is to lay out their story with clarity; but who knows, let's say, when they will be hustled out of the palace? When we got all the detail but at speed, I knew we were set up well for the first half, the engine purring; when not, worryingly not. Helena came drifting down one of the grassy banks, not necessarily at the moment Lysander and Hermia would have chosen; we decided her shock was recent, even that very day, so she had her letter from Demetrius with her. When she left, the bazouki theme was heard as Quince and Philostrate briefly met and a bottle of ouzo was seen to change hands; Quince, having made a successful investment in his friends' future, could announce jubilantly that his team was at least in with a chance.

The curtain the Mechanicals had left half-swagged on a post in the first scene dropped to reveal Puck. This magic didn't always work: even when the wind wasn't up, the curtain was hard to control, and there were unsettled nights when it had to be abandoned altogether and

Puck simply made an entrance. (By the time of *Pyramus and Thisbe* the wind had generally dropped and the curtain could be reinstated.) Puck was a little depressed by the deadlock in his and Oberon's life caused by Titania's intransigence, and his discontent gave him something to play rather than having to introduce himself with comic demonstration. Oberon appeared out of the sun-disc; his row with Titania left him furious and tearful at his failure, and Puck, the child for once father to the man, soothingly took charge of him.

Demetrius and Helena arrived through the auditorium, and Demetrius, still in his city suit, wiped a piece of statuary clean before sitting on it. He was frankly overcome by the sheer unfairness of Helena – she even punished him by grazing her knee painfully as she dropped on it to become a dog. This of course added to her feeling of hopeless clumsiness: sometimes an actor needs a small physical trigger for a big emotion. Lysander and Hermia arrived with camping gear and map, and Hermia laid out her sleeping mat for the night. As Puck dropped the juice into Lysander's eye he half-rose to meet it as if levitated; later, in the fog, he would become so light in his entranced sleep that Puck could just blow him out of the way. Positively discriminating as usual, Puck chastely kissed the sleeping Hermia and took a necklace from her which he wore for the rest of the play. The notion half-worked: Puck seemed himself to be a kind of changeling, yearning to return to the human world. But the necklace was too small for the audience to see in this theatre, and since Hermia says nothing about losing it and Puck never mentions it, the idea didn't earn its keep.

When Hermia awoke, her fear was accompanied by murmurings from deep in the wood and stray animal cries (the latter magnified when Puck chased the Mechanicals through bush and briar). The unnerving atmosphere remained as the Mechanicals gathered for their rehearsals, cautiously emerging from the bushes with lanterns and torches: Bottom's 'are we all met' made Quince jump out of his skin. Bottom's transformation was treated by his colleagues as largely his own fault, the result of hubris. His ass's head, a form of half-mask, allowed his eyes to be completely visible; it was cast in plastic and painted to match Peter Forbes's skin tone, like a prosthesis. Yak hair was knotted into it, and its light flexible ears were made from piano wire. At first Bottom's voice was rather muffled, but the addition of a harder surface to the upper palate in the head restored the crispness of his sound. He ended the act by plunging headlong with the fairies through our constructed hedges – the first intimation that they weren't real;[6] this dive was as close to a vanishing trick as we could get.

We had rehearsed the lovers' quarrel on long Saturday sessions when I too would have liked to go home. In the end, Hermia's most dangerous weapon became her rolled-up bedding, with which she assaulted Demetrius: despite the mildness of the attack, Demetrius, ever a little precious, reacted as if it had been a medieval mace. Seeing no other way out of her difficulties, Helena plunged towards the audience and had to be rescued at the very edge of the stage, almost at take-off. Hermia clawed at her like a tiger held by its tail and clung to Lysander's leg so that he could only walk like a man with a huge limp carrying a sack. The men prostrated themselves on the ground in parallel lines to do obeisance to Helena; and with some difficulty I dissuaded them from taking the exit line

> Nay I'll go with thee, cheek by jowl

too literally. Puck was furious at again being criticised by Oberon, then collapsed in abject terror at the approach of day. In the fog of Acheron, fairies' disembodied heads appeared through the hedges like road-blocks to change the men's direction of flight. Hermia crossed herself as she prayed for Lysander's safety.

Bottom lolled in Titania's bower upstage centre, a little too far away really for such an intimate scene: beneath his ass's head he still wore his rather childish red V-necked sweater, sleeveless and a little small for him. We heard the tongs and bones as he called for them. Nothing becomes a verse rule like the breaking of it, so Oberon was allowed a large and reflective pause on

> And now I have the boy

while he considered what he felt about his barren victory. When Bottom awoke, his first instinct was to use his mobile phone to make contact with Quince, before the full wonder of his dream dawned on him. This was part of a running gag built on the tradition that such an idea has to be seen three times to complete its effect. When the theatre's public address system had announced no smoking or mobile phones at the start of the play, Bottom had been seen to turn his off

---

6. They were mounted within a frame on vertical belts of elasticated fabric, which could therefore split at this moment.

(and Snout to pocket his pipe); now he failed to get a signal. So that was two.

At the risk of asserting national stereotypes, I had to note that the choice of an Irish actor for Flute made waiting for Bottom's return work specially well. At first he stormed through the scene as if he was going to hit everybody, but Quince's obscene slip of the tongue ('paramour' for 'paragon') completely disabled him: his chaste inability to say what a paramour was was like the sexual shyness of the young Celtic male you keep encountering in James Joyce's *Dubliners*. Starveling was deaf, so he missed most of this, and Quince had to yell in his ear to find out if Bottom had come home; Bottom could shortly be heard racing round the circumference of the auditorium as if on a full circuit of Regent's Park's Inner Circle. The red curtain came into its own even before *Pyramus and Thisbe*, as a background for Theseus in white tie and tails, and Hippolyta, who for her wedding wore a sequined evening dress and beautiful shawl, topped off with what we came to describe as 'My Big Fat Greek Necklace' – made to order, chunky and ancient-looking. She looked a little like Christine Onassis. The court wore designer clothes, Paul Smith and Ted Baker for the men and Agnes B and Paul Costelloe for the women. To launch *Pyramus and Thisbe*, Quince did his Prologue like Noël Coward, or perhaps the wartime newsreader Alvar Liddell: he was the only one who thought you should put on a special voice for acting.

Snout remained imperturbable, pipe in mouth; in fact it never left it throughout the show except to allow him to make the occasional sententious pronouncement. As Wall he was completely unaffected by nerves and blissfully unaware of any difficulties, ready to explain himself several times over if necessary, with a private extra runthrough afterwards for Hippolyta, whom he was rather taken by. Having completed his main part so successfully he became a little absent-minded and had to be prompted repeatedly to offer up Wall's chink for Bottom, which is perhaps why Bottom then beat him up in an evidently unrehearsed way. This wasn't the worst for Snout: he didn't much care for the lovers' saliva on his chink either. Bottom became equally infuriated by Thisbe's mantle not being left in the right place – as enraged as Quince was at hearing 'Ninny's tomb' for the third time so soon after emphasising the correct pronunciation in his Prologue. Now he flung his hammers down on his dulcimer in a fine discord. Starveling was crestfallen at his treatment but remained dignified; he recovered his spirits well enough to drift helpfully back onto the stage just as Bottom told the moon to take flight, so that he had to turn round and wander disconsolately off again without breaking his tentative stride. Snug was petrified but managed. Flute started with a silence so terrifying that everyone wondered if he would have to be removed, and then his lines came bursting out of him like a flood. At one point the visor on Bottom's helmet closed on him so that he looked like a suit of armour. In the middle of his great speech to the moon his mobile phone went off – number three. His repeated 'die' gave him a Wolfit-esque opportunity for the most elaborate display of vocalisations, before he collapsed and died, like Mr Wopsle's Hamlet in *Great Expectations*, 'by inches, from the ankles upwards'. Flute ultimately silenced the audience with his grief, which completely took him over; but so that such a switch of gear should not be too crude, he also had to struggle to find Pyramus's sword, on top of which Bottom had collapsed.

The Bergomask was a knees-up for Court and actors, its stamping rhythm incorporating a donkey dance for Bottom, as if the ass was still in him. In the best Greek manner (a little like the nuptial party in *My Big Fat Greek Wedding*) it was completely democratic: Hippolyta and Theseus both danced with Bottom, and the audience finally surrendered to clapping in time. The fairies moved throughout the audience with lights. As Puck finished the play, an ass's bray swung through a hundred and eighty degrees round the auditorium speakers, as Bottom himself had as he raced to re-join his companions. Finally, Puck – in a homage to Harley Granville Barker that I wasn't aware of at the time – snapped his fingers to cut the lights. The curtain call reprised the pleasures of the Bergomask.

The production, I must say, was a great success, not at all indecisive as it turned out, and it played to packed houses throughout a glorious summer undisturbed by the rain. Except, of course, for the Press Night, a day which dawned in golden splendour and progressively darkened over between teatime and curtain up. This is where I realised that the true risk of working regularly at the Park might be a permanent upward crick in the neck. The rain began to spit during the interval, consolidated itself for a quarter of an hour afterwards (so that Puck and Oberon were the losers as the critics' umbrellas went up), but then held off, just, for the rest of the evening.

Buoyed up by great generosity from the cast (it was near enough my birthday and the First Fairy knew someone in the wine trade) I went off to Moscow, but a month or so later spotted an opportunity to revisit the show while en route back from Italy to Edinburgh. The first thing I saw was a fairy I didn't recognise: in my absence, her predecessor, pregnant, had found that the early stages of that happy event were not really conducive, and I had been unable from afar to advise on the re-casting.

What somebody once called 'taking out the improvements' is a desperate business for a director, and one of the reasons I don't do the job more often. For every actor who has nurtured his perform-ance across thirty repetitions so that it has gained in subtlety, authority and confidence, there is another – essentially no less talented – who thinks he is improving but is actually ruining his own work. The ability to become so at home in your part that you can turn a cartwheel in the middle of a line of blank verse may be proof that you are 'making it your own', but it probably means that you have stopped talking properly to the colleague you are sharing the stage with. Our show had always had an open-hearted, storytelling quality, an innocence even, that, within a little month, had been cor-rupted by approval. The honesty of it was disappearing, much of the comedy broadening, and in the wake of every good new invention followed a coarser one. Incidental pleasures were sprouting like wild-flowers, and there was a knowingness about where the sure laughs were. All of us need reminding to keep things simple, to maintain the precise heat of our stage relationships and always to assume that the audience has never seen the play before.

With a melancholy affection on my side and light self-reproach on the cast's, this was all sorted out soon. In a way the actors held a trump card: as if in gentle reciprocal criticism, they had themselves cut Bottom's mobile phone. This truly was an improvement: even in a highly organised production some things remain optional, and the cast instinctively knew that this change didn't need approval from me. The joke had only ever hung on by its finger-ends, but it hadn't been altogether silly. Bottom is so self-confident, so breezily sure he has right on his side at all times, that any uncontrollable thing that catches him out is worth considering. Shakespeare did it with his malapropisms and mistakes, but they are a bit hackneyed now – the phone had been a way of freshening up the same idea.

*

It is always a great thing to hear an audience gasping with laughter as if in pain, and as good to hear them silenced on an instant. In the

Dream I had been the beneficiary of one of the great comedy machines; and watching a midsummer audience on its feet, clapping to the Greek beat as if they wished they had some plates to smash, certainly did the heart good. Strange as it might sound, I hadn't realised quite what a force for good, for pure enjoyment, the play could be, with its dazzling effects and broad contrasts, its sheer unpredictability and its high music. Shows are sometimes praised, with a distinctly English Puritanism, as 'a good night out'. It is an interesting phrase that simultaneously gives the theatre its due and puts it firmly in its place, as if to be let out of custodial care too often to enjoy such a thing would lead to the breakdown of society. In this sense *A Midsummer Night's Dream* could become a very bad habit indeed.

In our efforts this summer I had to conclude that the Mechanicals were a complete success; in fact, I will always find it hard to think of Snug as anything but a South Walesian, or Flute as not an Ulsterman, or Bottom as not a Scot. But the new view of Theseus – a fourth comic element! – also seemed completely justified; while the lovers, faced with one of the play's hardest tasks, pulled off far more than they expected. But I had to acknowledge what in truth I had always known, that in the middle of all the pleasure was a large failure of my own. Perhaps Harley Granville Barker was right after all:

> Can even genius succeed in putting fairies on the stage? [They are] the producer's test. How should they look? One does one's best.

I might add that in the open air they are particularly difficult, as you can't pull any magic stunts in broad daylight, least of all at matinees – though directors more experienced in the Park have succeeded by at least knowing what to avoid. Our original idea had led to a series of beautiful drawings and watercolours – Titania, safely framed, is looking down from the wall at me now – but the colours and textures didn't travel as far as the middle distance from which most of the audience saw them. No more did the effect of their flesh-coloured shoes made by Gina (Victoria Beckham's favourite), which if you were close enough looked very much like strange, bare feet. As the first night approached, we could see that something more robust was needed throughout fairyland, and, increasingly desperate, added white-face make-up and wild shocks of hair, achieving a cross between something from Stratford in the 1950s and the Glasgow Citizens' Theatre in the 1970s.

The fact was I had given Paul Farnsworth an unrealisable brief, and also let down the actors, who were excellent and had done exactly what I had asked from them. In the rehearsal room Oberon and Titania had fought over the changeling like wild animals: their thrilling quarrel applied human sweat to a fanciful world, and I truly thought this was going to be the strongest part of the show. But these fine performances dwindled with every item of costume the actors put on. In the end both were slaughtered by the press, which was a particular blow to Titania, who had had a sudden and most serious bereavement a few days before the opening and had continued with an almost unbelievable stoicism. Of course the reviewers couldn't have known, but somewhere in there is an argument for a little civility in our yobbish critical climate.

It was a failure of imagination and technique on my part. But I assume that very few productions manage to pot all the balls: we so often hear the judgment, Ah, not the lovers this time, or, Theseus is so dull. In terms of casting, design and inventiveness a director has to get very lucky with this play, and at some point the flooded mind may close down in the face of it. Over-familiarity can be blamed, but the truth is more reproachful: most imaginations fall short of the gratuitous brilliance of the author's. Shakespeare's talent is not usually a problem in this way. You don't shrink from doing *Hamlet* or *Lear* because of the length or depth of its vision, since even in some small way you feel implicated in it; but the *Dream* is different – more esoteric, for all its popularity, and without quite the view of the human condition that makes the whole world kin. There is such a glut of qualities here that, as with some great architectural confection by Antonio Gaudí, there can be real difficulties of entry.

Having said that, I hadn't expected the play to be even as moving as it was. I thought I would be looking at an exquisite diamond, brilliant, multifaceted and shimmering with intimidating beauty rather than with the soulfulness of the later comedies. But Shakespeare is never inert, flowing around you rather than settling into a shape, and what is in one play is in some way in all of them. He was, all his working life, interested in much the same things. Everyone in *A Midsummer Night's Dream* is driven by love as helplessly as they are in *Twelfth Night* or even *The Winter's Tale*. Theseus, immured in lonely, unenviable self-regard, ends by at least respecting Hippolyta and, in a muddled way, beginning to care for her; Hippolyta gradually puts aside her resentment as she sees what he might become.

The lovers are so called because that is their whole reason to live, so that the men yearn indiscriminately and the women dote without stint. Her fairies love Titania so much they will minister to an ass-man. Titania loves Oberon, sure, but she also loves the oxen, the ploughman, her gossiping votaress, as if they were her wronged children. Oberon loves the humans as well as Titania and is at his best when he is helping them; he is distracted, as we all can be, by an obsessive relationship, and hugely relieved when it is stilled. Puck half-loves the foolish humans, perhaps because he half is one. The Mechanicals love what the theatre can do, even if they could never put it into words.

And yet, and yet: the play remains a little remote and complete to itself. This is not the Shakespeare from which people quote a therapeutic line in daily life, even if a director might, at some despairing rehearsal, mutter that you can never bring in a wall. In the Shakespearian community, Hamlet can be imagined having an interesting talk about life and death with Feste; Queen Margaret might discuss with Cleopatra how to reconcile love and power; Gertrude could advise Romeo. But there is really no character in the *Dream* who could sustain such a conversation. Certainly there is no hero, though Bottom occasionally looks like one, and no absolute heroine. Oberon's poetry pricks at the eyes but in another way means nothing; the comedy is relatively obvious, its charm complicated in the case of the lovers by self-conscious ingenuity; with the Mechanicals, apart from during *Pyramus and Thisbe*, it is more amiable than uproarious. The mature Shakespeare strikes resonant laughter out of honourable mistakes and self-deception – we know Rosalind and Viola are not boys and that Beatrice and Benedick are in fact attracted to each other – but the comedy that arises from the action of the drug in the *Dream* is of a swift and brutal kind, leading to no special revelation of character. There is also little of Shakespeare's mischievous socialism, his teasing at the status quo: when the Gravedigger encounters Hamlet he wins on all counts, and when, in *Measure for Measure*, the Duke plots to substitute one severed head for another to mislead Angelo, he is confounded by the fact that Barnadine, his victim, flatly refuses to be executed that day. The malapropisms of Bottom are not in the same class, and in the end *Pyramus and Thisbe* affects its patrons only a little.

However, the play is very good for the health. Best of course to watch it among strangers in the special intimacy of a theatre; but it is also possible to sit by an open window, watching a honeysuckle circling an elm tree, and marvel at what Shakespeare made of such things in this play. This is only to do as he did as he pounded the fields to Charlecote, weaved through Bankside or suddenly looked up from his desk to see the mulberry tree he had planted in his garden in New Place. (This is not fanciful: it was cut down a hundred and fifty years later, its wood made into tobacco-stoppers and sold to the first Stratford tourists by a Birmingham toy-merchant.) No wonder the mulberry is such a common tree in Shakespeare, and that its shade covers Thisbe as she draws her suicidal dagger.

In this natural way Shakespeare, an ordinary man rather than an intellectual, makes us all talented: there are moments when we can feel ourselves on the brink, just the brink, of seeing what he saw. With the *Dream* we are in front of a pane of glass on which the light plays variously. Sometimes, magnified, the pigments, textures and shapes of a hidden life can be glimpsed through it. More rarely, it becomes like Hamlet's mirror held up to nature, reflecting back something we know in the fumbling recoveries of the lovers, the widening eyes of Bottom or Starveling's patience under pressure.

This is also like a jig written by Beethoven, a child's picture by Francis Bacon; an early masterpiece by someone who felt growing within him the power to see further and deeper than any dramatist has done since. No wonder, rumbling at the back like a kettle drum, are the deeper notes. It is still – just – a young man's play, pretending to flippancy even when serious: you feel foolish trying to read too much into it but cannot quite believe that Shakespeare didn't mean something more. So it hovers between significance and sheer invention, parable and dance, mocking the attention it feeds on. In the end you walk away from the glass and feel the play still dancing around you. The fireflies fizz into darkness and the moon sits in an indigo sky; you remember a story long forgotten or a man recently dressed as a wall; or, packing up after the evening's work to go home, glance at the discarded prop of an ass's head, all straps and little hinges and smeared with make-up, a wardrobe basket of sweaty fairy costumes, a toy dog and a lantern. Away it flies again, swift as midsummer lightning; a very good piece of work and a merry, a brush with genius on the move, an open invitation to the best night out imaginable from the theatre's great dreamer.